James Payn

Carlyon's Year

A Novel

James Payn

Carlyon's Year
A Novel

ISBN/EAN: 9783337039523

Printed in Europe, USA, Canada, Australia, Japan

Cover: Foto ©ninafisch / pixelio.de

More available books at **www.hansebooks.com**

A Novel.

BY THE AUTHOR OF "LOST SIR MASSINGBERD," &c.

NEW YORK:
HARPER & BROTHERS, PUBLISHERS,
FRANKLIN SQUARE.
1867.

CARLYON'S YEAR.

CHAPTER I.
ON THE SANDS.

"THAT will do, Stephen, thank you. You may let us out here. A charming scene, is it not, Richard?"

The speaker was a young lady of nineteen; looking, however, not older, but far wiser than her years. A thoughtful face by nature, and besides, one upon which some sorrow and much care for others had set their marks. The hazel eyes, large and tender, were confident, without being bold. The forehead, from which the heavy folds of bright brown hair were not drawn back, but overflowed it from under her summer hat at their own wild will, was broad and low. The form tall and slender, but shapely; the voice singularly clear and sweet, and whose tones were such as seemed to give assurance of the truth they utter. She was certainly speaking truth now when she said, "A charming scene."

The persons she addressed were seated with her in a cart, in the middle of one of those bays upon our north-western coast, from which the sea retires, with every tide, for many miles, and leaves it a level waste of sand, save for two river-channels, besides several smaller streams, fordable in places, but always running swiftly. Some islands, oases in this desert, dotted here and there at no great distance, yet farther than they seemed, showed grandly with their walls of rock and crowns of foliage. The shores of the bay itself, miles away at the nearest point, were of a beauty singularly varied, considering their extent. To southward a range of round, green hills sloped down to a white fringe of coast, on which a tolerably large town could be distinctly viewed, with, behind it, a castle on a hill, which marked the site of a much larger town. Upon the spurs of these hills were almost everywhere to be seen a cluster of grey dwellings, and from the valleys thin blue smoke; the district, although somewhat un-come-at-able, was so fair that many came to dwell there, especially in the summer; but yet it was not densely peopled. Eastward, these signs of habitation were more rare, and the hills began to rise in grandeur, till, in the north-east, they culminated to mountains, a knot of which towered in the extreme distance at the head of the bay. Small coves and inlets indented the northern shore, which was, moreover, thickly wooded; a white village or two, from one of which the cart had just arrived, glimmered through the trees; and to the west a far-stretching promontory, with one beetling cliff, concluded the fair scene—that is, so far as the land reached. Upon the south was the sea, separated from them by no bar or bound of any sort, and roaring in the distance, as though for prey. It was this which formed the most striking feature in the picture, and indeed, to a stranger to the position—as was one of the three individuals we are concerned with—it was almost terrible.

"Well, Agnes," observed Richard Crawford to his cousin, to whom he looked junior by at least twelve months, but was really her senior by that much; "this is truly grand. I could never have imagined what a spectacle 'Over Sands' afforded, if I had not thus seen it with my own eyes. It is certainly the very place for a sketch. Now, jump, and I will catch you."

The young man had leaped lightly from the back of the cart upon the brown, firm sand, and now held out both his arms, that his cousin might alight in safety.

"Thank you, Richard, I am used to help myself out of this sort of difficulty," replied she, smiling; "am I not, Stephen?"

"Yes, miss," returned the driver, respectfully, but in broad north-country accents; "this is not the first time you have been in my cart, nor yet the second. She's as active as any deer in his lordship's park out yonder, that I'll answer for, Mr. Richard. Lor bless you! you don't know Miss Agnes; but then, how should you, you that has been in foreign parts so long!"

Richard Crawford had, it was true enough, been for many years in a far-distant climate, and one which had turned his handsome features to the hue of those of a bronze statue ; but he grew of a more dusky red than even the eastern suns had made him, when his cousin, touching one of his extended arms with her finger-tips only, lightly leaped upon the sand. She took no notice of his evident annoyance, but exclaimed gayly, "Now, Stephen, the chair and the campstool; then go your ways, and good-luck to your craam. I dare say Mr. Richard here does not know what a 'craam' is; so great is the ignorance that prevails in the tropics. See here, cousin." She drew out from the cart a sort of three-pronged, bent fork, used by cockle-gatherers for getting the little bivalve out of the sand, beneath the surface of which it lies about an inch. "There! that is the true Neptune's trident. No barren sceptre, but one upon whose magic movement, thus"—she deftly thrust it into the sand, where two small eyelet holes announced the presence of the fish, and whipped one out—"meat, and drink, and clothing are evoked for many a poor soul in these parts. Why, you need not go far afield, Stephen, since there seem to be cockles here."

"Nay, miss, there's nobbut but one or two here about," returned the man. "The skeer* lies far away out yonder. You'll not be afraid to bide here till I come back and fetch you?"

"Certainly not, Stephen. How many hours shall we have to spare, think you?"

"Well, with this light south wind stirring, perhaps not four, miss. But I shall pick you up long before that—just as usual, you know. A deal of company you will have upon Sands this afternoon, I reckon," added the man, as he drove off to the cockle-ground; "you have brought Mr. Richard out on quite a gala day."

The scene upon the wave-deserted bay was indeed growing quite animated; for, in addition to many carts, such as that in which they had come, the owners whereof were all setting to work with their craams, two long strings of horsemen and wheeled conveyances were beginning to cross from either side of the bay, making almost to the place where the two were standing, sketch-books in hand; each band, both from the east and west, were conducted by a guide over the first *eau* or river, after which their course lay plain enough across certain broad, but shallow streams, to the second, near the opposite shore, where the other guide was posted.

"I have seen nothing like this since I crossed the desert," ejaculated the young man, with admiration. "I can almost fancy that those horses are camels, and the trees on yonder island palms, only there are no thieves of Bedouins."

"But in Egypt there is no sea, Richard, like that which seems to hunger yonder for men's lives. Is it not strange to think that all this space now used as a safe road by man and beast will, in an hour or two hence, be landless sea? that not one of those black rocks that stand out so prominently yonder will lift its head above the waves. Folks talk of there being 'no sea to speak of,' in these parts, but if they mean that the ocean has here no elements of grandeur and terror, they are much mistaken. Its very retreat and advance so many miles are something wondrous; and when I see the crowds of people crossing thus during its short absence, I always think of the Israelites passing through the Red Sea upon dry land. Nay," added she, as if to herself, and with reverence, "it is only God's arm that keeps the waves from swallowing us up to-day."

---
* The local name for the large beds in which the cockles are found.

"Yes, of course," returned Richard dryly; "yet the tides obey fixed laws, I suppose, and can be calculated upon to within a few minutes; otherwise I should say these good folks, including ourselves, are somewhat fool-hardy."

"I have known the tide come in here more than two hours earlier than usual," returned the young girl gravely. "There was a ship wrecked in yonder bay in consequence; the men having gone ashore and left her, high and dry, and feeling confident of returning in time. A strong south wind will always bring the sea up quickly."

"There's a south wind to-day, Agnes," laughed her cousin. "I think you must be making experiments upon my courage."

"Nay," returned she, "the breeze is very light. Besides, the guides and the cocklers all know very well what they are about. It is very seldom any one is lost, and when they are, it is through their own folly, poor folks."

"They get drunk a good deal in these parts, don't they?" said the young man, carelessly, as he sat down on the camp-stool and began to sharpen a pencil, "and being half-seas-over before they start, why it's no wonder if the tide—"

"Hush, Richard, do not jest with death," said the girl, reprovingly. "Men and women have sins to answer for here as in other places; but I have ever found them an honest and kindly race."

"Well, I only hope in addition to kindliness and honesty your friend Stephen reckons sobriety among his virtues. What! he *is* a little fond of tippling, is he? Phew!" here the young man indulged in a long low whistle, and his black eyes beamed with sly laughter.

"Stephen is weak," replied Agnes Crawford, gravely; "though not so bad, even in his weakness, as some say."

"There, I see it all," cried the young man, clapping his hands so sharply that the half-dozen gulls that strutted on the sands a little way off rose heavily, and wheeled in the blue air, ere alighting at a greater distance; I see it all quite plainly. My Cousin Agnes, who is so good herself that she can believe evil of nobody, employs this Stephen because no one else will employ him; she trusts him because every body says that he is not trustworthy."

"I believe he would risk his life to save mine," rejoined Agnes, simply.

"Of course he would, my dear cousin; for without you he is probably well aware that he could not gain a living. Don't be angry now! I am only delighted to find you are so unchanged; the same credulous, tender-hearted creature that I left when I was almost a boy, who never allowed herself the luxury of going into a tantrum, unless one of her dumb favorites was ill-treated. Now let me tell you a secret—that is, something which is a secret to you, although it is known to every body else who knows you. My dear Agnes, you are an angel."

"Don't you rumple my wings, then," replied

the young girl, coolly, as Mr. Richard Crawford concluded his eulogistic remarks by patting her on the shoulder. "See! yonder is a drove of cattle about to cross the eau. Are they not picturesque? Now, if you were an animal painter instead of being, like myself, only able to draw immovable objects—to shoot at sitting birds, as it were—we might by our joint efforts make a very pretty picture of this scene."

"You make a very charming picture alone, I do assure you," said her cousin, admiringly.

The remark evoked no reply, nor even a touch of color on the young girl's cheek. Her brow just clouded for a moment, that was all.

"We have secured an excellent position for our sketches," said she, after a pause, and each took their seat.

"Do people ever cross the sands on foot?" inquired Richard, presently, in a constrained voice. He had parted with his somewhat free and easy manner, and manifestly felt that he had been going too fast or far with his compliments.

"Very rarely," returned she. "There are always some places tolerably deep, as yonder, where, as you see, the water is above the axletrees of the coach. The poorer sort of cocklers, however, sometimes come out without a cart. Once no less than eight people were lost in that way, and on a perfectly windless day. It happened before we came to live here, but I heard the story from the guide's own lips. A sudden fog came on, and they were all drowned; and yet it was so calm that when the bodies were found at the next tide, the men's hats were still upon their heads. A little girl, he said, with her hands folded across her bosom, lay dead beside her dead father, just as though she slept."

"Even if they had had carts, then, the poor folks could not have been saved," observed Richard.

"Yes, it was thought they might," returned the young girl, sadly. "The guide has a trumpet which carries his words, or at all events the sound of them, to a great distance. It was supposed they were making for the right direction when the waters overtook them, but being encumbered with women and children, and on foot, the party could not hurry on."

"What a repertory of dreadful stories your friend the guide must have, Agnes."

"Yes, indeed," answered she, gravely. "There's one church-yard I know of in our neighborhood in which have been buried no less than one hundred persons, victims to these treacherous sands."

"And the quicksands themselves are the graves of many, I suppose?"

"No, never; or, at least, almost never. They are quicksands in the sense of instability; but they do not suck objects of any considerable size out of sight, or at all events they take some time to do so. The bodies of drowned persons are almost always found."

"Upon my word, Agnes, you make my blood creep. Talking to this guide of yours must be like a business interview with an undertaker."

"Nay, Richard," rejoined the girl, solemnly, "such stories are not all sad. Death has been sometimes met, as it were, with open arms by those who knew it was eternal life. And, besides, there are narratives of hair-breadth escapes from peril sometimes, too, which instance the noblest courage and self-sacrifice. I wish, however, that there was no such road as Over Sands."

"Nay, then we should never have been here with our sketch-books," returned the young man, gayly. "See! I have put in the three islands already."

"So I perceive, Richard; and the largest of them in the wrong place. Where are you to sketch in yonder village?"

"Oh! bother the village. The picture is supposed to be executed when the country was not so overbuilt. What are those little trees sticking up above the river? Every thing here seems so anomalous that I ought not to be surprised; but nothing grows there surely."

"They are only branches of furze called 'brogs,' which are set up by the guides to mark the fords. It is their business to try the bed of the stream every tide—for what was fordable yesterday may be quicksands to-day—before folks begin to cross. There goes the coach."

"Yes, and how the passengers do stare," returned Richard; nor, indeed, is it to be wondered at, if it is their first experience of this road. I think some of them will be glad when they find themselves on *terra firma*. Perhaps you might have seen me arrive rather pale in the face, Agnes, if I had come home this way, instead of by sea, to Whitehaven."

"No, Richard; to do you justice, I think you are afraid of nothing."

"I am afraid of one thing, and that is of you, cousin, or rather, of your displeasure," said the young man, sinking his voice, and speaking very tenderly.

"If you are, you would not talk such nonsense," rejoined his cousin, quietly.

"Dear Agnes, don't be cruel, don't; nor affect to take for jest what I mean with all my heart and soul. Thousands of miles away on the wild waves the very likeness of your face has comforted me, which you gave me when we parted, boy and girl, so many years ago. Think, then, what happiness it is to me to gaze upon that face itself, a child's indeed no longer, but with all the innocence and purity of the child beaming from it still. You used to tell me that you loved me then, Agnes."

"And so I tell you now, Richard," returned the girl, changing color for the first time, as she bent over her drawing, and forced her trembling fingers to do their work. "I love you now, very much indeed, dear cousin."

"Cousin," repeated the young man, slowly, "yes; but I don't mean that, as you well know, Agnes. I only wish you could have seen me in my little dingy cabin, reading your letters by one wretched candle stuck in a ginger-beer bottle—don't laugh, Agnes; I am sure you would not have laughed if you really could have seen it. I quarreled with the only one of my companions whom I liked, and knocked him backward down the companion-ladder because he put his stupid foot upon the desk you gave me. You are laughing again, Agnes. True, I was only a poor lad in the merchant service, and poverty is always ridiculous; but I would have shown my love for you in other ways had it been possible. Heaven knows I thought of little else than you!"

"Look here, Cousin Richard," said Agnes, rising quickly from her seat and speaking with some severity, "I will not hear this talk: you are well aware what my father thinks of it."

"I can not help my uncle's not liking me," said the young man somewhat sullenly.

"Nor can I, Richard, or you know I should make him esteem you as I do myself. But you are under his roof now; he is your host as well as your uncle—and my father. That is reason good—independent of other very valid ones upon which I do not wish to enter—why you should not address such words to me. I think you should have seen they were distasteful, Richard, without obliging me to tell you so."

The young man did not utter a reply: he only bowed, not stiffly, however, and held his hand up once and let it fall again with a certain pathetic dignity that seemed to touch his companion's heart, and indeed did so. Her large eyes swam with tears.

"Forgive me, Richard, I am sorry to have pained you," said she, in soft low tones, inexpressibly tender; "very sorry."

"I am sure you are, cousin." That was all he said; his handsome, clear-cut features appeared to have grown thinner within the last few minutes, as she watched his side face bent down over his sketch-book. They were both silent for a long time, during which they plied their pencils. Draughtsmen know how quickly the hours pass in this way without notice. Presently Richard lifted his eyes from his work, and looked around him. "Agnes," said he, "why does not Stephen fetch us?"

She looked up too, then started to her feet with agitation. "My God!" cried she, "the carts have all gone home."

"Don't be frightened, dearest," said the young man, confidently. "There are two carts still, and Stephen's is one of them. My eyes are good, and I can recognize it plainly, although it is a great way off. He is running the thing very near; that is all."

"Alas! he has forgotten us altogether, Richard. Both those carts are making for the other side; he could not now cross over to us even if he would. Do you not see how the sea has stretched its arm between us and him?"

Richard Crawford uttered a tremendous imprecation.

"Do not curse him, Richard. They have given him drink, and he knows not what he is doing; or perhaps he concludes that we have gone home by other means, as indeed we might have done. Poor fellow, he will be sorry to-morrow. Curse me, rather, my poor cousin; for it is I who have murdered you in having brought you hither."

"No, no!" ejaculated the young man, vehemently. "Do not think that. I swear I would rather die with you like this, than live without you. But is there no hope? Hark! what is that?"

"It is the guide's trumpet; they see our danger from the land, although they can not help us."

"Let us hasten, then, in God's name!" exclaimed the young man, bitterly; "and if He has ordained it so, let us die as near home as we can."

CHAPTER II.

BY THE WATERS OF DEATH.

THERE was no necessity for the words "let us hasten." Both had left chairs and sketch-books, and were running as swiftly as they could toward the western shore; but the sand, lately so hard and firm, was now growing soft and unstable—the flowing tide already making itself felt beneath it; their progress, therefore, was not rapid.

"The thought that I have brought you hither, Richard, is more bitter to me than will be these waters of death," said Agnes, earnestly. "You can run where I can scarcely walk; leave me, then, I pray you, and save yourself. Remember, you can not save me by delaying, but will only perish also. Why should the sea have two victims instead of one?"

"If the next step would take me to dry land," answered the young man, vehemently, "and you were deep in a quicksand, lifting your hand in last farewell—like the poor soul you told me of yesterday—I would gladly think that you beckoned to me, and would turn back and join you in your living grave."

She reached her hand out with a loving smile, and he took it in his own, and hand and hand they hastened over the perilous way. Richard, because he knew his cousin and how little likely she was to be alarmed, far less to despair, unless upon sufficient grounds, was aware of their extreme danger; otherwise, a stranger to the place would at present have seen no immediate cause for fear. The sea was yet a great way off, save for a few inlets and patches which began to make themselves apparent as if by magic; moreover, the shore to which they were hastening had become so near that they could plainly perceive the knot of people gathered round the guide, and hear the words, "Quick, quick," which he never ceased to utter through his trumpet, with the utmost distinctness. It seemed impossible that two persons should be doomed to perish within sight and hearing of so many fellow-creatures, all eager for their safety. And yet both were doomed. Between them and the land lay the larger of the two rivers that emptied themselves into the bay at high water, and ran into the open sea at low. The current was setting in by this time very swiftly, and the swirling turbid waters were broadening and deepening every minute. The banks of this stream, instead of being firm sand, were now a mass of white and slippery mud, a considerable extent of which lay between the *eau* and the shore; so that it was impossible to carry or even to push down a boat upon its treacherous surface to the river's edge. The bank upon which the two unfortunates were standing was not as yet so much dissolved as the other, but they could feel it growing more and more unstable beneath their feet, as they now stood on the brink of the *eau*, not fifty yards from their would-be rescuers. The scene was only less terrible to these than to the doomed pair themselves. Women could be seen among the crowd wringing their hands in agony, and strong men turning their heads away for the pity of so heart-rending a spectacle. Once, either moved by the entreaties of others, or unable to restrain his own feverish desire to be doing something, a horseman spurred his steed upon the ooze, as though he would have crossed the river to their aid; but the poor animal, well accustomed to the sands, and conscious of danger, at first refused to move, and when compelled, at once began to sink, so that it was with difficulty that either man or horse reached land again.

"Swim, swim!" cried the guide, through his trumpet.

"Yes, swim," echoed Agnes. "How selfish it was of me to forget that. It is very difficult, but to a good swimmer like yourself it is not utterly hopeless. Let the tide carry you up yonder as far as the island, Richard, then strike out for that spit of land; there is firm footing there. Take your coat off, and your shoes; quick, quick!"

The young man looked mechanically in the direction indicated, then smiled sadly, and shook his head.

"We are not going to be parted, Agnes; we are to be together for ever and ever. You believe that I love you now?" added he with grave tenderness.

She did not hear him. Her eyes were fixed on a high-wooded hill, close by the promontory I have mentioned, with the roof of a house showing above the trees. This was her home.

"Poor papa, poor papa!" murmured she; "what will he do now, all alone?" The tears stood in her eyes for the first time since she had been made aware of their danger. Both had now to step back a little, for the bank was crumbling in; the increasing stream gnawed it away in great hunches, which fell into the current, making it yet more turbid than before. There was still a considerable tract of sand, firm to the eye, although in reality quite unstable, lying between them and the sea; but the latter had now altered its plan of attack. It no longer made its inroads here and there, running slyly up into creeks and coves of sand, and holding possession of them until reinforcements came up, but was advancing boldly in one long low line, with just a fringe of foam above it like the sputter of musketry. In addition to the threatening growl noticeable so long, could also now be heard a faint and far-off roar.

"It will soon be over now, Richard," said the young girl, squeezing the hand that still held her own; "that sound is our death-knell."

"What is it, Agnes?"

"It is the tidal wave they call the Bore. It may be half an hour away still; it may be but a few minutes. But when it comes it will overwhelm us."

She raised her eyes to the blue sky, which was smiling upon the scene of despair and death, after nature's cruel fashion, and her lips, which had not lost their color, moved in silent prayer. Suddenly a great shout from the shore, echoed by another from Richard, drew her thoughts again to earth.

The crowd of people on the shore were parting to admit the passage of a man and horse, both so large that the guide and the animal he bestrode seemed by comparison to become a boy and pony.

"What are they shouting for, Agnes?" asked the young man, eagerly.

"Because," said she, "yonder is the man who can save us yet, if man can do it."

She spoke with calmness, but there was a flush upon her cheek, and a light in her eye, which the other did not fail to mark.

"Who is it?" asked he half angrily. For if men can be angry on their death-beds, how much more when, though in view of death, they are still hale and strong.

"It is John Carlyon, of Woodlees," said she.

CHAPTER III.
THE ROAN AND HIS RIDER.

IT might well have surprised and shocked a stranger to have seen that cluster of village folks watching for so long the approaching doom of two of their fellow-creatures, without making—with the exception of the attempt we have mentioned—a single effort to save them. Their inaction, however, really arose from their thorough knowledge of the fruitlessness of such efforts. It was not the first time, nor the second, nor the fiftieth that the sea had thus marked out for itself prey in that same bay hours before it actually seized it, quite as certain of its victims as though its waves were already rolling over them. Hundreds of years ago it was the same, when the guides were paid with Peter's pence by the old Priors of Mellor, and were prayed for during their perilous passage together with those entrusted to their guidance by the monks on Lily Isle, the ruins of whose oratory could yet be seen. As *Ave* and *Kyrie* had failed to save those who had delayed too long upon that treacherous waste, so good wishes availed not now. And they were all which could be given in the way of aid. It was very doubtful whether Richard Crawford could have saved himself by swimming even at the moment when it had been suggested to him. The strength of the tide of the eau was very great; "the furious river struggled hard and tossed its tawny mane," and firm footing there was none on either bank. It was this last fact which the stranger was slow to comprehend.

"Surely," he would say, "a good swimmer has only got to wait for the water to come up." But long before it could do so the victim found himself in something which was neither land nor water, and in which he could neither stand nor swim. Neither could boat nor horse get at him under such circumstances.

When the two cousins had first made toward the shore, they had to traverse only wet sand, which somewhat clogged their footsteps. Some patches of this were more watery than others, and through these, progress was more difficult. Presently the whole surface of the bay assumed this character, and then where the patches had been, appeared shallow strips of water, as yet unconnected—superficially at least—with the sea. Through these they had to make their way, ankle-deep in sand, knee-deep in water. The bank upon which they now stood was higher than the surrounding space, and as I have said, had only suffered the first change, from sand to a sort of white mud. The people on shore were as perfectly aware of what these two had had to contend with, as though they had accompanied them in their useless flight; and they knew now, as well as Agnes knew, that their life was to be reckoned by minutes, and depended upon how rapid or how slow might be the advance of the Bore or tidal wave.

This wave which in winter or in storm was sometimes as tall as a man, was in summer very much less: but it never came up until the whole surface of the bay was under water, and all hope was therefore gone for them it found there.

It was to the menacing roar of this coming doom that both victims and spectators were now listening.

"It will be twenty minutes yet," said some among the latter; "Nay, not so long," said others; "The sooner the better, poor things," added one, to which many murmured a sorrowful assent.

All seemed to know how the sad mischance had occurred, and yet no one alluded to the man whose forgetfulness or more culpable neglect had caused the catastrophe. The reason of this was that William Millet, Stephen's only son, was among the crowd. His face was deadly pale, and twitched like one with the palsy. He would have given his life to have saved the victims of his father's folly, and, indeed, had almost done so, for it was he who had mounted the guide's horse, awhile ago, and strove to reach them. Every word that was spoken around him, notwithstanding the reticence above alluded to, went to his heart like a stab.

"How I wish we had brought them home in our cart," said one woman, who had been cockling upon the sands the preceding tide.

"Ay, or we in ours," returned another; "but there, how is one to know? Who could have thought—" and William knew, though his own eyes were fixed upon the cousins, that a glance from the speaker toward where he stood, concluded the sentence.

"The Lord will take Miss Agnes to himself, that's sure," said one in a solemn voice. "It is the poor folk who are to be pitied, rather than she, for they will miss her."

"Ay, that's true," murmured many voices.

"She will be in heaven in twenty-five minutes, or half an hour at farthest," continued the same speaker, with exactness—a good man, by trade a cobbler, but who, imagining himself to have the gift of preaching, was sometimes carried beyond his last.

"And the lad, too, I hope," returned a fresh-featured dame somewhat sharply. "Did you not see how he would not leave her when Dick called out to him to swim. That will be taken into the account, I suppose."

"We have no warrant for that," resumed the cobbler, shaking his head.

"God will never be hard upon one so young and so bonny as yon," rejoined the dame, with a certain emphasis about the words, implying that the cobbler was neither the one nor the other.

"I trust not," returned the other simply. "Let us all entreat of Him to be merciful to those who are about to fall into His hands."

If there had been time to reflect, not a few of those present would doubtless have hesitated to follow such a spiritual leader as the mender of material soles; but as he raised his voice in passionate pleading with the Almighty—using such texts of Holy Writ as seemed to him applicable to the circumstances—every man bared his head, and every voice joined audibly in the Amen that followed his supplication.

Never, perhaps, since the days of the Early Church, was any company gathered together by the sea-shore in act of worship more reverent and awe-struck than was that little handful of fisher-folk in those brief moments; but while the last solemn word was being spoken, and its sound growing faint and far overhead, as though already upon its way to the Throne of Grace, the clatter of a horse's hoofs was heard from the village street, and down the steep lane which led from it to the sea came a rider at full speed. His own height, as far as you might judge a man in the saddle, must have been considerably more than six feet, but the red roan which he bestrode was so large and powerful, that steed and rider together looked quite colossal; just as though a mounted statue had descended from its pedestal, as in the days of portents.

"Make way, make way," cried he; and as the obedient crowd parted to right and left, "A rope, a rope!" he added, then galloped right on to the white unctuous mud. So great and swift was the impetus with which he rode that he got beyond the place which the guide's horse had reached without much difficulty or hindrance. Here, however, the roan began to stagger and slide, and then as he sunk fetlock deep, and farther, into the impatient ooze, to flounder in a pitiful manner. Upon such unstable footing the weight of his rider was evidently too much for his powers. Ere, however, that thought could shape itself into words among the lookers-on, the man leaped from his saddle, and while obliged to shift his own feet with the utmost rapidity to save them from a like fate, he drew the animal by main force out of the reluctant mud, and led him trembling with sweat and fear, to the brink of the *eau*. Now the river, although swollen by this time to a most formidable breadth, and running very swift and strong, had about this spot a bed comparatively firm, and which seldom shifted; so that what seemed to the superficial observer the most perilous part of the whole enterprise—namely, the passage of the river—was, in reality, the least difficult. Horse and man seemed to be equally well aware of the fact, and when the former felt the water up to his girths, he for the first time ceased to plunge and struggle, and even stood still for his master to remount him.

"Up stream, up stream," roared the guide with trumpet voice to the two unfortunates, who were watching the heroic efforts of their would-be rescuer with earnest eyes; "he can not come straight across." And indeed, while he yet spoke, the current had taken man and horse, despite their weight and determination, many yards to the northward; and the two cousins hurried in that direction also, over the fast-dissolving ooze. If once the roan lost footing, himself and master would have been carried to a spot where the river ceased to be fordable, and where the banks were even of a less trustworthy nature than those between which they now were; and, but that his heavy rider kept him down, this would have assuredly happened. With such a weight upon him it seemed easier to the poor animal to walk than to swim; his vast strong back was totally submerged, and only the saddle visible; but his head showed grandly above the stream, the fine eyes eager for the opposite bank, and the red nostrils pouring their full tide of life in throbs like those of a steam-engine. But for that head the rider himself, half hidden by the tawny waves, might have been taken for a centaur. He looked like one quite as ready to destroy men's lives, if that should be necessary, as to save them; to snatch a beauty for himself from a Lapithean husband, as to preserve her from the ancient ravisher Death! He was by no means a very young man; but if he had passed the prime of life, he was still in its vigor, and that vigor was something Herculean. His hat had fallen during the late struggle with his horse, and the short brown curls that fringed his ample forehead showed here and there but scantily, although they had no tinge of grey. His large brown eyes, although fixed steadfastly enough upon the point he hoped to reach, exhibited little anxiety, and certainly no fear. Their expression, although far from cold, was cynical, and the firm lips, pressed tightly together as they now were, yet spoke of recklessness if not of scorn. The gallant roan, as he neared the wished-for shore, drew gradually out of water, until his girths scarce touched the stream: but his rider made no attempt to force him to climb the bank.

"Be ready," shouted he to those who awaited him; then leaving the saddle, he hastily motioned to Agnes to take the vacated seat. "No, no!" cried he, as she was about to put her foot into the stirrup-leather, "you must trust to me to hold you on," and he passed his huge arm round her dainty waist. "Hold fast by the other stirrup," said he to Richard, "and stand against the stream all you can." Then, leading his horse close under the bank to southward, so far as he judged safe in order to allow for shifting, he turned his head to land. A shout of admiration had burst forth from those on shore when he had succeeded in crossing the *eau*; but every voice was hushed as the horse with its fair burden, and the two men on either side her saddle, began the return passage. Nothing was heard save the labored breathing of the roan and the increasing roar of the ocean, enraged, as it seemed, at this attempt to deprive it of its lawful prey. Richard, who was upon the side next the sea, had trouble enough to keep his footing; but the stranger had allotted to himself a far more difficult task; his huge form leaned against the horse with all its strength, and so strove to neutralize the rush of the tide, which was bearing them all to northward.

"God bless you, Mr. Carlyon," said Agnes once, and then was silent.

The strong man bowed gravely and smiled—though his air was not so confident as when he had made the passage alone—but answered nothing. Indeed, he had no breath to spare. Clogged with his wet clothing, pushing through sand and water, and fighting against the weight of his two companions and the roan, as well as against the stream, his task was arduous enough, even for one of his enormous strength. The water deepened with every step, and the force of the current increased.

"Not so fast," cried Richard, staggering in vain to keep his feet.

"Faster or you are a dead man," was the stern response.

They were at the very worst by that time and in the centre of the flood. Richard almost neck deep; the horse still feeling ground, but with his very nostrils in the water; Agnes deadly pale, but bearing herself as resolute and quiet as though she were Undine herself. The great shoulders of John Carlyon still showed above the tawny waves. They had passed the centre, and were getting into shallower water.

The breathing of the horse was, however, growing very labored and painful.

"He will never climb the bank," said Agnes, calmly.

"I know it," returned the other; "but I shall save you, do not fear."

His eyes fell once upon her grave and glorious beauty, then turned anxiously to southward. The roaring of the sea was growing very near. As they reached the bank, and before the roan could lift his fore-feet, and so place the barrier of his neck and shoulders between his burden and the shore, John Carlyon's arm swept Agnes from the saddle and drew her up the bank. The poor roan, the bulk of his protector thus withdrawn, uttering a terrible snort of fear and anguish, was instantly whirled away. Agnes had stretched out her hand and caught her cousin by the collar of his coat, or he would assuredly have shared the same fate. As it was, the three together struggled on through the water, for all was water now. It was then, for the first time, that Agnes uttered a stifled cry of horror. The tidal wave was coming; within ten feet of them it reared its creaming crest. Carlyon saw it too, and stretched out one giant arm as though for help. As he did so something struck him sharply in the face, and his fingers closed upon a rope, thrown at him lasso-wise by some one on the land. The next moment all three were under water, with a noise in their ears like the roar of a broadside from a three-decker. But the line was being pulled taut, though not too sharply; and presently the three were dragged on shore in a tangled mass, like some great waif from a wreck.

The first to rise was Richard Crawford. He pushed his wet hair back with both his hands, and gazed vacantly at the other two, round whom the crowd was standing, although at some little distance, for they knew better, from long experience of like mischances, than to throng close about folks in such a plight, who need air above all things, and to whom at first all help is an incumbrance.

As consciousness returned, Richard's brow began to knit, and he strove feebly to unclasp the arm that still encircled his cousin's waist. But the powerful muscles mechanically retained their hold.

Presently Agnes opened her large eyes and gazed wonderingly about her; the color rushed to her white cheeks, and her hand, too, sought to release itself from that which held her. At the touch of her cold fingers those of her preserver began at once to relax their grasp; but the next instant, catching sight of the ghastly face beside her, she desisted.

"He is dying," cried she; "fetch the doctor. Fetch Mr. Carstairs. Quick, quick!" and taking one great palm between her small hands she strove to recall in it the warmth that seemed to have fled forever. Truly it seemed strange enough that this strong man, to whose Herculean force the pair were indebted for their safety, should be the last of the three to recover from the late shock. The fine face was pale as marble, except for a certain blue tint about the temples; the eyes between their half-shut lids expressionless and dim; the limbs rigid; and the still curved left arm lying motionless beside him, which had so lately borne her from death to life. He did not want for tendance: other hands were chafing his wrists, and had unloosed his neckcloth, and propped his stately head; but she knelt by him still, ceaselessly adjuring them to fetch the doctor. At last he came; a middle-aged, intelligent man, with a quick step and voice.

"Bring blankets," cried he, sharply. Then poured the contents of a phial into the unresisting mouth.

"Is he drowned?" asked the young girl, in an agonized whisper.

"No, ma'am, no, it is not that," returned he, hastily, but with an anxious look. "Here, William, you and three more take Mr. Carlyon to my house. Gently, gently; keep his head up. No, my dear Miss Agnes," said he firmly, as the girl strove to accompany the party, still clinging to the hand that hung down cold and lifeless, "your presence will be worse than useless. Go home at once, and·you, Mr. Richard, too"—for the young man had constituted himself one of the bearers of the inanimate body—"unless, that is, you wish me to have three patients to attend to instead of one. Stop!" The white set lips of John Carlyon began to twitch a little, and Mr. Carstairs bent down to listen. "Yes, Miss Agnes is safe, sir; don't disturb yourself, I beg. It was William Millet who threw the rope. There, I will answer no more questions; move on, men."

"He has spoken, he will live, then," exclaimed Agnes, joyfully. "Oh, tell me, we have not caused his death?"

"No, ma'am, *you* have not caused it. That is—what nonsense I am talking. You should never bother a medical man, Miss Agnes," said Mr. Carstairs, testily, "during his professional duties. Go home and get to bed. You are as wet as a mermaid. I will bring you word of Mr. Carlyon to-night."

"This Carlyon is a fine fellow, whoever he is," observed Richard Crawford, as the two cousins walked swiftly homeward by the side of the bay that had so nearly proved their grave; "but who *is* he?"

"He is the owner of Woodlees, the estate that lies between us and the earl's."

"A rich man, I suppose, then. Is he a married man, or a widower?"

"He has never been married, I believe," said Agnes, changing color in spite of all her efforts to prevent it.

"Oh, yes, I remember now," observed Richard, dryly. "He lives rather a queer life, don't he?"

Agnes threw at him a glance of reproach, almost of resentment.

"He has just saved our lives," said she.

"Yes, true; he is a fine fellow, as I said, whatever he is. I shall certainly make a point of calling upon him to thank him in person on behalf of us both. Carlyon — what an odd name. It's scarcely English."

"It was once French. The old family name, they say, was Cœur-de-Lion," answered Agnes, coldly; "nor can it be denied that its present inheritor worthily bears the title. He has shown himself a lion-hearted man to-day."

CHAPTER IV.

A TERRIBLE TURK.

"WELL, doctor, you are not going to send for Puce, are you?" was the inquiry addressed by John Carlyon, as he lay upon the horse-hair sofa in Mr. Carstairs's uncheerful little parlor. The two men were alone; those who had carried the patient to the doctor's house having departed, well pleased enough to see the large blue eyes of Squire John gaze upon them once more in their old kindly fashion. "It is not time to think about the Rev. Mr. Puce yet, is it?"

"No," returned the doctor, gravely; "it is not necessary to think about Puce, Mr. John; but it is always worth a man's while to think about God."

Mr. Carlyon turned his yet pale face very sharply round upon the speaker. But Mr. Carstairs was gazing through the wire blind upon the dusty village street, and he could gather nothing from the expression of his shoulders.

"My good friend, you are rather like Puce yourself in one thing," resumed the patient, dropping his eyelids, partly from weariness — for he was still very weak — and partly because it was his wont so to do when indulging in sarcasm; "although his trade is to cure souls, he dearly loves to recommend all sorts of patent medicines, which he protests have done him good; so much so that I sometimes think he is a paid agent of Parr or Holloway; and you in the same way, and perhaps in retaliation for his conduct, I have observed to take *your* opportunities of dropping in a word or two of religion."

"It is not so altogether unreasonable, Mr. Carlyon, as you seem to imagine; if I had made an investment which produced a very tolerable percentage even now, and which promised to pay a thousandfold at some future time, is it not natural that I should give a hint to my friends that they also might lay out their money to so great an advantage?"

"Very good, doctor. It is extraordinary with what a gift of imagery the profession of religion seems to endow its advocates. They take up their parable at the shortest possible notice, just as a mere infidel might pick up a stone. There is Puce, for instance, who when pushed by simple folk like me, will envelop himself in a mist of metaphor, like any cuttle fish, and so escape. When a man becomes a parson it really seems as if he could no longer speak straight. His words begin to wheel about the subject supposed to be next his heart, 'like doves about a dove-cote,' but never alight upon it. He studies to say the least he can in the most words."

"I don't think you are much worried by sermons, Mr. Carlyon," returned the other, dryly.

"Well, it is true, I don't give Puce much opportunity for punishing me in that way. But I heard him preach only last Sunday."

"You were not at church, were you?" ejaculated the other, turning a face of great amazement upon his patient.

"Not *in* church, but I was just outside, so that not a single trope was lost upon me. Berild and I were wandering about in the sunshine, and while he cropped a little churchyard grass, I thought I would get some spiritual provender for myself. We were quite alone out there, for the earl was at church — he never fails to go once a year, you know, and not a soul (worth saving, that is) in all the parish but was there. Not only a great muster of carriage people and gentility, but all the fine-wooled sheep from the cobbler's fold. You may talk of the dangers of dissent, but if they get to be serious you have only to ordain half a hundred of the junior nobility and send them into the disaffected districts, and not a female saint but will return to her allegiance forthwith. The attention of the congregation — nobody thought of looking at *me* when I peeped in — seemed to be about equally divided between Heaven and his lordship; but that of Puce, I will do him the justice to say, was entirely concentrated upon the crimson pew. 'Now,' thought I, 'here is our reverend friend's opportunity for saying a word in season. He has this chance but once in twelve months, and surely he will not fail to take advantage of it. There will be something in the discourse for his lordship's particular ear (as, indeed, there was, although scarcely of an edifying kind), or else he is even a more pitiful sneak than I take him for.' I confess I was curious to hear the elegant periphrasis by which he would delicately refer to the existence of Mademoiselle Debonnaire, the latest acquisition to our respectable neighborhood, and whom I had just met, with two of his lordship's grooms sitting behind her, driving a pair of the prettiest little cream-colored ponies in the world. An allusion to this particular weakness, if not to the object of it, might surely have been hazarded, considering the very advanced age of the noble sinner, and the extreme probability that Puce would never catch him at church again. And yet what do you think that sermon was about? From first to last it was a denunciation of the unpardonable crime of poaching. The snare of the wicked one was represented in the literal form of a wire and horse-hair springe; his net was a partridge net; and the human agent he found most ready to his hand was an uninquiring game dealer."

"The fact of Puce happening to be a mean skunk—which I grant very readily," observed Mr. Carstairs, cheerfully, "does not invalidate the claims of religion. Of course it is very sad that a clergyman should pander to his patron in the manner you describe, and I have no doubt truly, for I heard that his lordship congratulated him on his discourse. But the man is not aware of his own degradation. Many persons who fill our pulpits are quite ignorant of the true nature and beauty of the thing which it is unhappily their lot to preach. You might as well expect to find in an organ-grinder, nay, in the monkey whose mission it is to sit upon the organ, an appreciation of Mozart."

"It appears to me, doctor," observed Mr. Carlyon, slyly, "that that last remark reflects upon the Church as well as the parson. You don't think much of hurdy-gurdies, I suppose?"

"I think a good deal of Mozart," answered the other, coldly. "Man's attempts to express his religious sentiments may fall very short of what he feels; his apparatus of worship may be exceedingly incomplete; but to deny the necessity for an operation merely because our means are inadequate to perfect success, seems to me illogical; and, if you will forgive me, rather ungenerous."

"Now, don't get angry, my dear doctor," observed Mr. Carlyon, laughing; "*I* have no objection to the monkey and the organ, I do assure you. I even pay them what is customary without a murmur, although they are far from pleasing to me. I am not like the cobbler who is always refusing to pay his church-rates."

"No; nobody accuses *you* of being a hypocrite, Mr. Carlyon," returned the doctor, not unwilling to exchange argument for agreement, even if only upon the demerits of a ranter. "That Job Salver is certainly a most offensive humbug. I understand the fellow was singing a psalm-tune on the shore yonder, within hearing of that poor girl and boy, instead of stirring a finger to help them. Both would have solved the problem long ere this which you and I have often so vainly contended about, had their safety depended upon that whining charlatan, who ventures to oppose himself to all authority, speaking evil of dignities and things that he understands not."

"And yet," said Mr. Carlyon, thoughtfully, "it is very curious—but the singing of that very hymn did, in point of fact, save those two lives. Red Berild and I were going slowly home, and had even reached the cross-roads, when the sound of the psalm-singing reached us; whereupon, instead of riding down the hill to the Hall, I cantered up the rise to see what they were making such a noise about. Then, thanks to poor Berild, who did the half mile in about a minute, we got down just in time. It was a precious narrow thing even then; and if it had not been for William Millet and the rope, we should all have been in kingdom-come by this time—that is, if your views are correct. If otherwise, we should have been, as the jockeys say, 'nowhere'—out of the human race altogether."

"And the thought of that gave you no uneasiness, Mr. Carlyon, eh?" inquired the other sharply, and regarding his patient with great earnestness.

"I did not think about it, doctor, for there was no time for thought, but only for action. If I had been quite certain that I was going to my death, I don't quite know how I should have felt. All change is disagreeable to a man who has reached my time of life; if you were to tell me, 'You will die in an hour from this time exactly'—as in certain cases you doctors are acquainted with—it would 'give me a turn.' If I know myself, however, I should certainly entertain no fear. There is nothing terrible to me in the idea of annihilation."

"What? to lie in cold obstruction and to rot?"

"In other words, to go to sleep and not to wake again, my good doctor. What is there objectionable in that? That is one of the ideas which it is conventually agreed upon among religious people to shudder at. I am very much mistaken, however, if nine-tenths of the good folks, who express themselves so strongly upon this subject, would not gladly welcome extinction rather than run the risk of a much worse thing."

"What! would men be content to die like dogs?" exclaimed Mr. Carstairs.

"Ay; and most of them would think themselves lucky in so doing. I am as certain of that as that I am lying upon this sofa. Many who are not absolutely terror-stricken, are conscious that they have been more fortunate in this world than they deserve; and are afraid of matters being righted in the other to their own disadvantage. A few, such as my lord up at the park yonder, justly conclude (with some character in one of Bulwer's novels, I forget whom or which,) that it is doubtful whether, in any other state of life, they can possibly be so well off as they have been in this. For my own part I sympathize with none of these people; but I have not found life so pleasant as not to have got over my first love for her. It is only the young who are in reality enamored: for though the old cling to her oftentimes with impotent desire, it is not because they love her, but because they fear the shadow that is beckoning them away. As for myself, I have said I have no fear, and what loss can death inflict upon me? You and I are very good friends, doctor; but we can endure to part from one another though it even should be forever. Observe, for yourself, how absence cools the friendship of the very best of friends; the materials of it being generally far from lasting. Love, indeed, is said to be 'forevermore;' but I am not in a position to offer an opinion on that delicate matter; and as for the ties of blood, I am sure I could bear to part from my only sister, Margaret, with equanimity; and I rather fancy that both she and nephew George would suffer such a calamity with equal resignation, provided they got Woodlees."

"Mrs. Newman does not behave to you in a very sisterly manner, I must own," said the doctor, grimly; "but there is one excuse to be made for her; she is a bilious subject. Without revealing matters that should be sacred, I can assure you, as her medical attendant, that she has a great deal of bile."

"Has she?" returned the other, shrugging his shoulders. "I thought it was religion: the symptoms of both are often much alike to the unlearned."

"My dear Mr. Carlyon," said the doctor, earnestly, "I am no bigot; I don't print texts round the wrappers of my physic bottles as some do."

"What moderation!" exclaimed the other.

"But, I do confess," continued Mr. Carstairs, without heeding the interruption, "that nothing annoys me more than these ill-natured carpings against what is, to me, a great truth. From your lips they are especially obnoxious. Here is a man who has just risked his life—nay more, put it in the most eminent peril—to save two helpless fellow-creatures deserted by all other human aid—"

"Tut, my friend, you make too much of a small matter," interposed the other, with an air of some annoyance; "and besides, you know," he added gayly, "I have no right to any credit; it was not even a good action in your eyes."

"I am d—d if it was not!" cried Mr. Carstairs, slapping his hand upon the little round table till the phial danced in the tumbler.

"Nay, the condemnation falls on *me*," replied the other bitterly. "What, have you served the office of church-warden, and yet not learned that works done by unbelieving wretches (like me, my dear sir,) lack grace of congruity, and even have the nature of sin? It would have been wrong for me *not* to have assisted those two poor tide-bound fellow-creatures, and it was also wrong for me to do so. Hit high, hit low, we can never please you theological gentry."

The speaker's face was very stern and pale, and his voice shook with passion.

"I do not deny," he continued, "that there are worse churches than the Church of England. There is one that says 'For the manifestation of the glory of our Creator, some men are foreordained unto everlasting death;' and yet they say the nation that invented *that* dogma has no sense of humor. Well, sir, *your* Church is only a little less barbarous than this."

"John Carlyon, you ought to be ashamed of yourself," returned the doctor, walking swiftly toward the couch. "To say such words within sight of yonder church, where your poor father is lying in his grave, is shameful. You should have respect for his memory, if for nothing else. What an example of faith, of piety, of goodness, was thrown away upon you in that excellent man's life; how you disgrace his teaching; how you insult—"

"That will do, sir," said Carlyon, coldly, raising himself with difficulty from the sofa; "I congratulate you upon having discovered a method for shutting my mouth. I can walk alone, sir, thank you, very well."

So saying he seized his hat and staggered to the door. His countenance wore the same leaden hue as when he lay upon the beach, an hour or so ago, just rescued from the sea, but it had not the same vacant expression. He looked angry, and pained, but also something more and worse. If it had been possible in a man of such calibre—both mental and bodily—as John Carlyon, one would have said that he looked panic-stricken.

"I am sorry," began the doctor, pleadingly; "it was cruel and unfair, I own."

But holding up one hand as though to deprecate all farther talk, Carlyon groped about the door with the other, and presently getting it open, felt his way along the passage like a blind man, and so into the street, and took his way toward home.

"I am a beast," exclaimed Mr. Carstairs, self-reproachfully, standing in his little porch and watching his departing patient move slowly and painfully away. "And the beast which I am is an ass. I have done him more harm than good in every way. Matters could scarcely have been worse, had I told him the truth at once, although he did say it would have 'given him a turn,' and yet how could I have known that the mention of his father would have put him into such a state! it was a mercy he did not drop down dead at my very door. Such a gallant, honest fellow, too! He will be a loss to the world, although, may be, the world, as he says, will be no loss to him: but as for you, Robert Augustus Carstairs, F.R.C.S., and late overseer of this parish, when *your* turn comes to be grassed over, you will be a loss to nobody, being an ass."

CHAPTER V.
COMING HOME.

THE short, yet straggling street of the village of Mellor was always very quiet. There was but little traffic through it, and still less in it, for it contained but one shop, full indeed of the most various commodities, from Bath note-paper to lamp-black, from Dutch cheese to Lancashire clogs, but not much frequented by customers. Most people stopped at the window, and turned away again after dropping their letters into the slit beneath it, for it was also the post-office; and there were not many folks even to post letters at Mellor. The houses on the north side of the street, which was built on a hill, made the most show, standing back from the road, and at a considerable elevation above it, with neat little gardens, spread apron-wise before them; eye-shot from the windows of these dwellings flew over the heads of passers-by. On the south side the houses all looked out to seaward over unseen gardens of their own, and turned their backs to the road, so that it was quite possible, providing only that he escaped the notice of the lynx-eyed post-mistress, for a wayfarer, however remarkable in his personal appearance, to pass through Mellor street without being observed. During the dispatch of the mails at 5 P. M., a ritualist in full vestments, or the Lord Chief-Justice of the Queen's Bench, in wig and gown, might have very possibly made a progress through it from end to end (if only they maintained a dignified silence), without any Mellorite being the wiser.

It was about 5 P. M. that John Carlyon took his way through Mellor, and that he was not spoken with by any one after what had recently occurred was a pretty convincing proof that he was not seen. The village inn, indeed, had more than its usual fringe of idlers about it, eagerly discussing the very occurrence in which he had so distinguished himself; but it stood apart from the road, on a little plateau of its own, and was avoided altogether by those who took the turning to the right which led to Mellor Church. Mr. Carlyon took this way. The church tower, being very highly placed, could be seen far out at sea, and was even used as a landmark for ships. The church-yard itself stood much above the village, and, indeed, was the highest point save Greycrags (whereon the house occupied by the Crawfords was situated, and after which it was named), within some miles of Mellor; it was therefore free from all overlookers. Something tempted him, as he passed by, to push open the wicket and enter that great green resting-chamber, where no sleeper turned uneasily on his pillow, or longed with impatience for the morning. Very many generations lay beneath those grassy mounds, or in the vaults of the old church, which was almost coeval with the abbey, the ruins of which could be seen from where he stood. Another phase of Christianity had succeeded to the ancient faith, but little change had been made in externals. Two stone images in lichen-covered niches stood on either side the porch, but time or the sea-winds had deprived them of all recognizable features; they might be meant to represent saints or demons. The stoup for holy water still had its place in the wall. Within lay many a cross-legged crusader—

> Knights, ladies, praying in dumb orat'ries,

or

> Emprison'd in black, purgatorial rails;

the dead representatives of a dead form of creed, lying, unargumentatively enough, beside Protestant lords of the manor, and other modern worthies of high degree. In the superior sanctity of the chancel, under what looked like a four-post bedstead of marble, hung with 'scutcheons, and sculptured with heraldic emblems, reposed the long line of ancestors of Charles, Earl Disney, whose anxiety for the preservation of game had been so recently sympathized with from that moth-eaten pulpit.

"All silent and all damned," quoted Carlyon, thoughtfully, as he gazed through the iron gate which suffered the cool evening air to purify this sanctuary, while it kept more substantial intruders out. "There is nobody at least to contradict it. What thousands of years of death have these good folks to tell of, yet not an hour's experience will the greatest gossip among them reveal."

He turned from the dark porch, where a certain musty flavor of mortality seemed to make itself apparent, and set his face to the sea-breeze, fresh as on the day when it first blew from the gates of the sun.

The wavy west was one great field of gold, with just a ripple upon it like corn at harvest-time that smiles to find the sovereign wind its wooer. A few white sails flecked its glittering surface, and a faint black line of smoke above one outgoing steamship blurred the red sky. From the village beneath thin blue smoke ascended for a little way, till it mixed with the bluer air and was lost; and far off, on the other side of the bay, wreaths of grey marked the unseen spots where man was living and laboring. Here was death—yonder was life; you seemed to step from one to the other at a single stride. Both hushed, for not a sound could be heard, save the dreamy lap of the sea, less like sound than silence; yet the one so chill and hopeless, the other so bright and busy!

"There seems certainly something in what Carstairs says," mused Carlyon; "that is, at times. To lie here forever, first bones, then dust, has truly little charm; and if it be so, death is a bathos, and the scheme of creation—that is the proper phrase, I believe—a total failure. Perhaps it is: who knows?"

It was not, however, for purposes of philosophic speculation that the speaker had sought this place of tombs; and the mention of Mr. Carstairs seemed to remind him, although indeed he had not forgotten it, but purposely procrastinated the matter, of what had attracted him thither. He walked with a quick step toward a secluded corner of the church-yard, and black with the shadow of an enormous yew; within a square of small stone pillars, not unlike mile-stones, and connected by iron chains, stood a huge monument of granite.

"Thanks to him, I have never set foot here save last Sunday, since the day we buried him; so this will be new to me," muttered the visitor, as he held aside a layer of yew and let the sunshine in upon the gilded letters of the inscription, now fast fading and almost effaced—

TO THE MEMORY OF
RALPH CARLYON,
OF WOODLEES,
A DEPUTY LIEUTENANT FOR THE COUNTY
AND JUSTICE OF THE PEACE.
A Prudent Father,
A Pattern Husband,
A Perfect Christian.
He closed a Life of Piety, Feb. IXth, 1840.

"Those are Meg's adjectives," muttered the intruder, grimly; "but what is this in Latin? I did not give her credit for the classics.

'Gone to join the majority.'

That was not Meg's, I'm sure. Ah! I remember now. He told me something of his wish to have a certain sentence placed above her grave, and I—thinking it was some pious text—bade her let it be done. Well, this is truth, at all events, and consistency likewise, for this perfect Christian and deputy-lieutenant always held with the majority while he was alive. But, silence, bitter tongue. *De mortuis nil nisi bonum;* and moreover, this dead man was my father. Let me try to feel pious and regretful at the tomb of my parent. Alas! I can not do it. But the doctor was wrong too when he accused me of undutifulness to this man. His example of faith has *not* been thrown away upon his son. I have *not* disgraced his teaching. I *have* had respect for his memory, if for nothing else, heaven knows! Ralph Carlyon," murmured he, after a pause, "I forgive you; and if what these grave-stones preach be true, God himself can scarce do more. You have placed a gulf between me and all good folks, dead and alive, as broad and impassable as that which is said to separate the wicked from the blessed in the world to come. Thanks to you, I have no happiness in the present, nor hope in the future. Forty years of wasted life lie already behind me; there may be as many still to come, for I am very strong. Is it likely that these will be more tolerable than those already passed, with youth exchanged for age, and strength for weakness? It is idle to suppose it; the years must soon draw nigh of which, even good men say, they find no pleasure in them. I have no friend in either heaven or earth. My kindred wish me dead that they may possess my goods. They are welcome, I am sure, although I doubt whether old Robin and the rest would like the change of dynasty. I wish they had had their desire this very day. I wish that William Millet had been a little less ready with his rope. But no; I don't say that, for then there would have been an angel less in the world—Agnes Crawford. I believe in angels so far. It would have been worse for others, if better for me. She is every body's friend—every body's, that is, who is wretched—except mine. They have told her lies about me without doubt, and even the truth would make her shrink from me as she never shrinks from mere pestilence and contagion."

He was leaning over the wicket gate and looking northward, where Greycrags, clothed and crowned with its verdant and noble trees, rose from the margin of its little bay like one green tower.

"No woman loves me, or will ever love me, being what I am," he went on; "and least of all, one like her." A far-off noise—the beat of a horse's hoof—struck upon his ear. "Even my horse is lost; the only living thing that cared for me. Poor Berild! you died doing your duty, good nag, and if there be a heaven for horses—why, surely I should know that footfall; and unless there are equine ghosts that haunt the way to their late stables, this is my own Red Berild coming home!"

He passed swiftly through the gate, and, standing in the middle of the road, clapped his hands together and whistled shrilly. Immediately the trotting sound was exchanged for a canter; and as the coming steed turned the corner and came within sight, a faint but joyful whinny proclaimed his recognition of his master. He never stopped till he had his nose in his human friend's hand, and was rubbing his tall, stiff ear against his bosom. There was nothing wrong with him, as Carlyon's anxious inspection soon discovered; but he had evidently gone through great exertions. His heaving flanks were dripping as much with sweat and foam as with salt water; his broken bridle trailed upon the ground; his saddle was half turned round; his legs were covered with black mud and sand up to the knees.

It was a touching sight to see the meeting between those two old friends.

"My brave Berild!" cried one.

And the other, though he could not speak, answered, "Dear master!" with his eyes.

Then setting the saddle straight, and knotting the bridle, so that his favorite should not be incommoded, John Carlyon once more resumed his way toward home, man and horse walking together side by side. The former seemed for the time to have recovered his usual spirits, whistling snatches of melody, or even occasionally trolling out a patchwork of song; but as he began to descend the other side of the long hill, and to lose sight of all the glorious landscape, and of Greycrags with the rest, his depression returned.

Woodlees was not a place to create high spirits. It was a fine mansion, with a small deer-park attached to it, and no less than three terraced gardens. But the house itself was in a hollow. Notwithstanding that the sea lay so near, not a breath of its fresh clear air ever visited it. It seemed to have an atmosphere of its own, odorous indeed, but faint and oppressive, in which it was an effort to breathe. For size and antiquity, it was an edifice of which the proprietor might reasonably (if there is any reason in such pride) be proud. The hall, with its huge painted windows—the spoil, it was said, of Mellor Abbey—and splendidly carved chimney-piece, was undoubtedly very fine, if somewhat dim and cheerless. The grand staircase of polished oak had for its every alternate baluster a twisted column of vine or briony, but then it was a very sunshiny day on which they could be seen without a candle. There were only two cheerful rooms in the whole house. One, the large drawing-room, now never used, the French windows whereof opened immediately upon the Rosary, and over the huge fireplace of which was a vast sheet of glass, so that you could sit in the warm glow and watch the snow-flakes whiten the broad carriage drive,

B

and deck the evergreens in bridal raiment. The other, the octagon chamber in the tower, John Carlyon's smoking-room, whence could be seen Mellor Church and Greycrags, and, far to the south, a strip of distant sea that was never sand.

Mr. Carlyon made straight for the stables, and saw the wants of his four-footed friend attended to with his own eyes, then strolled across the garden toward the house. At the open front door stood an old man with a scared face.

"God 'a mercy, Mister John! what is it now?"

"What is what now, Robin?" echoed the squire, in an amused tone.

"Why, your masquerading, sir!"

"Oh yes! I had forgotten. I could not think what made them stare so in the stable. I have got Mr. Carstairs's clothes on, that's all; and they don't fit."

"Well, well, sir, you are the squire now; you do 'is you please. But I don't think my old master would ever have exchanged clothes with the parish doctor."

"I dare say not," returned Carlyon, dryly. Then, after a pause, he added, laying his hand upon the old man's shoulder, "I know it is undignified, Robin; but I could not help it. Red Berild and I were caught by the sea, and so got wet through. Mr. Carstairs was good enough to rig me out."

"Ah!" sighed the butler, shaking his white head as he made room for the squire to pass in, "my old master never *would* have been caught by the sea, not he."

CHAPTER VI.
A COUPLE OF VISITORS.

WHILE Mr. Carlyon was yet arranging himself in garments more adapted to his six-feet-three of bone and muscle than the habiliments of the little doctor, Robin came up to say that two gentlemen were waiting for him down stairs —Mr. Crawford and Mr. Richard Crawford.

"I will be down directly," said the squire, with a flush of pleasure; "into which room have you shown them?"

"Into the master's room, of course, Mr. John. Where else?" inquired the domestic.

"Very good, Robin," was the quick reply.

John Carlyon particularly disliked that room, and the old butler knew it; but at the same time thought it his duty to combat so unnatural an aversion. It had been the favorite chamber of John's father, and ought, one may suppose, to have been agreeable to his son on that account. Otherwise, it had certainly few attractions of its own, being the gloomiest of all the reception-rooms. A small apartment shut within an angle of the building, into whose old-fashioned, diamond-shaped panes the sun rarely peeped, and when it did so, could throw no cheerful gleam upon the cedarn wainscot, or the few family pictures disposed—and not happily disposed—upon its sombre surface. It seemed as though the old gentleman had preferred the company of the worst favored among all his ancestors with one exception. This was the full-length portrait of a young girl, whose short-waisted attire and tower-like arrangement of her long fair hair, could not deprive her of the admiration due to great natural beauty. Seldom as it was that a sunbeam struggled in so far, when it did reach that exquisite face the whole room was lit up with its loveliness. Those luxuriant locks glittered as though gold dust—the meretricious fashion of a much later date—had been scattered upon them; the peach-like cheeks glowed with bashful innocence; the blue eyes gazed at you with a tender simplicity that was inexpressibly touching. This portrait faced the fire-place; and when the fitful gleams of flame fell upon it, the mobile features seemed really instinct with life. Nothing else was bright in this room, except the silver hilts of a yataghan and dagger that hung over the chimney-piece, and were kept untarnished by the butler's careful fingers. They had been brought by his old master from the East, where he had traveled (not without some strange adventures, it was whispered, in which those mysterious weapons had borne their part) in his far back youth. Here, day after day, for many weary years the old man had sat, too feeble to stir abroad; and here, night after night, had lain when near to death. At last, upon a sofa bed, with his back to the picture and his face to the fire, he had died here. Perhaps it was its association with that last event which had made the cedar chamber distasteful to his son.

However, John Carlyon now entered it with a winning smile, and a courteous greeting for his two unexpected guests. With one of these, Richard Crawford, we are already acquainted; the other, his uncle, was a very tall old man, of distinguished appearance; one, who, though manifestly hale and vigorous, and as upright as a May-pole, gave the idea of extreme age, unless some sorrow had done the work of years in emaciating his lengthy limbs, and deepening the caverns of his eyes. These last were very bright and black, and shot from under thick, white eyebrows one swift, suspicious look as the squire entered, then gazed upon him frankly and gratefully enough.

"This is my uncle, Mr. Carlyon," said the younger of the two visitors, "come in person to thank you for your noble devotion in saving my dear cousin—".

"Nay, Richard," interposed the old gentleman, with dignity, and stretching forth an arm almost as long as Mr. Carlyon's own, though wasted to one-half its thickness, "I must thank him for *that* myself. You have preserved to me, sir, the dearest thing left to me in this world: my beloved and only daughter. Accept the gratitude of one who, but for you, would have found the little remnant of life he has still to live very miserable and barren."

, Mr. Crawford," an-
rning the pressure of
ngers, "to have been
;, not only to yourself,
'e experienced her un-
e so priceless as Miss
ou, sir," here he turned
vas giving utterance to
pressions of gratitude
I am sincerely glad to
given you a helping
: certainly might have

the old gentleman,
s me that death stared

ncle," answered Mr.
. Carlyon makes light
use he is used to risk
. Directly Agnes saw
s the man to save us,
ice before, as I hear,
"
ear young sir," inter-
" your good-will makes
or else you have been
rst place, Miss Agnes
nger to any one who
vho has ears to listen
ondly, possessing unu-
xcellent steed, I should
tot to have used them
n. Had I done other-
t would have been the
he, turning toward his
men who are over six
be courageous, should

e of his host's invitation
ord had been standing,
his visit was intended
; at these words he sank
earest chair, as though
) it by main force, and
long limbs trembled as
hin face grew more wan
cept that in the centre
'e was a spot of burning
leavored in vain to ar-

ar uncle is ill," cried
with violence; "what
— Wine — brandy?—

ould reply, the old man
a tolerably firm tones,
and needed no refresh-

r Mr. Carlyon, this in-
anned me. I am very
ese many years I have
be sight of a stranger is
Thank you: since the
take a little."
that he scarcely put his
hat while he spoke his

bright eyes once more flashed forth such glances of anger and suspicion as certainly showed no lack of vital power.

"There, I am better now already," resumed Mr. Crawford, with cheerfulness. "Certainly, if there is an *elixir vitæ* for the old at all it is French brandy. I have some in my cellar at Greycrags—and I trust you will come and dine with us shortly, and take a *petit verre* of it after dinner—which numbers as many years in bottle as I myself have been in the flesh; in other words, it is three-quarters of a century old."

"That would be a great attraction," said Mr. Carlyon, gallantly, "to any other house but Greycrags, which, however, possesses a much more priceless treasure. You have so overwhelmed me with your generous, but really exaggerated, gratitude, that I have not yet been able to ask after Miss Agnes herself. I trust she has escaped all consequences of her late adventure."

"Yes, I think I may say, that, except for a little fatigue, which it is only natural she should feel after having gone through so much excitement, my daughter is none the worse. She is used to cold, and even to getting wet through, in her perambulations among the poor. Richard and she walked home at their pace, so she has not felt even a chill. She was exceedingly anxious, however, upon your account; and indeed, from her statement, I scarcely hoped to find you so completely yourself again. So, as soon as Richard was ready, he and I drove to Mr. Carstairs's house, and finding you had gone home, ventured to follow you hither. We should have welcomed a much less valid excuse I am sure. What a charming place is this Woodlees of yours."

"It is picturesque," said Carlyon, shrugging his shoulders, "viewed from without; but a lonely and cheerless place to live in."

"That must be the fault of its proprietor, surely," observed Mr. Crawford with a meaning smile.

"No, sir, his misfortune," returned the other dryly. "However, my butler seems to have resolved you should be as unfavorably impressed as possible, by showing you into this sombre room."

"Ah! there I differ from you," answered the old gentleman. "For my part, I like gloom. The worst of Greycrags is, that it is so exceedingly light; its uniform cheerfulness oppresses one like a too lively talker—a companion who is always in high spirits. In the whole house there is no quiet little den like this, where an old man may sulk by himself out of the sunshine. Not, however, that any room can be gloomy with such a glorious picture as that in it. Richard and I were agreeing, before you came down, that we had never seen a more charming face on canvas. Woodlees could not have been so lonely at one time, if, as I conjecture, that beautiful creature was once its mistress."

John Carlyon bowed gravely.

"What tenderness of expression, Richard, is

there not?" continued the old man, rising and approaching the picture. "It is almost painful in its pathos. Now, what epoch can this lady have adorned?—not your own, of course, and scarcely mine."

"She was my mother, sir," observed Mr. Carlyon, dryly; then, after a pause, he added, "I should be sorry, Mr. Crawford, for you to carry away with you an impression of Woodlees derived from this apartment only. Let me persuade you to step up so far as the tower room, where perhaps you will take a cigar."

With these words he opened the door like one who would have no denial.

"My smoking-days are over," replied the old gentleman, smiling; "I am a worn-out profligate in that way, and can only partake of the mere flavor of vice from the snuff-box: yet I will gladly visit your sanctum. But what a long way up it is; why, it's quite an eyric."

"Yes, and here I sit, a wretched, middle-aged bird, all alone and moulting."

"It should be a nest full of eaglets; the very room for a nursery, sir," observed Mr. Crawford, unheeding the other's remark, and standing in the centre of the spacious chamber with its three huge windows. "What a beautiful prospect! See, Richard, yonder is Greycrags. My daughter and I have often wondered, Mr. Carlyon, to what use this tower which never shows a candle was put, and I think we must have come to the right conclusion, to judge at least by this telescope." He touched a large instrument standing on a brass tripod and turning on a pivot. "This is your observatory, is it not? You sit in the dark here and watch the stars."

"Not I," returned Mr. Carlyon, smiling; "you give me credit for much more learning than I possess. But to keep a lamp burning here is very dangerous to folks at sea. It has been mistaken more than once for the light at Mellor Point; and so, as I don't want to hold the candle in whose flame human moths may shrivel, I sit here in the dark. But as for the stars, I do not trouble myself with them."

"No: I see this is not a night-glass," observed Mr. Crawford, turning the instrument to southward. "But what a field it has! This must have cost you a great deal of money."

"I see you are a judge of telescopes, Mr. Crawford. Yes, this was really a great piece of extravagance for me to indulge in; but it forms my only amusement. This is my watch-tower, from whence I survey the world, both land and ocean. I can sit here and sweep fifty miles of sea. The least white speck out yonder, I can recognize, or know at least whether she is friend or stranger. Look now, to that sail in the southeast, hugging the land; that is his lordship's yacht, the *San Souci*—very much misnamed, by the bye, if all tales concerning her proprietor be true. One would think she would never weather the point yonder."

"She never will," observed Mr. Crawford decisively, who was watching her through the telescope.

"Not weather it! Permit me to look one moment. Ah, you don't know that yacht. She can sail nearer the wind than any craft in the bay. She is rounding it even now."

"She is doing nothing of the sort, sir," said the old man, smiling, and tapping his snuff-box; "look again."

"You are quite right, sir," cried Carlyon much astonished; "she has missed stays. And yet I would have bet a hundred to one. What an eye you have: why one would think you had been born a sailor.—Good heavens! Mr. Richard, your uncle is taken ill again. It must be the tobacco smoke; I am afraid it was wrong of us to light our cigars."

Mr. Carlyon threw up the north window, the opposite one being already open, and so created a strong draft.

"I am better now," said the old man, feebly; "but it was not the tobacco smoke."

"My uncle sits with me while I smoke, every night," said Richard, coldly; "it must have been the exertion of coming up so many stairs."

"Yes, that was it, no doubt," added Mr. Crawford. "I am a very old man, Mr. Carlyon, and you must excuse me."

"My dear Mr. Crawford, I only reproach myself for my thoughtlessness in having persuaded you—"

"Don't mention it, don't mention it, I beg," answered the old gentleman, hurriedly; "but if you will allow my nephew to ring for the carriage. We shall see you soon at Greycrags, Mr. Carlyon? I shall behave better, I hope, as your host than I have done as your guest."

Leaning heavily upon his nephew's shoulder, he slowly descended the uncarpeted and slippery stairs to the great hall; then, holding out a hand cold and clammy as that of a corpse, he bade Mr. Carlyon adieu, and climbed into his carriage. Richard also shook hands in as friendly a manner as he could assume; but the effort was sufficiently evident.

"I am sorry that I don't like Mr. Carlyon," observed the young man, after a long interval of silence, during which they had rolled through Mellor.

"Indeed," replied his uncle, in the dry and cynical tone which was habitual to him when there was no necessity for politeness. "That is of no great consequence; I beg, however, you will take pains to conceal your dislike while you remain under my roof."

CHAPTER VII.

ON THE ROAD.

THE day after that on which the events which we have narrated took place, John Carlyon took a ride toward Mellor; although at first he had turned his horse's head another way. On his road thither he met with an interruption. Scarce had he left his own gates, when he came upon a knot of cocklers, just returned from the bay, and apparently making up for their superstitious abstinence from quarrel on the sands* by "having it out" on dry land.

"What is the matter, my friends?" cried Carlyon, good-humoredly, interposing the huge bulk of Red Berild between two combative ladies who were contending for the possession of something that seemed to be all legs. "Have you found the spokes of one of Pharaoh's chariot wheels?"

At this, all burst into a guffaw, for Squire John was an immense favorite with this class, and his jokes always certain of acceptance.

"Well, sir, it might be," returned one; "at least, it's like nothing as we knows on; it seems of no manner of use, unless it's for pinching your fingers."

"Hulloa!" observed the squire, examining this curiosity with interest. "Where did you find this?"

"In the middle of the bay, sir, stuck in the sand," answered the same comely dame who had held contention with the spiritual cobbler on the previous evening. "It might have floated away but for this great pad as it had hold of, just like a crab."

"My good Mrs. Mackereth, this is a camp-stool," explained Mr. Carlyon. "The pad, as you call it, was once a drawing-book, the weight of which, as you say, without doubt prevented its wooden companion from going to sea."

"Lor, sir, why then they're Miss Crawford's!" ejaculated one of the late combatants. "I am sure if we had known, we should not have thought of keeping them. Directly after we have had our sup o' tea we'll take them round to Greycrags, won't us, Dick?"

"Stop; I am going there myself at once," said Carlyon, after a pause, "I will take the book with me. Here are two half-crowns for your trouble, and I dare say you will not leave the house empty-handed when you have taken the camp-stool."

"No, squire, that's not likely; God bless her! yes, bless her!" returned the cockler, dividing the spoil with her rival. "Miss Agnes has as open a hand as your own; long life to you both."

"And I wish that them hands was joined, and that that was your marriage blessing," observed Dame Mackereth, boldly. This good lady was deficient in delicacy as some of her sex and age not seldom are. The rest seemed to feel that their spokeswoman had gone a little too far, so her observation elicited no mark of adhesion. The situation was rather embarrassing for every body but herself, who pleased as a gunner who has sent a shell plump into the enemy's magazine, notwithstanding that it has destroyed a score or two of innocent non-combatants, indulged in a very hearty fit of laughter.

"Good-morning, my friends," said Carlyon, coldly, moving slowly off with his prize under his arm. He did not venture to ride fast, for fear the merriment should at once become general. On the other hand, he could not help hearing the following observations:

"There, now, you have angered the squire, dame; your tongue is just half an inch longer than it ought to be."

"Nay, it's just the right length," returned that indomitable female; "and as for angering him, I'll be bound he's as pleased as Punch. I have not come to my time of life and been wooed and wed by three proper men—all in the grave, poor souls, worse luck—without knowing what a man likes said to him and what he don't."

And certainly John Carlyon wore a smile upon his face, as he trotted up the hill.

"I think I shall call *now*," said he to himself; "it will be only civil to take this drawing-book." He regarded it doubtfully enough, though, and indeed it had a rueful look. "One might almost think that Browning wrote of this identical article—

There you have it, dry in the sun
With all the binding all of a blister,
And great blue spots where the color has run,
And reddish streaks that wink and glister
O'er the page so beautifully yellow.

What a fool I am to be taking it back to her in all this hurry! Nobody can ever draw upon it again. It has become a mere blotting-pad, as that old woman called it. She was right there, though not when she gave me her good wishes. What is the use of my crying for the moon like a great baby? Mr. Crawford may be willing enough to have me for a son-in-law, and, indeed, I think he wished me to see that. But even if her affections are not engaged to her handsome cousin—and why not? he is half my age and has twice my good looks (if, that is, I have any left); and he has opportunities which I can never have; and he loves her. I could see that when they stood yonder upon the brink of their grave. The young bantam showed no white feather, that I will say. And Agnes—was ever such a courage seen in woman? I remember a picture at Antwerp, where they are binding the arms of a beautiful maiden before they cast her into some roaring flood—a Christian martyr, of course—and she wore just such an expression as this girl did last night when the sea was craving for her, and death within a hand's breadth. One would have thought that she had been in heaven already. And it is a saint like this that you have set your mind upon, John Carlyon, to have for your wife, is it? No less will serve your infidel turn, eh? But this is no Margaret to be won by the aid of any Mephistopheles. Faust, Faust, let me recommend you to stick to your profession as a country gentleman; hunt, shoot, drink, and die."

Here he arrived at the fork of the road leading down from Mellor Church, and pulled his horse up.

"No," added he, grimly, after a pause, "I will send this book by hand, and then be off to

---

* The cocklers never quarrel "on the sands," being under the impression that if they do so, the cockles will leave their usual haunts with the next tide.

London, where I have so many kind friends; some of them female ones. Then, when the invitation comes to dine at Greycrags, I shall escape temptation, or rather, what is much less pleasant, certain disappointment. Yes, I'll go home and pack my portmanteau, no matter how old Robin may purse his lips; or suppose," continued he, after a pause, "I let Red Berild decide the matter, as the knights of old used to do, letting the reins fall on the neck of their steed, and following his guidance rather than using their own judgment. But then that would be scarcely fair to—to the Greycrags alternative, since Berild is sure to take the road to his stables."

His fingers were yet playing irresolutely with the bridle, when a young man came suddenly upon him from the direction of the village, walking very fast, and with his cap pulled low over his brows, as though to avoid observation.

"Ah, William!" cried Carlyon, cheerily; and it was curious to note how very cheery his manner at once became, when addressing others, no matter how sombre might have been his previous meditations while alone; "the very man I wished to see!"

"And I was on my road to Woodlees, sir," returned the other, gravely, "expressly to see you, Mr. Carlyon."

The voice was subdued and low for a man's voice, but with that earnestness and resolution in its tone which bespeak deep convictions in the speaker.

"Coming to *me*, were you, William? well, I am always glad to see you, but I think it was my business to come to *you*. When I looked in the glass this morning, and saw this bruise on my forehead, I said to myself, 'I have William Millet to thank for that.' The rope struck me just over the eyes; exactly the spot where they lasso wild cattle on the prairies. There must be no touching of hats; you must give me your hand-my friend, this morning. John Carlyon owes you his life."

The young man hesitated; then diffidently reached out his hand to meet the other's.

"You are mistaken, sir," said he, "except in the bare fact that it was I who threw the rope; though Miss Agnes is good enough to make as much of that as she can. But, indeed, so far from your being indebted to me or mine, it was through—it was through my poor father, sir," (here the young man fixed his eyes upon the ground) "that the mischance happened at all. His old enemy tempted him and he fell."

"That's religion, William, and therefore unintelligible," returned Carlyon coldly; "how was it, in plain terms?"

"Miss Agnes and her cousin went out in father's cart, to take a sketch of the bay from the middle of the sands."

The speaker had enunciated his words with painful difficulty, notwithstanding that he evidently strove to be distinct and collected, and now he came to a full stop altogether.

"Well, she was on the sands and sketching," said the other, impatiently; "I know that much already, for here is her drawing-book."

Under any other circumstances precise William Millet would have smiled to hear a gentleman and lady thus spoken of as a single individual, to whom moreover was attributed the sex that is ungallantly stated to be less worthy than the masculine; but he was full of a great trouble, and had no sense of any thing else.

"It was arranged as usual, for he had been out, with Miss Agnes at least, on such expeditions before, that father should call for them on his way back to Mellor, and in good time. But while at the skeer he met with an old comrade, living on the other side of the bay, who not content with drinking the devil's health on shore—for that's what a man does every time he puts his lips to the whiskey bottle—must needs take out his liquor with him upon the very sands. Sir, my father could not resist it. God forgive him, he drank till he scarce knew where he was; drank till he had clean forgotten his promise to Miss Agnes; and at last, went home with his companion quite unconscious that death was drawing nigh to the best friend he had in the world, (for Miss Agnes had been his guardian angel, sir), and all through his own fault, his own folly, his own crime."

"What a cursed fool the man must have been!" cried Carlyon, angrily.

"A fool, sir, indeed, but I trust not cursed," returned the young man solemnly. "He is sorry enough now, is father. It is terrible to see his grief. But for you, Mr. Carlyon, he feels that he should have been a murderer. He will never hold up his head again, I doubt."

"Well, the sense of the mischief he so nearly wrought, will at least have this good result, I suppose, that Stephen will leave off drinking," said Carlyon. "That will be good coming out of evil—isn't that the phrase?"

"God grant it may be so," returned the young man, without noticing the other's cynical tone; "and that this awful lesson may save his soul alive."

"Humph," said Mr. Carlyon, dryly; then murmured to himself, "How characteristic all this is. To save a soul that is not worth saving, two *other* folks are put within a hair's-breadth of being drowned. And after all, the salvation is not with certainty effected. This sot will probably have to complete a murder before that satisfactory result is achieved. The calmness with which pious folks talk of sacrificing the lives or interests of innocent people to benefit the spiritual condition of scoundrels of this sort, is most curious. It is like making a blood bath from the veins of children in order that some jaded voluptuary may become rejuvenescent."

"I see you are very angry, sir," resumed the young man, humbly; "and I am sure I can not blame you. You are the third person whose death would have lain at my father's door. It was your forgiveness that I was coming to ask for him, sir. He dursn't come himself. I think he would rather die than meet Miss Agnes just at present, although the dear young lady was very anxious to assure him of her pardon. He can look in no man's face. Oh, sir, he is bowed down to the earth with shame and sorrow."

"Well, William, you may tell him he has my free forgiveness as far as what he has done to me is concerned."

"But not as respects Miss Agnes? You will never forgive him that. That's what you mean, is it not, sir?" said the young man, looking up with flushed cheeks, for the first time. "That's what they all say, sir. They will point at father as the man that nearly murdered Miss Agnes; and yet she—Mr. Carlyon, if you are going up to Greycrags, ask her what *she* thinks they ought to do. What she thinks *you* ought to do. She says for her part, that if she had been downright drowned, and that through that circumstance—"

"That will do, William," interrupted Mr. Carlyon, harshly. "Don't speak to me any more, or you will put me in a passion, and I shall say things that will hurt your feelings. You are an excellent fellow yourself (although you are a fool in some things) and I have always had a good opinion of you. I am bound to be your friend for life, for what you did for me twenty-four hours ago, and you may depend upon me at all times. Good-bye."

"Stop, sir, stop!" cried the young man, laying his hand imploringly upon the other's bridle rein, and speaking in earnest, but rapid tones; "if, as you say, I have deserved any thing at your hands, let it weigh with you now. The man that I speak of is cast down to the very dust—a broken man without hope; it lies in your example to give him one more chance among his fellow-creatures here or not; and, oh, sir, he is my own father!"

A spasm passed across Mr. Carlyon's face, the index of some mental struggle within, and he did not speak for some moments. Then, with a very gentle voice, he said—"What a good fellow you are, William. You may tell this man that I forgive him from the bottom of my heart, and I will do my best to persuade others to do so—for his son's sake."

"Thank you, sir; though I wish it had been for God's sake," returned the young man, fervently. "May He prosper you in all your undertakings, and call you home to Him at last."

But John Carlyon had already touched Red Berild with his heel, and did not wait for that reply. He had turned his horse's head toward Greycrags.

CHAPTER VIII.

EXPLANATORY.

THE residence occupied by Mr. Crawford (for it was not his own) was as secluded as Woodlees itself, although in a different fashion. It was a house that stood on a hill, and yet it was hid. Trees environed it almost wholly, although not growing so near as to give the outlook any appearance of gloom. Curiously enough, the view of the sea, an advantage generally so desiderated in those parts, was altogether shut out from the mansion, the principal rooms of which faced the north-west, and commanded a grand inland prospect. In that direction, hill rose behind hill, until in the distance their summits were usually mingled with the clouds; but on very bright days indeed this highest range stood grandly out against the clear blue sky, and in the late autumn, when the snow began to hoar their tops, afforded a really glorious spectacle. A still better view, of course, was gained from the summit of the hill from which the house was named, and hence it had at one time been a great resort for parties of pleasure during the summer months. This, however, was long ago; ever since Mr. Crawford's tenancy of the place a rigorous exclusion of all strangers having been maintained. Nay, it might almost be added of all friends, in such solitude had the old man lived for the whole five years he had passed at Mellor. So far, therefore, from enjoying its ancient reputation as a place of amusement, it was now in no very pleasant repute. Being shut out from Greycrags, its poorer neighbors affected (like the fox pronounced the uncomeatable grapes sour) to shun it; or perhaps they really had got to believe the tales which they had themselves invented against its proprietor when he forbade their making use of his grounds. What did the old curmudgeon mean by such conduct? People did not hedge themselves in, and keep themselves *to* themselves in that sort of way without some very good reason for it; or rather for some reason which (like the spirits at the Mellor Arms) were strong without being so very good.

What should induce an old gentleman of seventy years of age, with an only daughter of fifteen or so, to come and live at such a place as Greycrags—a man, one would think, to whom society would have been most acceptable, since his sole establishment upon his arrival had consisted of his daughter's attendant, and she a black woman! He had engaged the few other servants his simple mode of life required, in the neighborhood, and dropped down, just as it might be (except that the black woman was credited with having hailed from what I may venture to call the opposite locality), from the skies. It was nothing less than an insult to the intelligence of his neighbors, to behave in this unaccountable manner. Many of them would have forgiven his having closed the grounds, if they could have only found out why he did it. Even Mr. Puce, the parson, a man who had the reputation of knowing a great deal of the world (some even said that for a clergyman he had too exclusively given his attention to it), could make nothing of Mr. Crawford. He had called, of course, not without some thirst for information, and had found the new-comer pretty much as we have seen him five years afterward at Woodlees; with a curious look of suspicion about him just at first, which wore off before the visit was ended. A gentleman, without doubt; Mr. Puce was ready to stake his reputation (not his professional one, but the other) upon that fact; he was never mistaken as to whether a man had been accustomed to "move in the upper circles." He even expressed his opinion that Mr. Crawford was one who had been accustomed to habits of command. But this was going a little too far. The gentry of the locality who had not enjoyed the privilege of a personal interview with the mysterious stranger—they who had called and been "not-at-homed," and whose calls had not been returned—would not credit that much. It was only natural that Mr. Puce should make the most of his advantage; but after all, what Mr. Crawford had alleged about himself was probably correct. He had made a competency by commerce, and very late in life had married a young wife, who had died in childbed with his little daughter. At nearly the same time his only brother and his wife had been carried off by fever in India, and their infant son had been consequently consigned to his charge. The Ayah who had brought him over had undertaken the mangement of both children; and servants of all sorts were now required. Mr. Puce could doubtless recommend some among his parishioners.

In short, Mr. Crawford had been as business-like as polite throughout the interview; but although thus far communicative about his own affairs—indeed evidently anxious to explain his position—there was nothing to be got out of him by cross-examination. Attired in deep mourning, his wasted form and cadaverous features fully bore out his assertion that both as concerned health and spirits he was totally incapacitated for mixing with society; and this he hoped that Mr. Puce would be so good as to make known to any families who might be kind enough to entertain the design of calling upon him. He was not even at present well enough, he added (and during the last five years he had never been sufficiently convalescent to attempt the experiment), to attend public worship.

Indeed, notwithstanding the not unpromising character of that first interview, the rector had never got speech with his parishioner again. He had called perhaps half a dozen times at Greycrags (for he was piqued at having been so foiled in his dexterous home-thrusts and anxious to retrieve his reputation as a farsighted investigator into social millstones), but the answer he constantly received was that Mr. Crawford did not feel himself equal to see him—that is, except from a distance; for as the rector walked away discomfited it sometimes happened that the ancient invalid was watching him through his telescope from some umbrageous portion of the elevated grounds. As time went on a governess of mature years was provided for Agnes; and whether from the admirable "system" employed by that lady (and quite peculiar to herself as every body's "system" is), or from her previous training under some one else, no more satisfactory female pupil was ever turned out of the educational workshop. Her accomplishments, however, were far outshone by her kindliness and charity. Even Mr. Puce was compelled to confess that the Church had no such servant in his parish as the daughter of the recluse of Greycrags. She was humble, too, and submissive to authority; not like that pestilent Job Salver, who blasphemously conceived that he had received the gift of preaching; nor even that William Millet, who carried his religion into every affair of life like some nursing mother who embarrasses her neighbors by considering the baby is included in all invitations.

Agnes Crawford, unlike her father, "went out" (as the phrase goes) a good deal; but not into what is generally called society. She was on excellent terms with the ladies of the neighborhood, who had no worse term to apply to her than "very peculiar;" but she did not often visit them. No person (with any sense of propriety) could blame her for that, since having parted with her governess in her eighteenth year, she had no longer a "chaperon." Old Mrs. Heathcote, of Mellor Lodge, had indeed offered her services to "the dear girl," in this matter—including some very appropriate personal properties, item: a front as black as the raven's wing; a splendid turban, with an ostrich feather in it; and a portrait of her deceased husband, worn as a stomacher, and almost the size of life. But Agnes, with grateful thanks, had declined her protection. She did not even care for either of the two county balls (one civil, the other military); and therefore it may be easily imagined that the ordinary evening parties of the neighborhood failed to attract her. Dinner parties were not given about Mellor—a neatly-written statement that the pleasure of your company was requested to tea being the favorite form of invitation—but it is my belief that Miss Crawford would not very much have cared even for going out to dinner. She only took other people's dinners out to them in a basket; and when they were sick, supplied them with little comforts—made inexpressibly more comforting in their ministration. Thus it might have easily happened that not moving in the best local circles (to borrow Mr. Puce's imagery) Agnes had never so much as spoken with John Carlyon, although so near a neighbor.

The fact was, however, that Mr. Carlyon did not move in them either, or rather had not done so for many years. He had flown off from them at a tangent of his own free will, or perhaps, as they themselves averred with some complacency, they had made him fly. The squire at Woodlees had very much overrated his social position if he imagined that he might think as he liked, or at all events might express his opinions. Because the Earl Disney thought fit to absent himself from public worship fifty-one Sundays per annum, that was no excuse for Mr. John Carlyon's absence therefrom for fifty-two. Nor had he even the decency, like Mr.

Crawford (an old man whose case was shocking to contemplate, but who had yet some sense of shame), to frame an excuse. The squire was the picture of health, and might be seen, Sunday after Sunday, starting for his gallop on the sands, while all the other gentry of the neighborhood were proceeding with demure faces to listen in the proper place to the clergyman of their parish. These gentlemen, his sometime companions in the hunting-field, would look up in rather a sheepish manner and say, "How do, Carlyon?" as he met or overtook them on such occasions; but their wives never vouchsafed him a nod. Nay, as soon as he had passed by on his ungodly errand, they would often anticipate Mr. Puce's discourse by a little sermon of their own, or even bring the tell-tale color into their lord's cheek by stating their belief that he himself would rather be on horseback at that very moment like yonder wicked man, if the truth were known. It is fair to add, however, that it was not merely Mr. Carlyon's absence from church which caused him to be thus sent to Coventry (not a wholly disagreeable place, he averred in his cynical way), but also a very deplorable habit he had of speaking disrespectfully of religion. He protested he never did so unless in self-defense, and when belabored with the weapons of the dogmatic; but not only was this denied, but the defense, such as it was, was disallowed. He ought to have been thankful for the correction; and at all events, even in war, folks are never justified in poisoning wells or using Greek fire. What aggravated the matter, too, above all things, was that John Carlyon's father had been one of the best and most orthodox of men. While he lived no evidence of his son's depravity had been afforded; but no sooner had his example been withdrawn than the young squire had thrown off the mask, and appeared in his true character as infidel and scoffer. For the rest he was a man of daring courage, and open-handed generosity; but these virtues, of course, only made his irreligious opinions the more to be deplored. Every body in Mellor did deplore them, and especially Mrs. Newman, his widowed sister, a lady of most unimpeachable views in spiritual matters, although in worldly affairs she had the reputation of being overprudent. With regard to money, of which she had a plentiful supply, she was even called close-fisted. The shrewd husband of one of the poor women whom it was her pleasure to edify, once observed of Mrs. Newman that "You might get a ton of texts from her easier than an ounce of tea," and it must be confessed that the remark was not without foundation.

John Carlyon and Agnes Crawford, then, except for those terrible minutes on the lessening sand, had never met, although each had been made well aware, by report, of the character of the other. "She will thank me," mused the squire to himself, as he rode up to the front door at Greycrags, "and then she will shrink from me as from an adder."

CHAPTER IX.

GREYCRAGS.

"Mr. Crawford has not at present left his chamber, being unwell," was the reply given by the servant to Mr. Carlyon; "but Mr. Richard is somewhere about the grounds, and I will let him know you are here. Miss Crawford is in the drawing-room, sir, if you will step this way."

Twice or thrice, but not more, Carlyon had had an opportunity of observing Agnes with attention, but he thought that she had never looked half so lovely as when rising hastily, though with grace, from a table at which she was putting some finishing touches to a drawing, she came forward to meet him with heightened color, and outstretched hand. On the day before, her beauty had struck him indeed as wonderful; but then it was something out of nature, if beyond it. The expectation of immediate death had glorified that charming face, and changed it to something celestial; it had presented the chastened and unearthly loveliness which the moonbeams cast upon some fair landscape. To-day, though radiant as a sunbeam, she looked

A creature not too bright and good
For human nature's daily food.

"Mr. Carlyon," said she, "I have to thank you for my life; what words shall I find in which to do so?"

"None, my dear madam," returned he. "Words are unnecessary: indeed they are. I read in your face that gratitude which a generous mind is so prompt to pay with usurious interest."

She smiled and shook her head. "As you please," said she. "True courage, it is said, always makes light of its own acts; but when we left you yesterday at Mr. Carstairs's house, you were scarcely recovered. I trust you are now yourself again."

"Unhappily, madam, yes;" here he released her hand, and sighed. "They tell me I was under water a few seconds longer than yourself and your cousin: otherwise a great hulking fellow like me ought to be ashamed of himself to have been the last to get his breath."

"And your horse, Mr. Carlyon—I trust that noble horse has come safe to land?"

"He is standing in your stables at this moment. If I could but let him know that you had asked after him, I am sure that Red Berild would be better pleased than with a feed of corn. His nature is chivalric—except," added Carlyon, smiling, "that he never earns the spurs."

"I have had another visitor this morning, Mr. Carlyon, to whom, next to yourself, Richard and I are indebted for our preservation yesterday; and for fear I should forget it, I will tell you at once that I have a favor to ask you in connection with him. When one owes one's life to a fellow-creature, it does not matter what one owes beside; the weight of obligation can not be increased; so you see I am quite shameless."

"Whatever the favor may be, it is granted, my dear Miss Crawford. You speak of William Millet, I suppose, whom I have just met upon the road."

"Then he probably asked you himself?" said Agnes, eagerly.

"No; although, of course, I would have obliged him in any way. But he is very modest, is William."

"Very modest and very good," replied Miss Crawford, thoughtfully. "I don't know any one *so* good in all Mellor."

"He does not seem a happy man, however; at least, he has always a melancholy go-to-meeting sort of air about him." There was the shadow of a sneer upon this last sentence, cast by the speaker's self-contempt, not contempt of his subject. Carlyon felt that he was in danger of playing a hypocritical part to please this beautiful girl, and he resented his own weakness.

"If William Millet has sorrows," replied Agnes, confidently, "they are not his own. His heart, like the pelican's breast, bleeds for others, not for himself."

"Yes; he has a worthless, drunken father, poor fellow," said Carlyon, abruptly; "that must be a bitter bane to any man."

"Yes, indeed, Mr. Carlyon; you and I can not know how bitter. I say *you* from hearsay only; but if what every body agrees in must needs be true, you were exceptionally blessed in your father."

"He was a man of the strictest religion and piety," returned Carlyon.

The extreme coldness of his tone could scarcely have escaped her—and indeed it was intended to be observed—but she went on as though she had not heard it.

"In that case, you ought to feel pity for those who are less fortunate in their parents."

"I do pity William Millet, Miss Crawford. If you ask me to pity Stephen, a man who for a glass of gin has put a life like yours, to say nothing of your cousin's and mine, in deadliest peril, I can not do it."

"I ask you to forgive him," said Agnes, pleadingly.

"William has asked me to do that already, and I have done it. I have promised also to try my best to get the old man forgiven, although that will be no easy task in Mellor, where, if you had perished, they tell me every household would have lost its truest friend."

"No, sir, no," said Agnes, hastily; "poor folks are thankful for small kindnesses, and magnify them in their talk. But to *this* household—that is, to my poor father—my loss would have been doubtless great. The very nearness of such a calamity (for such it would have doubtless been to him) affected him very deeply; he showed himself far from well at Woodlees yesterday, Richard tells me."

"Yes, he was twice overcome, although I did not understand the cause; but at your father's age there is nothing surprising in such seizures, particularly since he has been such an invalid so long."

"Just so," said Agnes, in low earnest tones; "there is nothing surprising. You will not be disturbed therefore, if, when you come to see us, as he hopes you often will, he should occasionally give way in a similar manner. I am afraid he is scarcely well enough to see you to-day, although I know he counts upon the pleasure of your dining here on Thursday—indeed, I had, at his request, written you this formal invitation—which, as you see, only awaits the postman."

"I accept it very gladly," said Carlyon; "notwithstanding which, oblige me by not tearing up the note. It will remind me—although, indeed, I am not likely to forget it—of the engagement. Do you always act as your father's amanuensis thus, Miss Crawford?"

"Always: I have done so for some years. Even his business matters—except just where his signature is necessary—are entirely transacted by me. You smile, as though you doubted my fitness for such a post; but I assure you, I am very exact and methodical."

"Nay, I was only envying the attorney whom Mr. Crawford employs," said Carlyon, simply. Tone and gesture were both wanting, which should have accompanied a compliment so highflown. The young girl blushed deeply, and there ensued an embarrassing pause.

"That drawing of yours reminds me," resumed Carlyon, pointing to the table, "of the pretext on which I have ventured to intrude upon you. This sketch-book was found upon the sands this morning, as well as a campstool, which the finder will bring with him before night; it is yours, I conclude, although I am afraid it can be of no farther use."

Miss Crawford looked very grave at the sight of this memento of her late peril. "I thank you much, Mr. Carlyon. It is useless, as you say, for its original purpose; but I am very glad to have it. It will serve to remind me of the Providence which mercifully preserved me in so terrible a strait; as well," added she, with frankness, "of the brave gentleman who risked his life—nay, almost lost it—to save that of mere strangers. My unfinished sketch, I perceive—" here her voice faltered in spite of her utmost efforts at self-command—"has vanished from the block. Surely the sea could not have taken all the color out."

"I assure you, dear Miss Crawford, on my honor," exclaimed Carlyon, earnestly, "that *I* have ventured to take no such liberty. The book is just as it came into my hands."

"Nay, there would have been no great harm," returned she, smiling, "even had you committed such a theft. The wrecker, I am afraid, whoever he is, will have gained but a worthless prize."

"There I differ from you," said Carlyon. "I never before properly appreciated my manorial rights to Flottsam and Jettsam: I will punish the rascal who has thus deprived me of them with all the rigor of the law—that is, I would if I could. From whence is the sketch taken which you have just finished so charmingly? I should know those hills well enough: that is Wynthrop Pike, is it not? and that Cold Harbor Dod?"

"No, the Dod is here, in the middle distance; although I dare say it is my fault that it is not recognizable. It is taken half way up the crags; a most glorious place for a view. Come, I will show you the very spot."

"I should like that of all things," answered Carlyon, eagerly. "Greycrags has been so well preserved a sanctuary since your father's time, that I have quite forgotten the view from your hill."

She took up the summer hat that lay on the chair beside her, and, with the drawing in her hand, stepped out through the open window on the lawn, which sloped up to the wood-crowned height to southward. Two winding walks, to left and right, led to the top of this hill; and both of them had several little level resting-places, or plateaus, provided with seats either for rest or enjoyment of the extensive prospect afforded from them. On one of these, which commanded the windows of the drawing-room they had just left, Richard Crawford was seated reading, or, at least, with a book in his hand. He did not seem to observe Carlyon and his cousin. He had taken up his position on the left-hand walk; and when the point was reached where the two diverged, Agnes, after a moment's hesitation, took the other.

That, certainly, was a fair spot from which the good folks of Mellor had been shut out by Mr. Crawford's veto years ago. Art and nature seemed to have vied with one another in adorning the scene. The luxuriance of the wilderness predominated; for Mr. Crawford's out-door establishment was scarcely sufficient to keep in order such extensive grounds; but still the lawn on which you looked down at every turn of the shady zigzag, was kept smooth and shaven, and the flower-beds in their emerald setting glowed with harmonious hues. A terrace-walk — now diminished to a strip of gravel—ran round the house, and this was set with urns full of scarlet blossoms. As the moved higher, above the level of the house-roof, the prospect to the north-west, to which we have alluded, began to expand itself, and for the spectators an alcove had been erected at the most eligible point of view.

"This is the place from which I took this drawing, Mr. Carlyon," said Agnes; "and I think you owe me an apology for mistaking Windy Scar, yonder, for Cold Harbor Dod, whose hump, I flatter myself, I have represented with great fidelity. I have always been taught to prefer truth to beauty, independently of the fact that the former is always attainable, and the latter not."

"The poet tells us they are the same," answered Carlyon, "'Beauty is truth—truth beau-ty;' and when I look at *your* face, Miss Crawford, I do believe him."

"Mr. Carlyon, I am not used to listen to compliments," said Agnes, rising from the bench with quiet dignity; "and, to tell you the truth—or the beauty, since you say the terms are synonymous—it is a taste which I do not wish to acquire."

"You altogether misconceive my unfortunate observation, dear Miss Crawford," replied Carlyon humbly; "but pray sit down. I will take care not to offend again, even in appearance. You make light of my poet's dogma, it appears; I hope you do not flout at *all* bards, as Meg—that is, Mrs. Newman—does. A painter like yourself should surely be on friendly terms with the sister-art."

"I like poetry very much, Mr. Carlyon; but I must confess—making all allowance for my own lack of intelligence—that the claims which its admirers often put forth are somewhat extravagant. Poets seem to me to be the most thoughtful and suggestive of writers, touching with marvelous skill the innermost chords of our being; but as high-priests of our spiritual life I do not recognize their authority."

"You do not believe in the inspiration of the muse, then?"

"Yes, I do; but not in the same sense in which I believe in the inspiration of the Scriptures."

"Plenary?" asked Mr. Carlyon, smiling. "You surely don't believe, with Mr. Job Salver, that the Bible was dropped from Heaven in a lump, and in the vulgar tongue?"

"Oh, sir, I am an ignorant girl, and know nothing of what you hint at. But this I know, that when folks want comfort on their sick-beds, they only get it from one book."

"You are speaking of uneducated, simple people, such as you find about here."

"Yes; or in other words, of about nineteen-twentieths of our fellow-creatures. Of the other twentieth—the educated classes—about one-twentieth again, perhaps, have really any genuine poetic feeling. Thus the influence of the poets, however powerful, is restricted within very narrow limits. It is idle to speak of them as supplying the spiritual place of those inspired writers who address themselves to every degree of mankind."

"My dear Miss Crawford," returned Carlyon, laughing, "if it be possible that Doctor Samuel Johnson has been permitted to reappear upon the earth's surface in the form of a fair lady, she is certainly before me now. You make me believe in the doctrine of metempsychosis."

"I wish I could make you believe in something better and truer," returned the young girl, gravely.

"Well, try. I should like you to have as good an opinion of me as you have of William Millet."

"Nay, sir, but that is impossible."

"Dear me," quoth Carlyon; "why this is worse measure than I should get from Mr.

Puce himself. Surely he would estimate the Squire of Mellor above a cockler's son."

"Do you suppose, Mr. Carlyon, that God Almighty, who made the whole world, and ten thousand other worlds for all we know, cares whether a man is a king or a cockler?"

"No, Miss Crawford; nor, indeed, do I care, either. You are wasting your energies in preaching equality to one of 'the Mountain' like me."

"And yet I see a pride in this very humility of yours, Mr. Carlyon. Every man is equal, you say. You bend to no one, and you wish the humblest to treat you as man with man. And yet you are aware of your own superiority to the rest. When you rode down yesterday into the jaws of death—"

"Into the mouth of hell," interrupted Carlyon, finishing the quotation.

"Nay, I do not say that; God in his mercy forbid!" continued Agnes, fervently; "but when you saw yourself to be the only man of all that concourse upon the shore who would peril his life to save that of others, you must have known that you were braver, nobler, more generous than other men. Oh, sir, it is not well, I know, to say such things to your face; I see it embarrasses your nature to hear them; yet it is my duty to speak. Courage is good; but that is not courage which in the favored servant leads him to defy his master to whose forbearance he is indebted; that is not courage, but an ungrateful audacity, which moves a man to defy his God."

"Miss Crawford," returned Carlyon, slowly, "I thank you. I am not so willfully blind but that I can perceive you mean to do me a good service. We will talk of these things some other time together, as procrastinating Festus said to Paul. My visit to Greycrags has already been unconscionably long; in remembrance of it, however—especially of this interview—may I beg for that chalk drawing, that admirable half-length of my old friend, Cold Harbor Dod. Come, or else I shall think you vexed because your eloquence has not converted me upon the instant. You know it is quite the custom for those who would gain spiritual proselytes to bestow material advantages. 'Come to church, and you will get coals and blankets at Christmas,' says Mr. Puce to the disciples of Job Salver."

"As you will," said Agnes, sighing; "you are very welcome to my poor drawing, sir."

Her cheeks were pale, the light which had glowed in her earnest eyes awhile ago had quite gone out. Carlyon, on the other hand, looked flushed and pleased. He rolled up the little sketch with tenderest care, and placed it in his breast pocket.

"I will make a frame for it with my own hands," cried he, joyfully; "no carver and gilder shall touch it. Like the good old emperor of old, you may say to yourself, Miss Crawford, that you have not misspent this day, since you have made a fellow-creature happy."

Agnes did not reply. Slowly, and in a silence broken only by one or two conventional phrases, the two descended the hill. Richard had deserted his bench, and was nowhere to be seen. When they reached the drawing-room, and the horse had been ordered to be brought round—

"I must go out and see Red Berild!" exclaimed Agnes.

"Ah, do so," said Carlyon; "although he never looks so well, so powerful, and yet so gentle, as when he is carrying a lady."

So she went out to where the noble creature stood, pawing the gravel, and patted his arching neck approvingly, and whispered in his pricking ears how grateful she felt to him.

"On Thursday we shall see you at dinner, Mr Carlyon," were her last words.

"Without fail," answered he, with a warmth that contrasted with her quiet tones; and so they shook hands and parted.

Rapt in happy thought, and ever and anon touching his breast pocket as though to assure himself that his treasure was safe, Carlyon rode slowly away; and when he and his steed had come to a retired part of the road, and out of eyeshot of the house, he leaned forward and kissed that neck upon which Agnes Crawford's hand had lingered so lovingly.

———

CHAPTER X.

CUBRA'S TEACHING.

WHEN Agnes returned to the drawing-room, having bid adieu to her guest, she did what was with her a very unusual thing indeed—that is, nothing. Instead of working, or reading, or drawing, or attending to matters of the house, she sat in her old seat, with her hands on her lap, looking thoughtfully out upon the flower-bordered lawn, but only seeing the pictures in her brain. How long she might have thus remained in dream-land it is impossible to say, for that locality, seductive to all, is particularly so to those who, like her, are comparatively strangers to it, and find themselves there only occasionally; she was soon startled into consciousness, however, by some one moving in another part of the room which lay in shadow.

"Richard!" cried she, in astonishment. "What, are you here?"

"Yes, Agnes. I would not have disturbed you if I could have helped it; but I got the cramp and was obliged to move a limb."

"You frightened me very much, Richard," replied she, with a touch of annoyance in her tone. "Why did you not speak?"

"Because I had nothing to say which would be pleasant to you, or at least one-half as pleasant as the thoughts which were occupying your mind."

"You can not have read them, Richard, very correctly, if that is the conclusion you have arrived at."

"Yes I have, Agnes. I can tell you what you have been dreaming of, for it *is* a dream which can never have any reality, thank God! You have been dreaming of converting John Carlyon—into a husband."

"Richard!" She had risen to her full height, with flashing eyes and flaming cheeks. "How dare you insult me thus—you that are my own kith and kin! I blush for you."

"No, you are blushing for yourself, Agnes. You have seen this man but an hour or so, and yet the mention of his name turns you scarlet. I saw you when you stepped out with him yonder on the lawn together. You both looked up to where I sat, and then he asked you a question. An inner sense told me what it was as surely as though it had been whispered in my ears. You said that though my manner might have struck him as strange, that I meant no harm. That you really had a great regard for me, being your cousin, and lest he, Mr. Carlyon, should misjudge me, you would confide to him at once that I had had a sunstroke in Barbados."

"Heaven is my witness, Richard," interrupted Agnes, earnestly, "that I never uttered one syllable of all this; that even the idea of uttering it never entered into my mind. You will believe my word, Richard, I suppose, in opposition to this inner sense you speak of. Oh! cousin, cousin, for shame."

"How gentle and kind you are with me in consideration of my infirmity!" observed the young man, bitterly. "I dare say you have made up your mind that there shall always be an asylum for me in your own home—that is, if he has no objection—when you are married and settled."

He thought she would have flamed up again at this, but her face was now still and pale. Her large eyes gazed upon him in wonder and in sorrow. His fiery dart was turned aside by the shield of pity.

"Yes, you can afford to be patient and forbearing," he went on; "or at least you think you can; though do not be too sure."

A speck of color came into each fair cheek, then vanished instantly as a spark; but her eyes, suddenly stern, retained their firmness.

"I do not wish to threaten you, Agnes."

"Threaten *me!*" Unutterable scorn never took a more graceful shape than in that face and form. "You are mad, Richard."

"No—not mad, but wounded, vexed; that I allow, Agnes. Forgive me. I will school myself to better manners. Why did this man come hither? Why did he ask for *you*, not for your father? Why, as though this room was not sufficiently private for him, did he lead you to yonder arbor?"

"I deny your right, Richard, to ask any such questions; but they are easily answered, thus: Mr. Carlyon came to return me this sketch-book left on the sands on the day when he saved your life and mine. My father has not quitted his room, and therefore could not see him. It was I myself who proposed to take Mr. Carlyon up the hill."

"Good. The rest I know. He asked you for your drawing, and you gave it to him, and he said you had made him happy. I was behind the alcove and heard it all."

"What! *you* played the eavesdropper!"

He had approached her, but she waved him off with a gesture of supreme contempt.

"If you were a poor man, sir, I tell you what you would have been—you would have been a thief!"

"We do not despise the man—the Bible says it—who steals for bread," replied the young man, passionately. "*I* starve, and therefore steal. You, Agnes, are to me the bread for which I hunger; the fire for lack of which my blood runs cold; the drink I thirst for; the atmosphere in which alone I breathe. Oh, listen to me—listen to me, if you have a heart not stone."

He cast himself before her on his knees, and clasped her dress, for she was about to leave the room in terror at his words.

"You are all I have to live for—all. I love you as no woman ever yet was loved. Look you, you have given that man a drawing, and he says that he will prize it; but not as I prize this, although it was no gift at all. I tore it from your sketch-book yesterday, when I thought we had but a few minutes to live. So dear even then was every thing belonging to you. I wish we had both died together. Not I alone, for then you would have married this man—which you never shall—no, *never*. Yes, I had rather see you angered thus than pitiful. You never shall."

"Richard!"

"Nay, Agnes, do not look like that—I then feel without heart or hope. Oh! pity me."

From menace to appeal, from love to hate, his mood thus shifted; yet all his face was bright with changeful beauty, like some Eolian harp whose strings obey the tempest or the whispering summer wind as happens, but harmonious to each. Now he lay prostrate on the floor with his face hidden in his hands, and to judge by the movement of his shoulders, sobbing with hysterical violence.

"For shame, Richard! That is not the behavior of a man but of a spoiled child denied some plaything of which, if it were given him, he would tire in a little time and fret for something else. I can not stay, and will not, to see you thus conduct yourself. I will send Cubra to you, for I am sure you must need a nurse."

Thoroughly roused to wrath, Agnes disengaged her dress from his now yielding fingers, and left the room. The young man, moaning in a restless manner, like some wild beast in pain, lay where he was.

"What, Master Richard ill again! What have they been doing to my darling?" cried a female voice, speaking with great rapidity, and in broken English. Then followed a torrent of Hindostanee. "Get up, my own, lest the sahib come in and find you thus."

He looked up with an angry scowl. "Let him come, Cubra; I know now how to deal with him. Let him take care."

"Hush, hush! The wise snake gives no rattle. Has Miss Agnes made you angry? She is always doing that."

"No, Cubra, no," replied the young man, rising to his feet, and giving the old black woman his hand, which she covered with kisses; "it is I who was in fault. You must not be vexed with Agnes."

"What! when she does not love my Richard?" She shook her head, its hair more intensely black even than that of her young master, though by a score of years his elder, and her eyes gleamed white with wrath. "No, no. Why no she love you, my beautiful? It is she who should lie there and say, 'Kiss me, Richard, be my husband, be my master.' Tell me how she help it."

"She cares nothing for me; nobody cares for me except you, Cubra. And what is worse, she loves another man."

"She — love — another — man!" echoed the ayah; first in profound wonder, and then with malignant ferocity. "She love another man. Take Cubra's knife—this one she killed the dog with, years ago, that kept my pet awake o' nights with its yelping. Take it and kill him. If Massa Richard is afraid, shall Cubra do it?"

"Certainly not. Never hint at such a thing again, I beg. Throw that knife away. It would be very wrong, very wicked, and would displease me very much indeed, Cubra."

"I always please Master Richard, not make him sorry," returned the black woman, quietly. "What shall we do then? kill *her?*"

"Murderess!" cried the young man, with fury, seizing the ayah by the throat. "Give utterance to that devilish thought again, and I will choke you. Touch my Agnes, injure one shining hair of her bright head, and I would—ugh! you black savage!"

Richard let go his hold and shuddered. The application of the homeopathic principle of like to like, passion to passion, for the time at least, had cured him. The exhibition of such instincts in another had made him sensible of his own unreasonable conduct.

He passed out on the lawn, and up to the alcove which Carlyon and Agnes had lately occupied. There he sat alone, watched by the eyes of Cubra from below, exactly as a man in some trouble, beyond canine sagacity to comprehend, is watched by his faithful dog.

The ayah had been Richard's foster-mother, although not in India. For some reason, best known to Mr. Crawford, the place of the black nurse in whose care he had been brought home had been supplied by Cubra directly the vessel arrived in England; but she loved him as though he had been her charge and comfort from the first. Great and wondrous is the affection which women often evince for the little ones who are indebted to them not for the gift of life, but only for the prolongation of it; but in Cubra's case, this feeling was devotion; nay, idolatry. Without friends, without relatives, without country, without a God, this poor, ignorant creature had found a substitute for them all in Richard Crawford. She was ready to shed her heart's blood for him, and she had given him all that she had to give him short of that. Some of her gifts had better never have been bestowed. He had inherited from her the vehement passions of her Eastern race, not mitigated, and scarcely skinned over by her long contact with the civilized world. His education, such as it was, had done him but little service. His uncle, moody, and at times morose, had never taken kindly to the boy, although he had always done his duty by him in what is falsely termed "essentials," that is, in material requirements. He had not spared money, (the child had inherited but very little from his own parents) and had sent him to a respectable school. He had then offered to give him a fair start in any profession, save one, to which he might take a fancy. And here occurred the first considerable breach between the boy and his guardian. Richard had that vehement longing to enter the navy which sometimes seizes upon our insular youth with an intensity not to be explained, and upon which as a nation we may well congratulate ourselves as a nation, but not always as parents and guardians. Mr. Crawford entertained a repugnance for the sea quite as great and as unaccountable as was his nephew's predilection for it. The contest was very violent, and bore bitter fruit. So far as the subject of dispute was concerned, Richard gained his point, inasmuch as he was sent afloat, but instead of being admitted into the royal navy, he entered the merchant service. His uncle never forgave him his obstinacy, and his own proud spirit deeply resented the being placed in what he considered an inferior branch of his beloved calling.

At the time of his departure on his first voyage—which proved a long one—and just before Mr. Crawford's removal to Mellor, a second ground of offense had arisen. The boy had fallen in love with his cousin—if one of his rash and impetuous nature could be said to fall, and not rather to have leaped headlong over the icy barrier of kinship into the fiery gulf of love. The passion of a youth of sixteen for a girl one year his junior is not generally a very dangerous matter, and especially when there is no sign of its being returned; but it naturally intensified his uncle's prejudice against him, at the same time as it properly forwarded his own views in the matter of his being sent to sea. After an absence of a year or two on the salt water, it was reasonably to be expected that such a cobweb would be blown away from his young brain; and no serious talk had ever been held with him upon the point. Yet now, after being away from the beloved object for no less than five years, the young man had returned home more enamored of her than ever. He had only been at Greycrags for a few weeks, and, as we have seen, he had already addressed his cousin in the terms of a passionate lover; and yet the duration of his stay at home was indefinite. This was a state of things the suspicion of which might have aroused the anxiety of any father. Mr. Crawford, however, was not ignorant of the relative position which the two cousins occupied. Not only was he confident of the dutifulness of his daughter, but the sisterly affection which she had at all times manifested toward Richard was evidence to the shrewd old man of her not reciprocating any warmer feeling. She had interceded for him with her father, a hundred times, but never when the favor sought would have been to the lad's hurt, albeit to his gratification. She had shown none of the blind fondness of one who loves, and none of the reticence. Mr. Crawford knew from her own lips that his nephew had offered her his hand, and been refused. She had confided it to him upon the understanding that poor Richard was to be treated none the worse for all that had come and gone. It was, doubtless, owing to this proviso that the young sailor owed the toleration which he enjoyed at Greycrags from his host and kinsman, notwithstanding his audacious aspirations.

Although accepting his position, Richard was by no means grateful for the sufferance. He knew, or thought he knew, that he possessed a claim upon the hospitality of Greycrags, nay, upon the possession of Agnes Crawford for his wife, that only required to be put forward to be allowed; a claim basely acquired, indeed, and base for a man to use—but still a valid one. Of the game he felt himself certain; whether it was to be obtained by honest play, or by the card which he kept in his sleeve, was the question that now agitated him as he sat in the alcove, endeavoring to nerve himself for the cheat's device by thinking how willingly she had lately sat there by another's side. It was not an easy task; for the young man, although unprincipled and reckless, was not a coward, as we have already seen. He had stooped to at least one meanness, besides that with which we are acquainted; but it was not his nature to be mean. The strength of his master-passion had overthrown all barriers of honor and good faith that interposed themselves to its current, and was now threatening to whelm his whole moral being. Out of the course of this stream there was much good ground and fertile; but, curiously enough, in pursuit of one of the purest objects human heart could desire, his own was indurating and being debased, just as the diamond-seeker burrows in the depths of the mine, or the modern Prometheus seeks the photographic fire with covered face.

"It is only a little less base than Cubra's knife," muttered Richard to himself, after much reflection. "She might hate me for using such a weapon, even though she became my wife. No, no! it can not be that she will always reject such love as mine. I was wrong to show myself so jealous of the visit of this stranger, although I can see how the old man favors him. Oh, Agnes, Agnes!" exclaimed he, passionately, as with a fervent and almost frenzied gaze, like some fire-worshiper in presence of his divinity, he gazed upon the western hills, now smitten with flame, "if I could only win you fairly, my beloved one!" Then, as he turned to descend, and his eye fell upon Cubra, still keeping her patient watch below, he added, "but fairly or not, Agnes Crawford"—and there was a bitter sneer in the tone in which he pronounced her name—"you *shall* be won, and that soon."

CHAPTER XI.
A LITTLE DINNER AT GREYCRAGS.

THE institution of dinner parties, admirable for mankind in many respects, and certainly superior to all other forms of entertainment, is not so advantageous with regard to our relations with the other sex. Man can have no better opportunity of cultivating acquaintance with his brother man, but scarcely a worse for improving his position with the lady of his affections. We may not be so fastidious as the noble bard who "hated to see a woman eat," but we still must acknowledge that we had rather see our beloved object doing almost any thing else. We do not know how it may be with chopsticks, but a knife and fork in woman's hands seem certainly inimical to the tender passion; the jingle of glasses, the clatter of plates, are not to be trusted to, as in any degree permanent; servants are not invariably noisy; and just as, under cover of a fusillade of this sort, you have hazarded a remark with meaning, a sudden silence may place you in the most embarrassing position. The attentive fair one poising a morsel upon her fork, presents a truly ridiculous spectacle, and you—with the sentence you dare not finish—how foolish *you* also look, as you plunge madly at your champagne glass, and wish it were an opaque pitcher in which you could hide your diminished head. And yet, how you counted beforehand on that evening when you knew you were to meet her, and that your good-natured hostess would see that your Arabella should be placed under your charge in the procession to the dining-room! For my part, I think the Eastern custom, which excludes females from feasts, is a most excellent one. The only exception should be picnics, which, indeed, would never exist except for women, who care not what they eat, or what they drink, but only wherewithal they shall be clothed.

However, as I have said, the lover still looks forward to the repast at which he is to meet his fair one, notwithstanding the not unrecorded experiences of the generations before him: and the Thursday on which John Carlyon was invited to Greycrags, seemed to beckon him to bliss.

His late interview with Agnes had filled his heart with hope—it must be confessed on but slight grounds. He did not take into account the depth of gratitude which she felt for the service he had rendered her, and which, of course, had placed him upon quite another footing than that of a stranger making his first visit of ceremony; the unconventional simplicity of her nature, too, so different from that of young ladies in general, gave to her manners a frankness and cordiality which he had construed, somewhat egotistically perhaps, into a liking for himself. But, he was at all events certain that she did not shrink from him as he had apprehended would have been the case, in pious horror. He did not at all dislike her remarks to him upon the question of religion. They evinced an interest in his future welfare, which perhaps might be extended to the present. Charity begins at home, but love may begin anywhere. Marriages themselves were said to be made in heaven. It was very foolish of him to leap to these conclusions; but the fact was, Carlyon was dealing with a person whose motives of action he could appreciate, and yet by no means understand. Nothing is more unintelligible to an irreligious man than the position of the truly pious. The quoters of texts, the wearers of long faces, the denouncers of fiction, the foes of the Pope, and all that rout of the vulgar and ignorant who make up so large a portion of what is called "the religious world," are very transparent to him, and afford him endless opportunities of scoffing at the Great Cause of which these foolish persons imagine themselves to be the advocates. But, brought face to face with those who spend their lives in doing good, from motives quite other than those of simple benevolence, and whose charity is of the heart as well as the hand, he is puzzled how to treat them. These "amiable enthusiasts," who show their faith by their works, are very embarrassing to him; but they are seldom met with in society.

Carlyon had long regarded Agnes like some star set far above him in a heaven of its own; but now that he had been admitted to her presence, and listened to her opinions, she seemed no longer out of his reach. Yet as soon might he imagine that the substance of the star was any nearer to him, because in some tranquil pool he had seen its reflex, and hung over it for a little unrebuked.

It is sad to think how soon with ordinary men, and especially with those who pay a somewhat exceptionable homage to women, the angel is lost in the wife, and the wife in the drudge; how lightly they value the prize once so humbly sought when they have become possessed of it. With one of Carlyon's generous and knightly nature such degradation was impossible, but he was not without some share of that vanity of his sex which translates the pressure of a woman's hand into "Persevere," and her smile into "You will succeed." A week ago, had his heart ventured to whisper to him that Agnes Crawford might some day be his, he would have laughed aloud for very bitterness. But now, as he was borne toward Greycrags, in the close car of the country, to dine in company with that no longer unapproachable young woman, the idea of such a union was by no means laughable, but eminently practicable and very nice. There was no dinner-party to meet him, of course. Not that there is any difficulty in the country in getting folks to dine with you, for they will cheerfully come six, and even ten miles, to do it in the depth of winter, but simply because Mr. Crawford knew nobody to ask. Mr. Puce, indeed, would have given five pounds (and he was not a recklessly extravagant man either) for an invitation to Greycrags; but Mr. Puce was not there. Mr. Carstairs was the only guest besides Carlyon, who was not an inmate of the house.

An apology for this circumstance was tendered by the stately old man, as he welcomed the young squire, who on his part rejoined, most truthfully, that he was glad they were to be so small a company. He might, with equal veracity, have added that at least one of the present party could have been well spared. Mr. Richard Crawford, offensively good-looking and objectionably young, was standing by his cousin's side, and continued there to stand while Carlyon and she shook hands and dilated upon the fineness of the evening—as though June were generally a series of pouring days alternating with snow-storms. It was quite a relief when cheery Mr. Carstairs bustled in late—("When a lady's in the case, my dear sir, and especially under certain circumstances—ahem—all other things must give place")—and fastened himself upon Mr. Richard, with some startling particulars concerning the right of fishing, which that young gentleman, it seems, had exercised of late in contempt of the lawful authority of Charles, Earl Disney. The doctor, indeed, was just one of those persons whose presence is invaluable in a small company, in which there are discordant elements. A common acquaintance of all, he seemed to be unaware of the existence of any antipathies. He rattled on at dinner from one subject of gossip to another in his good-natured way, insisting especially upon the attention of Richard as being a youth, and one who had never paid him his dues in any other form. In vain the young man replied to him in monosyllables, and never took his eyes off Carlyon and his cousin, who were conversing in reality innocently enough about ordinary matters; the doctor poured forth his cornucopia of news to the last item, and then took to science.

"By the bye, Mr. Richard, ever since I heard you have been to Peru, I have wanted to have a long talk with you about the cinchona plant."

And a long talk he had, lasting through half the repast, during which his unfortunate victim presented the appearance rather of one who was employed in *taking* quinine than of merely conversing about it. Mr. Crawford, senior, threw in a word or two, here and there, evincing considerable knowledge of the subject, but never at sufficient length to extricate his nephew from the discussion and set him at liberty to watch his cousin and her neighbor. If, in short, the whole thing had been planned for the discomfiture of the young sailor, and for affording his opportunity to Carlyon, the end in view could not have been more successfully attained.

When Agnes had risen and departed, the doctor, exhilerated by social success and some first-rate Madeira, was still the lion of the evening.

"I am glad to see *you* to-night, Mr. Carlyon," said the little man, good-humoredly; "the last time we parted, it was after rather an unpleasant discussion; but forgive and forget is my motto, as I am sure it is yours. And I am glad to see you *here*, sir, especially, where you will find precept and example too—for, if your excellent daughter, Mr. Crawford, does not convert him from his errors, neither would one who rose from the dead; that's my opinion."

"I too am extremely glad," observed the old gentleman, with a grave smile, "to see Mr. Carlyon here, although I was not aware that he stood in need of spiritual aid. But for him, sir, my daughter, of whom you are pleased to speak so highly, would not be now alive; nor, indeed, would this young gentleman."

"I have already endeavored to express my gratitude to Mr. Carlyon," rejoined Richard, stiffly. "Mr. Carstairs, I think I know what you have in your mind, and also in your pocket. I assure you my uncle has no sort of objection to your smoking a cigar."

"None whatever," responded the old gentleman, and the cigars were lighted accordingly.

Carlyon had not thought it possible that any observation of Richard Crawford's could have afforded him so much satisfaction. Armed with the benignant weed he knew that he would be permitted to dream as he pleased while the doctor talked; that he could conceal his thoughts in grateful silence as easily as he could hide his countenance in the fragrant smoke.

"You are very indulgent, Mr. Crawford," began the little man; "unusually so to us young folks—ahem" (the doctor was on the shady side of fifty); "and you don't smoke yourself, neither, which makes the permission doubly commendable."

"I was so smoke-dried in my—at one time in my life," observed the old gentleman coldly, "that nothing annoys me in that way."

Mr. Carstairs had it upon the tip of his tongue to say, "That was in the army, I suppose," but he did not feel quite equal to such an audacity, so helped himself to Madeira instead.

"One thing gives me great comfort," continued the little man; "without which, even with your permission, I should scarcely venture to enjoy myself in this way, and that is, that Miss Agnes has no objection to the smell of smoke. She never asks a poor man to put out his pipe when visiting his cottage, although the tobacco in Mellor is by no means like that of the young squire's here. What a difference there is in tobacco! When we go home together, Carlyon, I shall ask you for one out of your case."

Carlyon laughed, and they all laughed. This little doctor, who had dined and wined so freely, and was enjoying himself so much, was quite a godsend to the company. In the drawing-room after dinner he was still the leading spirit. At the conclusion (and sometimes a little before it) of Agnes's charming Scotch songs he led the applause, clapping his large hands together, like a dramatic critic of the pit. Once again he informed Carlyon that he was glad to see him in that house, and in such improving company. "Go and talk to her, sir, she will do you good," whispered he, with earnestness. Nor did he fail to give him the opportunity; for fastening vampire-like on the unhappy Richard, he sucked his brains for a quarter of an hour, with reference to the insufficient supply of lime-juice in the merchant service for the prevention of scurvy. In short, Carstairs was the guest of the evening; nay, it was Carstairs's dinner given by Crawford; it was almost Carstairs's daughter by a previous marriage.

Carlyon laughed aloud as he and the little man strode home together that beautiful night —having sent away their respective vehicles— each with one of those excellent cigars of the Woodlees brand in their mouths. He had not had much private talk with Agnes, but he was indebted to the surgeon for all that he had had. Her last words had been the sweetest. She had expressed a wish to take the portrait of her equine preserver Red Berild. He was to ride the gallant roan to Greycrags for that purpose the very next day. She had said, "any day," and he had replied, "To-morrow," and to-morrow it was to be. It would take a long time and many sittings (if such a term could be used for such a subject) to paint a horse. He saw no end to his opportunities of visiting Greycrags.

"What a charming evening we have had," exclaimed he, enthusiastically.

"Very jolly!" answered the surgeon, promptly. "I never enjoyed myself more in my life. Curious young fellow, though, that Mr. Richard; deuced hard to get any thing out of him. Wants a deal of pumping. But when I want to get the truth out of a man, I flatter myself I generally get it. How do you like Miss Agnes?"

"Stop a bit; my cigar's going out. Give me a light, Carstairs."

"No, it isn't. It is in a state of complete combustion. How do you like her, sir?"

"What, Miss Crawford?"

"Well, I don't mean the girl that helped to wait at table; I refer to our late hostess."

"I think she is a very—pleasant—agreeable —and certainly beautiful young woman."

This opinion, given with the utmost deliberation, and much of the conscious solemnity of a judge, seemed to satisfy the inquirer. They walked on for some distance in silence.

"Don't you think that young fellow, Richard, uncommonly handsome, Carlyon?"

"Very," returned the squire, unhesitatingly.

"And so young, too," continued the doctor. "One can not wonder that Miss Agnes is obviously weak in that quarter. Did you not notice how quickly she spoke in his behalf when the old gentleman was inclined to take him to task once or twice."

"Yes; she defends every body; and, besides, as you say, she is doubtless much attached to the lad. They are first cousins, you know."

They walked on in silence as before, except that ever and anon the doctor now stole a look at his unconscious companion, full of embarrassment and pity. His high spirits seemed to have quite deserted him. Carlyon, on the other hand, stepped gayly along, solacing himself, in place of another cigar, with snatches of song, according to his custom when well-content. They were drawing near to Mellor, where they were to part, before Mr. Carstairs spoke again.

"I say, Carlyon, did you observe a very singular thing that took place this evening while we were sitting and smoking in the dining-room?"

"Yes," answered the other, demurely; "I noticed you let Mr. Richard finish one whole sentence without interrupting him; it was a phenomenon no one could fail to observe."

"Pooh! pooh! I don't mean that; those young fellows want to be pulled up now and then. But did you see what old Crawford was doing while we smoked?"

"No; what?"

"Why, he was chewing tobacco. He kept moving the quid about in his mouth whenever he thought he was not observed."

"Nonsense. He was talking, only you would not listen to a word he had to say, so that he might have seemed to you to be only chewing."

"I will stake my existence, Carlyon, that he had a quid in his mouth. Was it not monstrous?"

"I didn't see it; and, therefore, can't say whether it was monstrous or not," rejoined the other, laughing.

"Now, do be serious, Carlyon. I mean, was it not monstrous for a person in Mr. Crawford's assumed position to be doing such a thing?"

"Assumed; why assumed?" inquired the other, sharply.

"Well, that's just the point," pursued the doctor. "Nobody knows who he is, or where he hails from. You have observed, I dare say, how shyly he fights off any question about his past history. Well, coupling that peculiar fact with the occupation in which I saw him engaged to-night — putting one and one together, you know—I should be surprised (notwithstanding Puce's opinion to the contrary) if this strange old gentleman has not sprung from a very low origin."

"Well; and what then?" inquired Carlyon, coolly.

"Well, a good deal *then*, I should think. I mean that this Crawford's relatives and antecedents are probably by no means what they ought to be."

"Yet he seems to me to speak very good grammar," returned the other, laughing. "If, however," added he, more gravely, " you refer to the possibly inferior social position of the ancestors of the gentleman with whom we have just condescended to dine, I honestly tell you I have no sympathy with such prejudices. A man's father may have been a sweep for all I care, so long as the color is not transmitted (I do stop at color). And, by the bye, did you happen to observe that dusky female who flitted like a bat up the staircase as we were lighting our cigars in the hall?"

"Yes; that was Cubra, young Mr. Richard's foster-mother. The only servant whom the Crawfords brought with them from the south. She never ails in health, or she might afford me an opportunity for a harmless experiment I have long had in view, in respect to the circulation of the blood. Very interesting subject that, Mr. Carlyon."

"Doubtless, doctor. That reminds me—since you are the medical attendant of Mr. Crawford, might I ask, supposing it is no breach of professional confidence, whether he has any thing the matter with his heart?"

The doctor's rubicund face grew almost white; he stopped suddenly. "What, in heaven's name, made you ask that question?" inquired he.

"Simply, because I have seen him start and change color in a very curious manner more than once, from apparently inadequate causes."

"No, sir, his heart is as sound as a roach," returned the doctor, abruptly; " I wish I could say as much for all my—patients. Well, I must wish you 'good-night' here, Carlyon."

"Good-night, Carstairs. Don't cut poor Crawford out of your visiting list because you are not sure if his family came in with the Conqueror. Make inquiries; or give him the benefit of the doubt."

Laughing gayly the young squire strode away up the hill. The church-yard cast no shadow of death upon him to-night as he passed it swiftly by. The moonlight sleeping on the bay had no power to make him sad. When a woman has passed the heyday of her life, she never deceives herself in respect to that matter, notwithstanding that she may use all her art to deceive others; but with us men it is different. There is an Indian summer in many a man's life; a period, always brief indeed, but of uncertain duration, which takes place after youth has fled, and its flight been acknowledged. It is fostered by the sunshine of a woman's love, often only to be nipped by the frost of her indifference. Then winter sets in indeed.

This second summer had suddenly befallen John Carlyon. He had never been in such high spirits, or felt so full of life since the time —a score of years ago—when he was a boy.

"I ought to have told him from the first," mused Mr. Carstairs, gloomily, as he lit the flat candle left for him as usual in his little hall. " My plan for that poor fellow's welfare has sadly miscarried. Instead of her doing him good she has done him harm. He has fallen in love with her, head over ears. What a *fiasco* have I made of it! All that I have done this evening is to leave an impression upon the company that Robert Augustus Carstairs, was exceedingly drunk. Well, I will tell Carlyon to-morrow at all hazards. I was a coward not to do it just now when opportunity offered; but he seemed so full of hope and life, poor fellow, that I had not the heart."

CHAPTER XII.
SKETCHING RED BERILD.

In pursuance of his previous night's resolve the doctor called at Woodlees first in his morning's round; he had taken one foot out of the stirrup, making sure of his man at that early hour, when Robin stopped him with, "The young squire's out, Mr. Carstairs;" then added, in a confidential tone, "he has ridden over to Greycrags." And his old eyes twinkled with unaccustomed mirth. "There mayn't be any thing *in* it, you know; I don't say there is," continued he, "but it would be a great thing for the old house, as you remember, in the old times, to have a missus, and Miss Agnes, by all accounts, is just the one to do him good."

"Yes, Robin, perhaps so," responded the doctor, thoughtfully, not at all astonished by the terms in which the ancient retainer spoke of his young master and his affairs. Carlyon's spiritual case was considered "interesting" by all the orthodox about Mellor, and as many different remedies had been recommended by all classes, as are volunteered for the whooping-cough. "I will call again to-morrow, or the next day."

Day after day went on, and Mr. Carstairs called and called again at Woodlees, but saw nobody but Robin, whose servile smirk was now exchanged for a broad and very unbecoming grin. "I have done my duty," murmured the little doctor to himself on each occasion; then cantered away, not sorry that his mission had ended where it did, like an unwilling churchgoer who duly presents himself at the sacred edifice and finds there is no room for him.

In the mean time Red Berild—very gradually, for Carlyon, when matters were going too fast, would make critical objections, and cause a whole leg to be rubbed out—was being transferred to paper. He was permitted to come upon the lawn, where he stood, now making futile efforts to crop the short-shaven sward, now advancing toward his master and the fair artist, to complain perhaps of the too great efficacy of the grass-cutting machine. Like the French Government when revolution threatens, Agnes always gave him bread upon such occasions, which she kept by her in necessarily large quantities for purposes of erasure. The three made a very pretty picture; Agnes sitting upon that camp-stool reclaimed from ocean, Carlyon stretched at her feet, with his fine face bathed in sunshine; and the great horse champing his bit, as though proudly conscious that he was being handed down to posterity. On the terrace-walk, half way up the wooded hill, sat Richard Crawford, always with the same book in his hand, and the same leaf of the book open before him.

At unfrequent intervals Mr. Crawford senior's skeleton form would stalk out of the house, and cast its gaunt shadow over the preoccupied pair.

"How good it was of Mr. Carlyon to give up his usual gallop on the hill-side, or 'over sands,' in order to indulge his daughter's whim in this fashion. What a very magnificent creature—although he (Mr. Crawford) for his part was no horseman, nor a judge of horses—was Red Berild! He did hope so much that Mr. Carlyon would honor his poor house (lunch being invariably over before the old gentleman put in an appearance), by remaining to dinner."

Thus matters went on—with the exception of the wet days, that are "neither few nor far between" about Mellor, and on which there was no excuse for Carlyon's coming—for weeks. The conversation between him and Agnes had hitherto never centred upon religious matters, since the occasion of his first visit to Greycrags. Each felt that that was the only ground not common to both, and, although one of them most earnestly desired that it should be made so, she shrunk from the contest for fear of its possible result. Not that she had any apprehension for her own firm faith; not that she was without hope of turning his noble soul to the truth; but, if she failed to conquer, something told her that they two would have to part; and she was so happy as things were. Happy always in his presence; but, out of it, when he had gone away no wiser than he came—not bettered, when she had had it in her humble power to better him, or at least to try to do so—her conscience, tender as a rose leaf, was pricked.

"Preach the word: be instant in season, out of season; reprove, rebuke." Had these words been addressed to Timothy only, or to all true professors of the faith? She would repeat them to herself, even while he was speaking to her in his low earnest tones, as though they were a charm against witchery. At last the opportunity long wished for, long shrunk from, offered itself.

He was speaking of Stephen Millet, now, notwithstanding his late lesson, and vehement protestations of amendment, become even a greater sot than before, and a source of poverty as well as wretchedness to his son.

"The poor fellow has had to sell his very furniture to support that old scoundrel," said Carlyon. "When I think of William Millet, and of my Lord Disney over yonder, it really almost seems that Providence, in applying the sacred precept of 'Love your enemies,' protects its own foes, while it persecutes its friends."

"That is indeed only seeming, Mr. Carlyon. The happiest man in all this parish, the richest (in all true riches), the wisest, the best, is William. Fret not thyself because of evil doers, of him who prospereth in the way, and bringeth evil devices to pass. Nay, do you believe in your inmost heart that such a man as Lord Disney is happy?"

"Most certainly I do, my dear Miss Agnes, in so far as his capabilities permit. He is not happy in the sense that you are happy, but he is happy enough for him. The middle classes of this country possess just so much religion as to make them uncomfortable. They have too little to constitute happiness, yet too much to permit of them enjoying themselves. Now, the aristocracy, to do them justice, are not restrained from indulging in any pleasure by considerations of its sinfulness. Nor do they lose the respect of society by so doing, for the Bible of the said middle classes is bound up with their *Peerage*, and merely forms a supplement to it, unless when they are at death's door, and the choice has to be abruptly made between their duty to the Lord of Lords, or to persons of title generally. Even the clergy are thus divided in allegiance; or else, like some we wot of, they boldly throw in their lot with the latter, and become, as it were, private chaplains to the hereditary aristocracy—than which occupation, by the bye, in the literal sense, I can fancy nothing queerer. Think of it: Paul accepting the post of private soul-keeper to a nobleman of the neighborhood; or still worse (since it would be a spiritual sinecure), to one *not* of the neighborhood! Upon the whole, I must say, for religious folks, that they have the smallest sense of humor, the greatest obtuseness with respect to their own anomalies and contradictions, and I may add, the least understanding of the principles of their own creed of any people I know. Have not the true faith with respect of persons—the whole chapter is addressed to these idiots; but it might just as well not have been written, we are told, since they grovel at the feet of any fellow-creature, however base, who happens to have a tag to his name. Look at the behavior of your religious folks about Mellor, in regard to his lordship, for instance. My sister Meg is almost charitable when she speaks of *his* little peccadillos. Mr. Puce himself dined at the greathouse last week, in company which I can not speak of before you."

He spoke with uncommon energy and passion, though never raising his voice beyond its usual tone; his cheeks flushed brightly, his eyes flashed scornful fire. Agnes, on the other hand, grew very white, and her hand, so cold that it could scarcely hold the brush, trembled exceedingly. She felt that the time was come for her to speak.

"This may be very true, Mr. Carlyon," returned she, after a pause, "concerning the professors of the truth—or at least some of them—because, as you say, they are ignorant of the very principles they profess. But if ignorant, why be angry with them? why scourge them with such terrible words, when they only (as you allow) need teaching? If we do not love our brother whom we have known, how can we love God whom we have not known?"

"Indeed, my dear Miss Agnes," rejoined Carlyon, smiling, "I think there is something wrong about that text, for I am sure I should have a much greater regard for sister Meg, if I had never had the misfortune to know her. Still, as you hint, my expressions were not charitable, and I retract them. Come, you see you are doing me good, reprobate that I am; and, also, please to observe that I might have behaved much worse by railing against religion itself, instead of its professors."

"I can not go with you there, Mr. Carlyon," replied Agnes, gravely. "I have always held that to speak evil recklessly against our fellow-creatures is worse than to speak blasphemy against the Most High. We can not hurt Him by any thing we say. He can redress his own wrongs in a terrible fashion; we are very sure of that, although He may not use the thunderbolt upon the instant. But Man, whom he has also bidden men to love, is weak; our words may injure him in reputation—in a thousand ways—nay, they may embitter his very soul."

"And do you say the same of deeds, Miss Agnes, in relation to man and his Creator?"

"Undoubtedly. Can any sacrilege be equal in guilt to an act of oppression, or rather is not oppression the very highest sacrilege against the poor, who are God's peculiar people?"

"Very good, and very true," said Carlyon. "Then the sin of unbelief, the intellectual misfortune of not being able to credit the statements of the Bible, you must allow is not to be compared in point of enormity to the sin of leading a wicked—that is, a cruel and remorseless—life"

Agnes was silent; her heart beat so strongly that she could hear it in that still sultry noon; she heard the horse cropping the grass; she thought she heard her ever-watchful cousin crumbling the leaves of his book as he leaned forward to listen to her reply.

"If faith without works is dead," continued Carlyon, earnestly, "faith with bad works must be surely rotten. Now what I want to know is this—I am not speaking of myself in the matter, for I do nothing to boast of, God knows—but are good works without faith in your opinion valueless, Miss Agnes?"

If he was not speaking of himself, it was, she well knew, of him that she had to speak, when she should answer. There were texts enough ready to her hand, crushing ones, final ones, such as Mr. Puce would have clapped on quickly enough, like hatches upon a mutinous crew in the Tropics, and yet she hesitated. A harsh and uncharitable dogma from her lips—that is, one that would seem so to this unregenerate man might do the very mischief it was her intention to avert. He had never given himself the opportunities of grace—what if she should throw away this chance by any spiritual indiscretion, and so through *her* (of all people) *this* soul (of all souls) should perish!

"You say you do not speak of yourself, Mr. Carlyon; but I can not affect to agree with you—at least, altogether—in that. Is it possible that you have no belief in religion?"

"I do not quite say that," returned Carlyon, frankly; "it is indeed impossible to be so rank an infidel in the presence of so pure a disciple—"

She stopped him with a reproving finger, and a face very stern and sad.

"Do not trifle with me, Mr. Carlyon; but answer me honestly, and like—if that is all I may adjure you by—and like a gentleman."

"Well, dear lady, I will say this much. Your religion is good for poor folks, I do believe, and admirably adapted for them, although, as I have said, the upper classes can make nothing of it. Your remark about William Millet, for instance, was in my opinion a just one. He comforts himself in the absence of earthly blessings, with dreams of heaven. The weightier his cross here, the richer, he thinks, his crown hereafter. The devout countrymen of our friend Mistress Cubra, who hope to gain Paradise by self-torture, present only an exaggerated phase of the same superstition. Don't be angry with me, Agnes," added he pleadingly, tenderly; "don't look like that. I was obliged to be honest with you. You would not have had me tell you a lie."

She shook her head, and her lips moved twice or thrice without sound.

"No," murmured she, presently; "I suppose a lie would have been worse even than what you have said. I am not angry, sir, God knows—I almost wish I were; but I would have given this right hand to have heard you answer differently. The Psalmist says that he never beheld the seed of the righteous begging their bread; but, how much more terrible is this, that the son of a righteous man should deny his God!"

She dropped her head upon her lap, and wept like one who feels she has lost forever him that is dearest to her.

"Shall I tell you, Miss Crawford," said Carlyon, in an altered voice, not moved by her tears, but cold and bitter in its tone, "shall I tell you how it was I became a heretic?"

"Became, sir! it is not possible that such as you can have once found God and then lost him. And yet I have heard of something of this before; with such a father it could not be but that you were brought up in the right way: and after that to go astray! Alas! alas! 'it is impossible,' it is written, 'if they shall then fall away, to renew them again.'"

The despair in the young girl's face was unspeakable, as though, with those tender eyes, she had herself seen the open door of heaven closed in his face.

"Miss Crawford, I am beyond measure shocked to have caused you such pain; I was about to say—not in justification, indeed, but in explanation of my opinions, that there had been reasons unguessed at—"

"But with God nothing shall be impossible," murmured Agnes, under her breath; "why did I not think of that before? Yes, yes—I beg your pardon, sir, you were saying—"

"I was about to tell you something that has been a secret between me and the dead for many a year. Promise me to keep it, when you have heard it, as though it had never been told."

"I promise."

"Listen, then."

CHAPTER XIII.
HOW JOHN CARLYON BECAME A HERETIC.

WITH hesitation and evident reluctance, with his face averted from the listener, and at first hammering the daisy heads upon the lawn with the handle of his riding-whip, John Carlyon began—

"My father, as no doubt you have heard, Miss Crawford, on all hands, was indeed a constant churchgoer, and he brought me up in the same path. There was no man more respected, although I do not think he was loved, in all this neighborhood. He not only never offended against the proprieties, but he was a steadfast upholder of them—what is called one of the safeguards of society. That was the general opinion of him to the day of his death; but it was a mistaken one. He was a hypocrite from first to last; his whole life was one huge lie."

"Mr. Carlyon!" exclaimed Agnes; "you make my blood run cold; not so much by what you say, which seems almost too terrible to be true, but at your manner of saying it."

"When, however, I first found out the truth, young lady, I was more moved than I am now. The student of anatomy faints at his introduction to the dissecting-room; but, after a while, he ceases to shudder at its revelations. He sees what lies behind the velvet cheek of beauty, and the keen eye of wit, but it affects him little. He knows that with all humanity it is the same. He has his advantage over me in that respect. If I could think that behind the veil of religion, the cloak of respectability, the infidel and the debauchee were inwardly concealed, I should loathe my own father less; but I know there are honest folks in the world. I know that you, Agnes, are as pure as you look, as good as you seem. But this man, that was my own flesh and blood, to whom I owe my being, to whom I was bound by Nature herself to respect and honor—oh, spare me! I can not bear to speak of it."

"Even a good man may err and give way to strong temptation," whispered Agnes; "yet if he repents—"

"This man did not repent," broke in Carlyon, almost fiercely. "He had nothing to repent of; for in his eyes nothing was sin, nothing was vice, nothing was wrong—unless it was found out. Then indeed he would have been sorry. He was a tyrant, and he broke my mother's heart. I will never forgive him that! She was beautiful, gentle, guileless as yourself, and he killed her. She prayed for him upon her death-bed, and he despised her prayer; I do believe that that was the bitterest drop she had to drain in the whole cup of her wretched married life. She made me promise not to tell him what I knew, and not to tell the world. I had to live on with this murderer for years, a participator in his acted lie, and hoodwinked, as he thought, like the rest. He deceived every body—yes, every body—parson, people, neighbors, servants. Robin, at home, believes him to this day to have been the best of men. A tyrant and a libertine, he was yet reckoned the most pious man in Mellor parish. This was the sort of father, Agnes, from whom I learned how to be religious."

"Mr. Carlyon," returned she, thoughtfully, after a long pause, "are you sure—are you quite sure, that in your great love for such a mother as you describe, and in your own tenderness of heart, you may not have taken sternness for cruelty?"

He shook his head impatiently.

"Some men," she went on, "not naturally cruel, I have known to be without tenderness of manner, even to those dearest to them; rugged and harsh even when their wives lay a-dying, and yet not heartless."

"No, girl, this man was not rugged. He knew how to frame tenderest words for ears that should have blushed to listen to them. Of some men, it is said, 'we never knew his worth until we lost him;' now *I* never knew how base a father I had got until he came to die."

"Ah! he confessed his sins, and the long catalogue appalled you!" exclaimed Agnes, clasping her hands. "You should thank God for that. Perhaps in that last hour, all was forgiven him. No one can fathom the infinite depths of Divine mercy. Let us hope, let us pray, that he may have been preserved from that awful state of which he stood in dread."

"Nay, Agnes, we Carlyons have no fear," observed her companion proudly.

"No fear!" echoed she, in scorn. "What! had this man, living, as you say, a lie, for fear of the opinion of his neighbors, no *fear?* Does cowardice, then, among infidels, solely consist in being afraid of the righteous judgments of God? If so, 'obtuseness with respect to their own anomalies and contradictions, is surely not entirely peculiar to religious people."

Carlyon bit his lip.

"It would surely be the rankest cowardice to be afraid of that in the existence of which one does not believe," said he, evasively. "The man I speak of died, laughing in his sleeve at the world he had cajoled. He had been a wanderer in many lands, and examined a hundred creeds, only to find one as worthless as another. His god was Self, and he had served him very faithfully. His last advice to me, his only son, was given when the grave was gaping for him; we were alone together, and he upon the sofa that was to be his death-bed, and he knew it; the very room has been hateful to me ever since. He bid me lie like him; be serious and devout; affect the virtues that I had not, for the very vices' sake which they concealed. So should I live a life of ease and yet of dignity, and die with honor, troops of friends, and all the regard that accompanies the close of a life well spent. He would, as it were, have bequeathed me his very mantle of deceit, having no farther occasion for it himself, like some poor conjuror, who teaches his tricks to his children while he lies a-dying, as the best legacy he has to leave them."

"Mr. Carlyon, this is too horrible to be believed," gasped Agnes. "Nature does not permit of such a father. I have seen many deathbeds, and when death is claiming us we are often not ourselves; the senses are disordered, the mind wanders; men impute to themselves sins which they have never committed."

"But not this man, Agnes. Do you suppose that I would not believe so if I could; that I have not exhausted every suggestion that could lighten this load which has so weighed down my life? No. He told me the truth at last. He left behind him only too ample corroboration of it. No one is so prudent that he can guard his memory after death. No man, who keeps a check-book, can dare say 'I do not keep a journal;' besides there were letters that came for him long after he was lying in his grave—but why all this? You know his secret now, which I have hitherto preserved inviolate. Do you wonder that I loathe religion; that 'the very name of Nazarene is wormwood to my Paynim spleen,' and synonymous with all that is false and fairseeming? That, from the instant that I found myself freed by this man's death from my promise to my mother, that I forsook his hypocritical ways and all belonging to them?"

"I do not wonder, Mr. Carlyon," said Agnes, sorrowfully; "I do not even say (as others would), why doubt the genuineness of that thing of which you have only witnessed a fraudulent imitation. We are molded, I know, by the iron force of circumstances—though not all of us. Your mother did not lose her faith in Heaven because your father had none?"

"My mother? No," answered Carlyon, in hushed and reverent tones.

"She was a Christian woman to the last?"

"She was an angel: to impute wrong to her would be to confuse wrong with right."

"And has the thought of her—of her long-suffering patience, and forgiveness — never moved you toward the faith your father professed, but which she practiced?"

"I have sometimes thought there should be an immortality for such as she; that so much goodness ought not surely to be allowed to perish. I have thought so lately of one other person also—of you, Agnes."

"Hush, sir, hush! I am very different from this saint in heaven. If she had lived, I can not but think her love, her teaching, her example would have won you to her creed, as to herself. You felt better—happier—when you were in her presence, did you not?"

"Yes, I did," replied Carlyon, eagerly; "as I feel when I am in yours. Yes, Agnes—do not shrink from me; I will do my best—only I will not lie—to learn better things of *you*. Will you teach me, even although I do not promise to learn?"

He looked up in her face for the first time, while she, the heretofore questioner, drooped her eyelids, and a fire burned in her cheeks.

"Can you not take compassion upon me, even though I am a heretic?" urged he with tenderness; but she heard him not.

"If any man love not the Lord, let him be anathema, maranatha," were the words which she seemed to hear.

"Go to some wise and holy man," said she, in a faint voice.

"To Mr. Puce?" asked he; "or to whom? No, I shall sit at the feet of this Gamaliel, Agnes Crawford, or of none. I love you with all my heart; nay, I can well believe—so wondrous is the change through all my being—with all my soul. I seem to have another life beyond myself, and if that be my soul, it is you who are its keeper, for to you it flies. Will you be my teacher? Will you be my wife? one word, one 'yes,' will answer both questions." But there came no answer. He could not even read one in her face, for it was hidden closely in her hands. She was speaking, though her speech was inarticulate, but not to him.

"I know you will never marry—an infidel," said he, slowly.

"Never, never," answered she, with eagerness. It was quite a relief to her to get so categorical a question, and one to which she could so unhesitatingly reply.

"Yet you will not reject my—proposition; you will not refuse to afford me an opportunity of being convinced?"

"I can not say," murmured she; "I must have time, Mr. Carlyon, to think of this. Do not press me for your answer—that is, just now. In your presence, I can not—I must be alone," added she, hurriedly. "I must ask guidance."

"I venture to think," interrupted Carlyon, respectfully, "that your father will be no obstruction."

Her face flushed from brow to chin. "I was not referring to my father," said she, coldly.

"I trust," returned he, earnestly, "I have not been too bold—not said too much and too soon. Pardon me, Agnes; do not let the greatness of my love be the cause of my undoing. If my presence is an embarrassment to you, you will write, perhaps?"

"Yes, I will write!" exclaimed she, eagerly; "to-night, to-morrow. It will be better so."

He rose at once, and took her hand in his.

"Whatever you may so write, Agnes," said he, slowly, "will be my law. If you decide against me, to have nothing to do with this wicked person, to avoid the touching of pitch, lest even your pure soul may be defiled, I shall understand it. It will be unnecessary to state reasons. The one word 'no' will suffice; I had rather that you wrote nothing more. I will never trouble you again. I shall have turned my back on Paradise forever. But if—if you think within yourself that I may be won to what you deem the right—mind, I do not say it is even probable, for I will not use lies to gain Heaven itself—and if won, that you might, in time, even stoop to love me, I shall understand that also, by one word, 'yes.'"

What would he not have given to have touched her white brow with his lips, as she stood close beside him, downcast, thoughtful, with her snow-cold hand in his! It was not because every window, for all that he knew, might have had its watcher, or because her cousin was playing the spy as usual, upon yonder terrace, that Carlyon did not do so. It was not for fear of *them*, that, having raised those fingers midway to his lips, he let them fall again, and turned away in silence, while Red Berild followed, docile, with a hasty farewell crop at the scanty grass. To have kissed her would have been very sweet, but it might have demanded its dread memories for years.

Heavy of heart, the strong man took the road from Greycrags homeward; while his good horse pressing his great nose against his hand, strove vainly to give his master comfort.

Agnes remained standing in her place, deep in thought, till a book fell heavily upon the terrace-walk, and a well-known step began to descend the hill; then, at it's first foot-fall, she started from her reverie and hastening in, sought her own chamber, where she remained for hours.

Her mind was torn with antagonistic emotions. She would never marry an unbeliever, that was certain; to that she clung, and reverted to it again and again; it was her sheet-anchor in the storm. But had she not grown to love one? Was she not paltering with her own conscience in this matter? and even with still more sacred things? Did she honestly believe herself to be a bearer of God's message to those unwilling ears; or was not her strong desire to convert the sceptic, alloyed with a wish to win the man? Agnes Crawford was not a student of Pope, or she might almost have applied to herself, the self-accusation of Eloisa—

Even then to those dread altars as I drew,
Not on the cross my eyes were fixed, but you;
Not Grace nor Zeal, Love only was my call,
And if I lose thy love I lose my all.

Hour after hour passed by; the luncheon bell rang, but she took no heed; but, late in the afternoon, a knock came to her chamber door, and a voice in mocking tones (or what, perhaps, she fancifully imagined to be so), reached her through the key-hole, saying, "Missie Agnes, you are wanted in the parlor; Mrs. Newman's come, and wish to see you very partickler."

"Mr. Carlyon's sister!" murmured Agnes to herself, while a sudden pain seemed to shoot through her heart; "why should *she* come here?" But she answered, in her usual firm, clear tones, "Very well, Cubra; tell her I will be down directly."

CHAPTER XIV.
MRS. NEWMAN'S ACT OF CHARITY.

It is not to be supposed that Carlyon's visits to Greycrags passed without notice among the good folks of Mellor. The appetite of that small community for gossip was absolutely insatiable; it was quite a trade with more than one respectable female to make it, and even to invent the materials. So that when a subject for it was found, that could be relied upon as fact, good solid substratum for all sorts of scandal, the public satisfaction was unbounded. But not in all cases the private. Mrs. Newman, of Mellor Lodge—a place that had been once termed the Priory, but it was not to be supposed that so good a Protestant would call her residence by *that* name—was by no means pleased with the reports that reached her from all quarters concerning her brother's proceedings. She had long "washed her hands of him," in a spiritual sense; she had excommunicated him in an almost episcopal manner, by throwing her hands up and shutting her eyes, at solemn conclave over many a tea-table; but she had never shut her eyes to his property, which was entirely at his own disposal. She anticipated with confidence the reversion of Woodlees for herself and Jed (short and loving for Jedediah), her son, when its present unworthy occupant should be—elsewhere; for Carlyon was her senior by five years. It was astonishing with what calmness and fortitude this excellent woman reflected upon the future fate—the terrors which she honestly believed to be in store—for so near a relative. Upon one occasion, while discoursing upon this particular topic, which was a very favorite one with her, she was rebuked by no less a person than the archdeacon of the diocese. For archdeacons, as such, she had no great reverence; but this one happened to be own nephew to my Lord Disney, and she had that admiration for noble birth which supplies the place of such a multitude of other virtues in minds like hers. He bade her not to make too sure of the eternity of the torments of the wicked, and explained to her the doubts entertained by the learned of the literal meaning of the word αιώνιος. "Not," added he, with a benignant smile, "that that much alters matters; for the duration signified doubtless extends to millions and millions of years."

"That is *some* comfort," quoth Mrs. Newman cheerfully, and with a sigh of relief.

But, notwithstanding this opinion of Carlyon's deserts, she had always counted upon his leaving Woodlees and the rest of his property to his own flesh and blood. Not to provide for one's family is (as is well-known) to be worse than an infidel, and Meg had never thought worse of brother John than *that*. Yet, lo! at an age when he might be supposed to have almost escaped the perils of matrimony, here was he visiting Greycrags daily, with a motive that it was easy to guess at. Jedediah, indeed, who was of a frank and open nature, even for eighteen, alluded to it one morning at breakfast in the following terms.

"I say, mother! Uncle John is after that gal at Greycrags—Miss What-d'ye-call-um—Crawford."

"Seeking to ally himself matrimonially with that young woman, Jed? Impossible!"

"Glad you think so," answered Jedediah, gruffly, and filling his mouth with muffin; he was rather gluttonous in his habits, and also a good deal spoiled. If his mother was stern to others, she was not so with him; he had always done as he liked from his childhood, and he had generally liked what was not good for him. He was vicious beyond what she had any suspicion of, and his good-nature was of the sort that only lasts so long as its proprietor is pleased. Mrs. Newman was getting, as all such mothers do in time, a little afraid of her darling son."

"You needn't be cross, Jedediah," said she, quietly; "I was only asking for information. The affairs of this world have, I am thankful to say, no great interest in my eyes, and those who know me do not much trouble me with them. I have, however, heard a rumor of what you speak of, although I have never suspected any thing serious in it. I am not one of a suspicious nature, Jed."

"Ah," said the young man, dryly—so dryly, indeed, that the tone would have suited "Bah" equally well; "I wish for my sake, then, if not for your own, that you'd just look alive and put a stop to it. It's a most disgraceful thing. Why, if uncle marries, there may be a whole kit of children, and then what becomes of those alterations that you are always talking about making when we come into Woodlees?"

Between Mrs. Newman and her brother, although their characters, and therefore the expression of their countenances were so different, there was a considerable personal resemblance. Although she did not dress becomingly, and, indeed, wore clothes of a texture much inferior to what is usual with women of her social position, and wore them threadbare, she always looked a lady; but when annoyed, her thin lips shut together unpleasantly close; her fine blue eyes seemed to harden, and she sniffed like the war-horse that scents the battle, only of course in a lower key. There had been a passage of arms between herself and Jedediah that morning in reference to a scarcity of marmalade at the breakfast-table, and he had carried his point and got a new pot. This had given her real pain, as extravagance always did. There were still a few stale strips sticking to the little glass dish, and she would have liked to have seen them eaten before being driven to the preserve cupboard for a fresh supply. Jed had even taunted her, at the height of the discussion, with those prudential habits which her enemies (for the good lady had enemies) denominated parsimoniousness, and when she had replied, "Ungrateful boy, it is only for you I save," he had replied, "It is for *me*, then, that I require some fresh marmalade."

He had taken butter, as well as that costly sweetmeat, with his muffin, on purpose to vex his parent, and had effected his object; and now he was choosing a subject of conversation very ill adapted to give her peace of mind. The relations said to be established between her brother and Miss Crawford were by no means a matter of such indifference to her as she professed. In fact, she had thought of little else from the first moment the rumor had reached her ears; but she had endeavored to shut her eyes to the full extent of the danger; it was very objectionable to have it brought before her in this inexorable manner, and she sniffed disapproval audibly.

"Yes, I know you don't like it," observed Jedediah, in reference to this signal; "but it is time to look matters in the face."

"What would you have me do, Jedediah?"

"Well, I'm sure I don't know; she is one of your own sort, this girl, and you ought to be able to stop it somehow. I only know this, that Uncle John is said to be getting on in that quarter uncommonly fast, and the sooner you set about putting a spoke in his wheel the better."

"I shall certainly consider it my duty," said Mrs. Newman, slowly, "to hint to this young lady at the injurious reports that are in circulation respecting her: she can not surely be aware of the peculiar opinions entertained by your unhappy uncle."

"She is probably aware that he is sweet upon her, and has a good two thousand a year," observed the practical Jedediah.

"No, Jed; I will not think so ill of any young person of religious principles as to suppose she is actuated by sordid motives."

"Bah!" exclaimed Jedediah, this time with a most unmistakable B. It was rude, but not altogether inexcusable. From the day from which dated one of the boy's earliest but strongest recollections, when his deceased parent had been carried to his long home in a coffin made out of an ancient piano-case (some enemies of the thrifty widow averred that it was too short for him, and that he had been decapitated to suit its dimensions), up to the present hour, when that stale marmalade had been almost foisted upon his reluctant palate, he had been familiar with the sordid devices of at least one saint, and had learned to suspect them all. Yet singularly enough, while mistrusting the genuineness of the profession of those among whom his lot was cast, this young man had imbibed their prejudices, and though greatly inclined to vice, was as intolerant of error as Mrs. Newman herself. It was an unspeakable comfort to her to reflect, that although boys would be boys, and you could not put old heads upon young shoulders (this in allusion to some very Bowdlerized edition of Jed's peccadillos which occasionally reached her ears), her Jedediah was a young man of the most excellent principles. For the rest, he was a very handsome young fellow, (except for a certain coarseness about the mouth, which it did not need a Lavater to translate), and there was no wonder that his mother was proud of him. Moreover, he was a sensible fellow, after a fashion—what Mr. Carlyle and the vulgar are both agreed to call "knowing"—and she did not despise his blunt but practical utterances.

Nothing more passed between them on the present occasion; their sparring—in which the hitting was all on one side—often ended in that manner; but the force of Jedediah's observations, backed as they were by Mrs. Newman's own secret misgivings, was not lost. She had made up her mind to follow his advice in respect to that peril so imminently impending at Greycrags, but in the mean time she did not neglect her usual precautions in the smaller matters of domestic economy. When her Jed had lounged out of the room to have his pipe in the stable—for the time had not yet come when he should rule the house and take his narcotic therein—she locked up the tea and sugar, and having scraped up the old marmalade and mixed it with the new, made a faint mark with her pencil outside the pot exactly at its highest level. Then she descended to the kitchen, discovered that there were sufficient bones and *débris* left from past meals to make excellent soup, without getting in fresh stock, as recommended by that extravagant hussy, the cook; sniffed violently in the larder over the carcase of a fowl, which did not appear to have so many legs as it ought to have had. "Mr. Jedediah had had *both* broiled for his yesterday's breakfast," said the hussy. "I only saw *one*," said her mistress. She shook her head when the kitchen-maid demanded another box of lucifer matches.

"How dare you require so many lucifer matches in the summer?" inquired she, as though, during that season, the kitchen fire might be lighted by a burning-glass. "What is the use of my having that admirable proverb hung over the dresser?" and she pointed to the spot upon the whited wall where " *Waste not, want not*" was inscribed upon a scroll, not in the illegible high church fashion, but in such a manner that one who roasts might read.

Next she dived into the pantry and delivered to the astonished foot-page—the last of a long but short-lived line of foot-pages—a lecture upon the use and abuse of plate-powder, with a few remarks upon the pecuniary penalties that await breakage in all well-conducted establishments. After which, ascending noiselessly to the upper regions, she came upon two housemaids making a bed and giggling, to whom she promptly issued a couple of tracts, entitled "The Crackling of Thorns; or, How Anna Thema and Marion Arthur were made to laugh on the other side of their mouths," with one (practical) illustration.

After thus performing the duties of a diligent mistress, she sat down at her desk, with a mind relieved of all lesser cares, and free to be concentrated upon the important subject forced upon her notice by Jedediah. Even then her habitual prudence and attention to minute affairs did not desert her; instead of spoiling half a dozen sheets of Bath post, as some persons do, who have a letter of difficult composition before them, she selected some waifs and strays of paper, backs of envelopes, and blank spaces at the foot of bills, and thus proceeded to concoct a letter on almost as many surfaces as the Sybil inscribed her oracles. "Dear madam," it began; then "Madam;" then "My Christian friend;" and once—but that she tore up into small pieces as soon as written, and sniffed so that she blew them all about the room—"My dear Miss Crawford."

She was still hanging over "My Christian Friend"—on the blue lines of a butcher's bill—like a poet in search of an impossible rhyme, when a shrill voice suddenly interrupted her with "Please, mum, the gardener's wife is a-waitin' for her bonnet."

"You wicked boy," cried she, starting to her feet; "how dare you enter the room without knocking?" and, with that, as if to apply the mnemonical system of association of ideas, she smartly slapped his cheeks. "Tell her to come up; that is, in a minute or two."

The page retired drooping, dogs' eared. Mrs. Newman instantly sought her own apartment, and opening the door of its hanging wardrobe, took from it a faded old summer bonnet, looking like an autumn leaf.

"I've promised it to the woman," mused she regretfully; "and I suppose I must give it her. And yet it looks almost as good as new. I am sure I might have had another season's wear out of it."

She gazed at the yellow bonnet-strings which had once been white, with lingering fondness.

"Well, I'll cut off the trimming, at all events; that is quite unsuited to a person in her station of life."

Suiting the action to the word, she regarded the mutilated article of apparel with some approach to resignation.

"There," said she; "the wires are all in shape. She could not have got such a bonnet as that, if it was new, under fifteen shillings. Fifteen shillings," she repeated, very slowly, as though she were reluctantly counting down the money, coin by coin. "That is a very large sum to give away. I think I'll tell her to call again some other time—but then I've done that twice already. How weak it was of me to promise it to her. How foolishly impulsive I am."

The mirror of the hanging wardrobe before which she stood did not reflect the features which are generally considered indicative of an impulsive character. The pinched-up mouth, the greedy eyes, the fingers clutching tightly at the threatened treasure, would have furnished a study for any painter who wished to symbolize (genteelly) greed. But presently the thin lips straightened themselves into a really pleasant smile, the eyes softened and even twinkled, and the white hand carried its burden of frail rubbish with a grace. She had thought of a plan to keep her word, and yet not lose her bonnet, or at least her bonnet's worth.

"Well, Mrs. Jones," exclaimed she, with cheerfulness, as she entered the drawing-room, "you see I have brought your bonnet."

It was very necessary to say this. For Mrs. Jones, a delicate nipped-up-looking woman, who had had half a dozen more children than was good for her, and was expecting another, regarded the object dangling from her mistress's fingers with considerable embarrassment. Could that wretched, half-stripped thing be the long-promised gift which she had already applied for to its unwilling donor twice in vain? It was no more a bonnet than a skeleton is a man!

But all of us are not in a condition of life to express our genuine sentiments; it is not so easy to be honest and straightforward as gentlemen of "culture" and independent means, who write philosophic leaders in reviews and newspapers, are apt to imagine. People who live by hard work, and have little ones to support, can not afford to lose their places; but must be humble and obedient to their masters (and mistresses) in a sense beyond that which (I hope) the Church Catechism contemplates. Thus, Mrs. Jones, the gardener's wife, bethinking herself of those near and dear to her, resisted the temptation of saying, "Where is the bonnet?" and dropped a courtesy before its *simulacrum*. Perhaps the expression of her mistress's face, beaming with conscious benevolence, persuaded her for the moment that the thing was really of some value, and induced her to murmur, "Thank ye, mum."

"I thought you would be pleased, Mrs. Jones," returned the lady, still maintaining her hold upon the article in question. "It will make a very nice bonnet after a little looking to."

Whatever this mysterious process of observation might have implied, the very mention of it seemed to enhance the value of that with which Mrs. Newman was about to part. "Now mind," she continued, "I don't wish to make a bargain with you, Mrs. Jones, for this is a free gift. A promise is a promise, and you shall have it whether or no."

Here the thing changed hands, and its late proprietress uttered such a sigh as only escapes from one who has resisted a great temptation.

"It's your wedding-day, is it not, Mrs. Jones?"

"Yes, mum, it be; it is twenty year come this very day that me and my husband have lived together, and a many crosses we have had, and its been a hard job all along to make both ends meet, but we *do* make 'em, thank God!"

"Very good, and very right; it's a pleasure to hear you say so, Mrs. Jones, and now, I dare say, you have a nice little dinner to-day—a leg of pork, or a bit of beef, perhaps—about one o'clock."

"Yes, ma'am, thank you, mum, we 'ave got a leg of mutton, although it is not every day as we sees even bacon, far less butcher's meat—"

"Just so," interrupted Mrs. Newman, with one of her sweet smiles; "and you will have no stint of potatoes, for your husband has permission to take as many as he pleases for his own use out of the garden."

"Yes, mum; that was considered in his wages."

But Mrs. Newman went on smiling as though no such remark had been interpolated.

"Now, what I was going to say, Mrs. Jones, was, that if you find the leg of mutton more than you require, one o'clock being my luncheon hour, if you choose to send a nice hot slice, with a few potatoes, between two plates—mind, I say if you have lots to spare, and I don't want to put it as any return for the bonnet (which, indeed, is ridiculous, for that was a very costly article)—I shall be very much obliged to you—there."

And Mrs. Newman smiled and nodded, and pointed toward the door, as though to preclude all expressions of gratitude upon the part of the gardener's wife, and really looked so lady-like and pleasant, that poor Mrs. Jones retired like one in a dream, doubtful whether she could have heard aright. But before she reached the bottom of the stairs, her doubts were resolved, for a sweet voice called softly to her over the bannisters—

"Let the potatoes be fried, Mrs. Jones, if it is all the same to you; and don't trouble yourself about the pepper and salt, for I don't wish to put you to expenses."

CHAPTER XV.
AGNES AND SISTER MEG.

DOUBTLESS it was with the elastic vigor that characterizes the acts of most of us when we have done a good stroke of business in whatever walk of life, that Mrs. Newman reverted to her epistolary labors, after having secured for herself a gratuitous luncheon. Yet none of her compositions seemed to give her satisfaction. But for her forethought in using scraps of paper for her rough draughts, she might have wasted two-penny worth of Bath note.

"I will go and see the girl myself," murmured she, impatiently; "that will be better than writing."

She would have started on the instant, for Mrs. Newman was not a person to let the grass grow under her feet when once a resolution was formed; but she could not bring herself to sacrifice, or, at all events, expose to possible miscarriage and loss, that excellent slice of mutton. And here she made a mistake. It is providentially arranged that very prudent and saving persons shall invariably, at one time or another, miss their mackerel, through an unwillingness to expose their sprat to possible loss; in their exclusive care of the pence the pounds occasionally take to themselves wings; their pin a day secures to them their groat a year, but in picking it up they sometimes neglect more important sources of income. Thus, in waiting for her gratuitous lunch, Mrs. Newman missed her opportunity of putting a stop to that conversation between her brother and Agnes Crawford, which we have had the privilege of overhearing. If she had started on her mission without waiting for that slice of mutton, she might (to use a culinary metaphor while speaking of a kindred subject) have cooked somebody's goose pretty completely. Imagine the effect of her appearance upon that sunny lawn; its abrupt interruption of the *tête-à-tête;* how she would have frightened the horse, and worried the man, that (would have liked to have) kissed the maiden all forlorn, that lived in the house called Greycrags!

As it was, Mrs. Newman did not start for that retired mansion until 2.30 p. m. She arrived in her basket pony-carriage, driven by the small foot-page: like a baleful fairy, who, though drawn by fiery dragons, guided by a duodecimo fiend, reaches the house of the young princess the day *after* her coming-of-age, when it is vain to wish her wall-eyed or web-footed. But, out of elfland, it is never too late to do mischief.

Agnes had a foreboding that evil was impending when Cubra hissed through the key-hole, "Missis Newman come, and wish to see you very partickler;" nor did her instinct deceive her.

Nothing could be sweeter than the smile with which her guest arose as she entered the drawing-room, and greeted her as a mother might greet a daughter. It was the first time that Mrs. Newman had visited Greycrags since the Crawfords had resided there, and she had a great deal to say about the improvements that had been effected in the mean time. At last she said—

"What a charming lawn you have, my dear Miss Crawford; but what a pity it is that you allow horses upon it, for surely I see hoof-marks?"

["Ah," thought the speaker, "it's all true. The hussy blushes. It's quite as well I acted upon dear Jed's suggestions."]

"Yes, those are Red Berild's hoof-marks;

the horse your brother rode when he saved my cousin and me upon the sands. I wished to take his portrait."

"My brother's portrait?"

"No, madam; Red Berild's." They were looking steadily in one another's faces. Agnes had quite recovered herself. Mrs. Newman felt that no easy task was awaiting her.

"It is all the same," said she, "whether it was the horse or the rider. I am an old woman—that is, comparatively speaking—and you, Miss Crawford, are a very young one. I am quite sure that you are unaware of the consequences — I mean of the construction which must needs be put, nay, which of late *has* been put upon my brother's visits to this house. In your exceeding innocence—" here Mrs. Newman placed a hand with a darned glove on it upon her young friend's shoulder, and her voice became even tenderer and more winning—"and in your happy ignorance of the ways of the world, you have unwittingly given this wicked creature—"

"The horse, madam?"

"Miss Crawford, I am astonished at you. This levity is most unlooked-for, most unbecoming. I say that you have unwittingly—as I *hope*, unwillingly—given this wicked and abandoned man encouragement. I am obliged to speak plainly."

"So it seems, Mrs. Newman, since you call your own brother by such names." She drew herself slowly away, so that her guest's hand, reluctantly slipping, hung by the darned finger tips for a second, and then fell.

"And is it not the truth, Miss Crawford? Can you pretend to be ignorant that John Carlyon is an infidel? And is not that to be wicked and abandoned?"

"We are all wicked, madam; but we can not tell whom God has abandoned."

"And I thought this was a Christian woman!" exclaimed Mrs. Newman, holding up her hands. "How we are deceived in this world."

"Yes, madam," returned Agnes, coldly, "it is only in the next world that a true judgment will be arrived at, and even then we shall not be the judges."

If Mr. Richard Crawford had been occupying his usual post (which he was not half way up the hill, or even higher, he could not have failed to hear Mrs. Newman sniff; it was like a hippopotamus who had just emerged from under water.

"Perhaps you think the infidel is only to be *pitied*, young lady," observed she, with what, had she been an irreligious person, would certainly have been termed a sneer. "Now pity, we all know, is akin to love."

"Mrs. Newman!"

"Yes; I can read it in your face. You love this man. You would marry him if he asked you to do so."

"That is false, madam, and I think you know it."

Notwithstanding this unpleasant imputation, Mrs. Newman was pleased. The girl was on her part evidently speaking truth. No irretrievable mischief had as yet been done. If he had proposed, she had not accepted him, although perhaps she might not have rejected him.

"I would never marry any man," she went on, "with the opinions you have, however uncharitably, described."

"But you are not without hope that his opinions may change," observed Mrs. Newman, quickly. "You believe in this man's possible conversion. Perhaps you believe that you yourself may be the happy instrument. You do; I see you do."

"If you have no other purpose in coming here than to insult me thus, Mrs. Newman," returned Agnes, trembling, "I will retire." Her courage, so high when it was *he* who was attacked, sank before these relentless blows aimed at herself alone.

"Not before I have told you the whole truth," exclaimed the other, stepping swiftly toward her, and grasping her by the wrist. "Your conscience whispers that you are looking beyond the convert for the lover. If you have hitherto deceived yourself, you can do so no longer now, for I have undeceived you."

"And you do not wish your brother to be converted?"

"By *you*, no," answered Mrs. Newman, fiercely; "that is," added she, recollecting herself, "because such a thing is out of your power; you do not know how strong he is—this man. It is you who would be perverted by him. Two precious souls lost in the endeavor to save one."

"He did not think of his own life when he spurred across the whirling river to rescue mine," murmured Agnes, as though to herself.

"A reckless man will do any thing for a pretty face, girl."

"You hurt my wrist, madam; please to let me go. A reckless man! A brave and noble man, I say, and one to be of the same blood with whom should make you proud."

"Those are strong words, young lady, and scarcely modest ones. If I must needs be proud of being this man's sister, how fine a thing it would be to be his wife. And it *would* be a fine thing to some people."

Up till now, Mrs. Newman had preserved the habitual smile and gentle tones that had stood her in such good stead through years of vulgar and penurious greed, but at these words her look and manner became those of a shrew.

"For a girl, for instance," she went on, "without money, without family—springing, in fact, from no one knows whom or whence, it doubtless would be a great matter to secure John Carlyon for a husband; that is to say, if she had no religious principles whatever, and was only bent upon attaining a position for herself in this world. But for you, Miss Crawford, no matter what the advantage you might gain by such a marriage, I will take leave to tell you—"

"Nothing more, madam," interposed Agnes, with dignity, at the same time ringing the bell sharply for her visitor's carriage. "I will not listen to another word. You have said enough already, far more than any gentlewoman ought to say. Any honor to be gained by alliance with one of your family would indeed be dearly purchased if it entailed intimacy with such as you."

Mrs. Newman courtesied deeply with her customary grace.

"Thank you, Miss Crawford," said she. "I have also to be grateful to you—" here the servant entered and received his orders, retiring, doubtless, with the impression that the two ladies were most uncommonly polite to one another —"for having exhibited to me, under the guise of a Christian young person, an unprincipled girl, and a designing fortune-hunter."

"She never can see him again after *that*," murmured Mrs. Newman, as, leaning back in her pony-carriage, she thought over that heavy chain-shot delivered at parting. "It was absolutely necessary that I should not mince matters; and what a comfort it is to think that I have acted for the girl's own good!"

CHAPTER XVI.
SENTENCE OF DEATH.

IT was on the morning after the interview between Mrs. Newman and Agnes that Mr. Carstairs, calling, as he often did, at Woodlees, was, for the first time, so fortunate as to find its proprietor at home.

"Mr. John is in to-day, sir," said old Robin, whose eye-twinkling upon this subject had become chronic; "he really is, for once."

"Oh," ejaculated the doctor, by no means with satisfaction, but rather like one who, having received certain information that his dentist is out of town, has gone to consult him respecting a troublesome tooth, and finds him *in*. "Not gone to Greycrags this morning, then, eh, Robin?"

"No, sir, but he's got a letter from the young lady. Leastways, one was brought to him five minutes ago, and if you had seen his face when he took it into his hand—oh, yes, we was right about that, bless you. 'There was no answer,' said the man as brought it over. Why, of course not; what's the need of answering by letter when my gentleman rides over every mortal day? Perhaps he's put off a bit, that's all."

"Perhaps," said Mr. Carstairs, musing.

"I tell you what, sir," went on the garrulous old man, "it will be a sore day for Miss Meg as was when the young squire marries. She counted upon Woodlees for Master Jedediah, bless you. But it's better as it is, to my thinking; for Miss Agnes, she'll win Mr. John to what's right, to the path as my old master walked in all the days of his life—a good man, Mr. Carstairs, if ever there was one—and that is all as is really wanting. If he had but piety and propriety, as our gardener says (and a remarkable long head has gardener), he would be perfect; and though I think it my duty not to let him know it, this I will say, never had servants a better master, or a kinder, than Mr. John. Whereas, you know, Miss Meg as was, she was always near—very pious and very proper, but most audacious near. Why, I remember, as if it was yesterday, when our Susan (she as was married to him as kep' the Disney Arms, and a sad drunkard *he* was, but they're both gone now) went out to wash some chitterlings in the millrace yonder and fell in. That was just after missis died, and Miss Meg she managed the house, and pretty nigh starved us for a matter of six months; we had to eat the innerds of every thing, such as we had been used to throw away before her time, and she set us an example by having chitterlings for breakfast; nasty, stinking things as ever you smelt. Well, Susan fell in, and the news came to the kitchen just as I was bringing in the urn, and I told Miss Meg at the breakfast table. 'Ma'am,' says I, 'while cleaning them innerds Susan Grives have tumbled into the mill-race.' '*Where are the innerds?*' cried Miss Meg. I never shall forget it, never. Without even asking whether the girl were drowned or not, '*Where* are the innerds?' Oh, yes, I do hope that Miss Meg as was will not be mistress here in my time."

"Well, that's not very likely, Robin, is it?" inquired the doctor, looking earnestly in the old man's face. "You surely do not expect at your age to outlive your master."

"At *my* age," grumbled Robin; "well, I'm sure, one would think I was Methuselah. And as to that, the young are taken, and the old ones left, oftentimes."

"Very true, Robin," answered Mr. Carstairs, nodding. "And now let me see Mr. John. I know my way, and needn't trouble you to come up stairs."

"Ah, but he ain't in the turret-room," ejaculated the other, still in rather a dissatisfied tone, for Robin was tender as a belle of eight-and-twenty upon the point of age, " he's in the master's room. He happened to be in the hall when the letter came, and just as though he couldn't wait for a minute, he shut hisself in there to read it, and ain't been out since; I dare say he's a getting it by heart," chuckled the old man. "You must knock louder than that, bless ye—"

But Mr. Carstairs, getting no reply to his summons, and finding the door made fast, stooped down and looked through the keyhole. "Fetch some cold water," cried he; "quick, quick!" and while uttering the words, the agile little man flew out at the garden door, and in at the window of the cedar chamber (standing open as usual to get what sunshine it could) like a bird. There was, indeed, not a moment to spare. John Carlyon lay upon the floor, still breathing stertorously, but with a face like that of a strangled man. His head had fortunately been caught by the sofa cushion, and remained higher than the rest of his body. His hand still clutched an open letter, the receipt of which had doubtless caused the calamity by some emotional shock, and a small book—it looked like a Testament—lay on the floor by his side. The doctor's quick eye took in all these things at a single glance, and sooner than the action could be described in words, he had freed Carlyon's throat from neckcloth and collar, and bared his arm. Then, throwing open the door to get a free current of air, as well as to admit Robin, he began to use the lancet. Would the blood never flow? Was he dead—this strong man, in the full vigor of his prime? No; very slowly, drop by drop, but presently in a crimson tide, came the life stream; while old Robin stood by, dazed with terror, and sprinkling the cold water as often on the floor as upon his young master's forehead.

"Is it a fit, doctor?" inquired he, in a hoarse whisper.

"No, the heat of the weather, that's all," responded Mr. Carstairs, hastily. "See, he is getting better now."

There was a deep drawn respiration, and the large eyes drowsily opened and closed. "You had better go away, Robin; he is coming to himself, and perhaps would not like to know that you had seen him in this state. Say nothing to any one of what has happened. Hush! go, go."

"Ay, ay, sir, I understand," answered the old man, moving reluctantly away. "It is not for me to tittle-tattle about my master's affairs." Then, as the door was pushed hastily behind him, he added, "But I knows a fit from a faint, I reckon. God forbid that Miss Meg as was *should* be mistress here in *my* time, as I was just saying; yet many's the true word spoken in jest. And he did look mortal bad, surely."

"What is the matter?" asked Carlyon, sitting up, and passing his hand wearily across his forehead. "Have I been ill, doctor?"

"Yes, my friend, very ill; but you are getting over it now. Let me help you on to the sofa; there."

"The letter! where is it?" inquired Carlyon, feebly.

"It is here," said the other, returning it to him, folded up.

"You have read it, doctor?"

"Yes; I could not help reading it—that is, seeing that one word."

"Ay."

The voice that was wont to be so strong and cheery sounded faint and hollow like the last boom of a funeral bell.

"Only one word, doctor, yet with a world of meaning in it. That 'No,' means for me No happiness, No hope. I wish you had not come and saved my life. What years of wretchedness may be before me ere I gain the shelter of the grave!"

"No, Carlyon," returned the doctor, gravely, "you have at least not that to fear. You will never be a long-lived man."

"How so?" inquired the other, incredulously. "I should be glad to be able to believe you; for somehow," glancing up at the strange weapons upon the wall, "I could never bring myself to hasten matters—to desert my post here, albeit I have nothing to guard, nothing to protect—"

Carlyon did not finish the sentence, but turned round with his face to the wall.

"That letter was from Miss Crawford, was it not?" said the doctor, very tenderly: "and its meaning is that she has refused you. I am deeply sorry, old friend, that you have been caused this pain, and I reproach myself because it was in my power to avert it."

"In yours?"

"Yes. If I had done my duty, I should have told you something weeks ago which would have spared you much of this. Can you bear to hear it now?"

"I can bear any thing," murmured Carlyon, wearily, "the worst that can befall has happened to me already. She is not like other girls; when she says No, she means it."

The despairing words had no such hopeless ring but that the other knew an answer was expected with some comfort in it. Yet none was given.

"Carlyon," said he, after a long silence, "if Agnes Crawford had written, 'Yes,' instead of 'No,' still, knowing what I know, learning what it would have been my duty to tell her, she would not have married you. And you, if you had known, you would not have asked her to become your wife."

"Would I not?" murmured Carlyon, bitterly. "Your secret must indeed then be a terrible one. Perhaps I have madness in my blood. I sometimes think I have."

"No. It is not terrible—at least, it need not be so—but only sad. Had it been what you hint at, I should have known it years ago, but this I only learned a few weeks back—on the day when you saved Miss Crawford's life upon the sands."

"I wish I had been drowned in saving it."

"You were very nearly drowned, Carlyon. It was only your fainting under water that saved you. Your case, I saw at once, was different from the other two; and when you lay insensible at my house, I found out this—you have heart disease, John Carlyon. You nearly died to-day; you may die to-morrow if any thing should cause you the least excitement. Your life is not worth six months' purchase. I do not think it possible that you will live beyond a year." There was a solemn pause, during which the lightest sound was heard; a butterfly brushed against the open window; a bee buried in some fragrant flower beneath its sill, emitted a muffled hum; far off on the other side of the high garden-wall, the mill-race roared; the rooks cawed sleepily from the elm tops in the park.

"You remember, upon the day I mention,"

continued the doctor, "that I began to speak upon religious matters. Doubtless it seemed impertinent to you that I did so; but you know the reason now. I thought—do not let us argue any more, my friend—I thought it my duty to do so, and I think so now. Science had passed your sentence of death, and it was surely meet that religion should comfort you. I saw that I was unfit for such a task, and yet I wished to be of some service to the son of your father. There, I will not speak of him again, since it pains you. But I have known you from a child, my friend, and I knew your dear mother, who gazes upon you from yonder picture with the same love and with the same fear (I did not understand it then, but I do now) with which I have seen her gaze upon her darling boy a hundred times."

"You understand it now?" said Carlyon, bitterly; "oh, no."

"I think I do," returned Mr. Carstairs, quietly.

Still keeping his face averted, Carlyon held out his hand, which the other took tenderly within his own.

"And why did you not tell me this—I mean about my heart—before, doctor?"

"Partly, lest the shock might hurt you at that time, which, from something that you yourself let fall, I thought it would; partly because I was a coward, and loth to be the bearer of such news; but principally, because I thought I saw in Miss Agnes one who would show you the road to heaven far better than I. I knew, of course, after what had happened, that you two must needs become intimate, but I did not look forward to—to this sad end of it all. Even that, however, lies in some measure at my door. I did all for the best, and nothing has turned out as I would have had it."

"Don't fret, my friend; don't reproach yourself, you good soul," said Carlyon, turning round and smiling upon the doctor, who stood dejected by his side. "It was not certainly your fault that I shut my eyes to the gulf that lay between me and Agnes. I am punished for my folly, that is all."

"It was I, however," pursued the doctor, mournfully, "who gave you at least one opportunity which has doubtless worked with others to this sad end. I knew that that hare-brained cousin of hers would be jealous of you. He suspects every body. I believe he is jealous of *me*, the self-willed idiot!—and so, when we were at Greycrags that night, I kept him to myself, solely that Miss Agnes might have some serious talk with you. I was an ass not to foresee what sort of talk it would be. I would have told her the whole truth, but that that would have been the betrayal of a professional secret. Now, if I had been a parson I should have done so for the good of your soul."

"Lost! lost! forever lost!" murmured Carlyon.

"No, no, my friend, not lost," returned the doctor, kindly. "It is never too late to—entertain more correct views upon religious matters."

"What are you talking about, man?" exclaimed Carlyon, fiercely. "I was not thinking of my 'miserable soul,' as you call it."

"I am sorry to hear it," returned the doctor, simply.

"And I'm not going to join your fire insurance society," added the other, scornfully. "The premium would, under the circumstances, be probably enormous."

"I have said what I thought it was my duty as a Christian man to say," said Mr. Carstairs, reddening, "and now I am here in my professional capacity only. Can I do any thing more for you, Mr. Carlyon?"

"Yes. That instrument which I see peeping out of your pocket is the stethoscope, is it not? Please to use it once more."

"I have told you what its answer will be," said the doctor, hesitating.

"Nevertheless," replied the other, smiling, "I wish to make 'sicker,' as Kirkpatrick said when he drove his dirk into the Red Comyn."

He opened his waistcoat himself, and watched Mr. Carstairs steadily as he applied the instrument.

"When I was on the grand jury at Lancaster last year, doctor, I saw a sad scene. A mother waiting for the verdict upon her son, who was being tried for murder, and had been caught red-handed in the very act. I am glad to think that when you pronounce *my* doom there will be none to lament for *me*, not one. Come, doctor, what is it? I know you are a wise man, who looks upon the bright side of things, and yet has the knack of telling the truth. You are putting your black cap on, I see. The sentence is death, is it?"

The kind-hearted doctor nodded. Perhaps he did not like to trust himself to speak.

"Good. And the stethoscope never deceives?"

"Never," returned Mr. Carstairs, firmly, and with some approach to indignation. "I will stake my professional reputation upon what I have stated with respect to your case."

Carlyon smiled in his old, pleasant fashion. "I would not damage your credit, doctor, by overliving my year, for all the world. And I may die in the mean time, of course?"

"At any moment. To-day—to-morrow. It is certainly your duty to lose no time in setting your affairs in order. I think you should see your sister, Mr. Carlyon. I met her only yesterday afternoon, and she spoke most kindly of you."

"Most kindly of *me?* Then she must certainly have been speaking very ill of me to somebody else. I have always observed that in Meg. After administering a great deal of scourge she sometimes applies a little balsam."

"You are uncharitable, Carlyon. She not only spoke quite enthusiastically of your heroism upon the sands the other day, but also very patronizingly (you know her way) about Miss Agnes, whom she had just been to see at Greycrags. Why, what's the matter? Excitement of this sort is the very worst thing—"

"Did my sister go to Greycrags?" exclaimed Carlyon, starting to his feet. "Did that lying woman speak to Agnes? It is she then whom I have to thank for this—this letter. I see it all now. She did not wish me to marry, lest Woodlees should not revert to her Jedediah; and to stop it she maligns me to Agnes. The hypocrite, the backbiter!"

"You are killing yourself, Mr. Carlyon."

"You are right; I will be very careful," returned the other, bitterly, and pacing the room with hasty strides. "I should be sorry to die within the next few days. Perhaps you will call to-morrow, and see how I am."

Carlyon took the little man by the arm and gently, but firmly, urged him toward the door.

"It is no use my coming to see you, sir," expostulated the doctor; "I can do nothing for you."

"Very well, then, don't come," returned the other, quietly. "I shall remember you all the same, as if you did."

"Sir!" ejaculated Mr. Carstairs.

"Forgive me, old friend; I am not myself. I do not know what I am saying. I thank you for all your kindness, and especially for your telling me the truth."

Doctor and patient shook hands warmly enough. Although widely different, each respected the other after his fashion.

"For God's sake keep yourself quiet," was the kindly and characteristic remark of the former, as he rode away.

Carlyon nodded, then turned to Robin.

"Tell James to saddle Red Berild directly, and then come to me."

"Red Berild, Mr. John?" returned the old man, scarcely believing his ears, for it was rarely that any one ever crossed that horse except his master.

"Did not I say so?" observed Carlyon, coolly, and, returning to the parlor, sat himself down to write. The note was finished before the groom came, and he began to fret and fume.

"You have been a long time coming, sir," said he, with unwonted sternness; "and Red Berild must make up for your delay. Do not spare the spur. I want this letter taken to Burnthorp, to Mr. Scrivens."

"The lawyer, sir?"

"Yes, the lawyer; who else? There is no answer; but he or his partner is to come at once. If the means of conveyance are wanted, lend him your horse, and you will walk."

"It is twenty miles," murmured the groom, thinking of the distance to be traversed by shank's, his (unaccustomed) mare.

"I shall expect him here in four hours," observed Carlyon, referring to his watch instead of to this remonstrance.

When sentence of death is pronounced by one's doctor, we think—that is, just at first— that it is going to be executed forthwith; and we are in a particular hurry to make our wills.

CHAPTER XVII.
MR. SCRIVENS'S LITTLE MISTAKE.

THOSE who collect the statistics of death-bed scenes, without the intention of confounding the sceptic, are aware that, for the most part, folks die as they have lived; that is to say, according to their several constitutions. Good Christians, if of a nervous temperament, are alarmed. Phlegmatic persons, even if they have no sure grounds of religious belief, are to the last (what their friends call) "philosophic." People little accustomed to thought of any kind, rarely feel, or, at all events, exhibit, any mental emotion. An old officer of experience once told me that he had seen upward of a hundred soldiers die in hospital, and not one of them was moved by the prospect of dissolution at all. At the same time it must be owned that much of this immobility may arise from the indefiniteness of the time when death shall be actually knocking at the gate. People talk of the uncertainty of life as a reason for repentance; but, in reality, its uncertainty is the great encouragement for procrastination. There may be no hope, but also the danger often does not appear immediate, until it has actually overwhelmed us. Criminals, it is true, when their day of certain doom draws nigh, are, in many cases, terribly agitated; but these last are exceptionably bad subjects for any such trial, since they have especial good reasons for feeling remorse, and for fearing retribution. The old are, as a general rule, least impressed with the nearness of dissolution. They have lived so long without dying, that it has become, as it were, a confirmed habit with them; and they can not picture to themselves, while still in tolerable health, so radical a change.

In Carlyon's case, if Mr. Carstairs had confined himself to saying, "You have heart complaint of the most serious character; you may die any day; your life is not worth six months' purchase," his patient would not, perhaps, have been much moved; but the addition, "I do not think it possible," or "I will pledge my professional reputation"—which was it?—"that you will not live a year," made the professional opinion very striking.

Carlyon sat alone in the dark little chamber, looking forth upon the many-flowered garden, faint and odorous in the hot noon, and strange thoughts indeed were busy within him. He had read long ago at school in some Latin author (he did not even remember that it was Cicero), "No man is so old but that he imagines he will live a year;" and this line, arising in his mind sudden and unsummoned as a ghost, began to haunt it. There was no man in health, then, in the whole world, so old but that he looked to live longer (by so much time as the doctor had already left the house) than himself. Curiously enough, while thus confining himself rigidly within the life-limit assigned, this man did not now consider the probability of dying in the interim. The apprehension that had caused him so hastily to dispatch the groom to Burnthorp was already gone. It seemed as though some warning such as is stated to have sometimes come to mortals from beyond the grave, had fixed his death at a certain date. Only a year, neither more nor less, save by a few minutes, to live. How strange it seemed to think that this self-same sunny hour would never return for him again. Thus, every succeeding day would be the last of its date for him. That, after a few weeks, no summer would shine for him more; no autumn after the next bear its fair fruit; no winter—this was his favorite season—afford its usual sports, save once. Then spring, which to all his kind was the welcome herald of so much, would come only to make the earth green for his grave; how strange it seemed that the occurrence of no one of nature's operations should (precisely) take place for him again; never to see the shadow of yonder dial begin to lengthen on the grass, exactly as it was doing to-day. Stay; would it ever do so exactly. His mind began to seek what little science was in it to imagine how this might be. Then it reverted to the dial, and thence, naturally enough, to the story of King Hezekiah.

"There will be no miracle done for my sake, I suppose," muttered he, with bitterness. Then, losing his scornful look, he added, tenderly, "When she hears this, how she will pray that I may improve my year of grace. Sweet soul!"

His hand mechanically sought the letter in his pocket, and at the touch of it his brow grew dark.

Only one quarter gone of the earliest time in which he could expect Mr. Scrivens to arrive. If hours were to pass like this his life would be a long one after all. He sat down to write, and occupied himself with certain papers, until there was a far-off sound of wheels: some vehicle was slowly entering the great gates; a craunch upon the gravel sweep. Yes, he was come.

A red little dapper man was Mr. Scrivens, bald, except for a rim of sandy hair, and with a ferret face half hidden by huge red whiskers, which it was his constant ambition to get both in his mouth at once. Holding one fast between his teeth, and coaxing the other with his white hand (of which he was very vain) toward the same trap, was his habitual occupation; and when he had succeeded in the double capture, he would let them go, and begin again. Notwithstanding this impediment to conversation, his words flowed like a river. He had not been at all put out by the suddenness of Mr. Carlyon's summons; quite the contrary; he was delighted, charmed, after so many years, to revisit Woodlees. The last time was—ahem—upon a very melancholy occasion. "A good man, sir, was your poor father, an excellent man. Yes, yes."

"I sent for you thus hastily, Mr. Scrivens, upon a business matter, which to me, at least, seems pressing," began Carlyon, without noticing these interjectional remarks. "At present,

I believe, in case of my dying intestate, all the property I possess would go to my sister—"

"Real *and* personal, sir, without doubt. And a very pretty property, too. Mrs. Newman is well, I trust, sir; Mr. Jedediah, your nephew, I had the pleasure of seeing—"

"I wish to make a will, Mr. Scrivens. Here are ink and paper, be so good as to take my instructions."

"Very right and very proper, my dear sir," observed the lawyer, encouragingly; "one of the first things that a man should do, upon emerging from what the law holds to be infancy, is to make a will—that is, provided that he has any thing to leave; otherwise the precaution is needless. Even in your case, a man in the prime of life, with what I may venture to call a constitution of iron—"

"To my nephew, Jedediah Newman, I wish to leave the sum of five hundred pounds, Mr. Scrivens."

"Just so, sir. Something for himself, as it were, independent of mamma, eh. Young men often stand much in need of such forethought as you display. Not that your nephew, let us hope, with the example of so excellent a mother before his eyes, so prudent, so—ahem—so discreet, would be likely to have embarrassed himself."

"My nephew is a scamp, I believe," observed Carlyon, dryly; "but that is no matter to me. I wish to leave him five hundred pounds."

"Just so, sir. No matter at all. Young men will be young men. Too tight a curb at home—we know the rest. Any other particular bequest?"

"Yes. Robin must have an annuity of fifty pounds for life; and the other servants—their names are written on this paper—of twenty pounds."

"Very considerate, I am sure, Mr. Carlyon," returned Mr. Scrivens, setting down these particulars, "service is no inheritance, as the saying is. Any more special bequests?"

"I wish a hundred guineas to be paid to Mr. Carstairs, of Mellor. That is all."

Perhaps Mr. Scrivens was secretly disappointed that that *was* all, imagining that the name of one's legal adviser as well as of one's family doctor might have appeared in the document; for this time he said nothing, and silence, with Mr. Scrivens, meant not consent, but disapprobation.

"The whole of my property, real and personal, with the aforesaid deductions only, I wish to bequeath to Agnes, daughter of Mr. Robert Crawford, of Greyerags."

"My dear Mr. Carlyon!" The imprisoned whiskers flew from their ivory jailers, for the lawyer's lower jaw had suddenly fallen.

"You are not in earnest, sir, surely?"

"Why not?" continued the client, gravely. "I, John Carlyon, being of sound mind, do hereby—you have dropped your pen, Mr. Scrivens."

"I beg your pardon, sir," observed the other, humbly: "the Carlyons have held Woodlees for three hundred years, and just at first I missed your meaning. As your family lawyer, I was about to enter a respectful protest; but, of course, when a lady's in the case, all other things give place. Ahem! Permit me to congratulate you, my dear sir, with all my heart. I have heard the young lady spoken of very highly."

Carlyon bowed with considerable stiffness, and signed that his companion should resume his writing.

"No, sir, no," said Mr. Scrivens, gayly, and with a whisker in each hand, "the thing can't be done—at least, not at present."

"Then I'll get somebody else to do it," ejaculated the other.

"My dear sir, you mistake me," pursued the lawyer, blandly. "I can, of course, do as you request; but it will all be labor in vain. Dear me, how ignorant you laymen are of the simplest rules of law—though it is not for me to regret it, far from it."

"Will you leave off making those damnable faces, and begin?" shouted Carlyon.

"My dear sir," explained the lawyer, with some precipitation, "these instructions are valueless: that is the simple fact. They will become waste paper upon the day of your union with this young lady. Marriage invalidates—"

"I am not going to be married, sir," interrupted Carlyon, in a voice that made the lawyer's blood run cold. "Now, your impertinent curiosity is satisfied, sir, perhaps you will do as you were told."

CHAPTER XVIII.

MR. RICHARD GETS SOME GOOD ADVICE.

SCARCE a week has elapsed since the incident recorded in our last chapter, but it has witnessed great changes, or what were considered such at Mellor. John Carlyon has broken up his establishment—not, however, without remembrance of those who had belonged to it—and Woodlees is advertised to be sold. These facts alone were dainty dishes enough to be set upon the tea-tables of the neighborhood; but there were a score of other strange reports respecting the young squire beside. Quite a glut of gossip, in short, and yet the market was very far from dull. The more immediate cause of this charming state of affairs was old Robin. In spite of his protest that he was "no tittle-tattle," there was no ancient female in the county so incapable of retaining a secret. Nature had ordained that he must out with it or burst. Was it not painful enough to have been the witness of his dear master's seizure, without the additional torture of having to conceal that most interesting occurrence? To expect silence was to be too exacting, too exorbitant. There was no "ambiguous giving out" either, in Robin's reference to this calamity. "Mr. John was in a fit, and Doctor Carstairs a-bleedin' on him."

Then followed the scarcely less exciting narration of the sending for Mr. Scrivens. After what had happened, this prompt measure could have been taken for no other purpose than that of preparing a will. Except as to details (which were sought after with feverish eagerness), no farther information was required by an intelligent public. They "put two and two together" with a rapidity unequaled even in the old coaching days.

John Carlyon had had a fit: apoplexy, epilepsy, paralysis; there was a great opportunity here for imagination, and that display of medical science so grateful to the human mind—nay, it was even darkly whispered by some folks, *delirium tremens*. With the prospect of immediate dissolution before his eyes, the sceptic had characteristically concentrated his thoughts upon his temporal affairs. Mr. Scrivens on his part had been, for the present, reticent enough, notwithstanding that Jedediah had ridden over to Burnthorp within the last few days, on pretense of "looking at a horse" which the lawyer happened to wish to part with, and had endeavored to pump him; but this announcement of Woodlees to be sold, spoke for itself. John Carlyon must have willed his property away in some direction other than its legitimate channel, else why was the family residence to be thus disposed of?

Mrs. Newman maintained a calm exterior—some people called it "malice at a white heat"—and only shook her head and touched her forehead when the subject was mentioned. She was understood to imply that her unfortunate brother was not answerable for his actions, and doubtless it would have afforded her great satisfaction if such had been indeed the fact, and the law could have been got to certify it.

Now, as is not unusual in such cases, the person whom all these rumors chiefly pointed to, namely, Agnes Crawford, was least aware of their existence. She knew that Carlyon had left Mellor, and that Woodlees was to be sold, and she had a suspicion, which gnawed the tender heart within her, of what had sent him away. Her conscience reproached her twenty times a day for having done the very thing which it had before insisted upon. Its old self, if I may say so, had now no ally except in those bitter words which Mrs. Newman had flung at her at parting. It was they which had turned the scale in the late conflict within her, and which now played the part of the metropolitan brigade upon the flame of love. But they no longer made head against the devouring element. Now that the goods had been removed and the fire was confined to the premises, the flaming serpents flickered over the empty rooms and the bare walls at their wild will. Now she had lost him forever, Agnes began to feel how deeply she had loved Carlyon. And how he must have loved *her*, since one word of hers had sent him forth, she knew not whither, and made his home so hateful to him that he had resolved to enter it no more!

Was it likely that he would make any use of that sacred book, which had accompanied an answer so curt and so unwelcome? True, its brevity had been agreed upon, nay, proposed by himself; but might she not, nevertheless, have becomingly added something to have made rejection at least less ungracious, considering too that she was addressing, probably for the last time, the preserver of her life? Her cheeks burned while she thought of this, not in self-reproach, but from the consciousness that she had acted thus through love for him. For she had not dared trust her fingers to write more. Ah! if he could have only known what it had cost her to be so coldly brief! But now he would despise her parting gift, even more than his scepticism would have prompted him to do, from contempt of the giver. She had had it in her power to move his unbelieving heart, perhaps to win it, to the truth, but she had refused to take advantage of so rare and blessed an opportunity. His errors, nay, his very condemnation, might lie at her door. And why? Because she feared, as Mrs. Newman had suggested, being herself perverted from the right way? No; but because she feared to have imputed to her the vulgar, sordid motives she was assumed by that plain-spoken lady to entertain. Such ideas had never so much as entered into her brain; it was only this woman who had thrust them there; but once admitted—like a vile image intruded on a pure mind—she could no longer be ignorant of their existence. Although she had not been influenced by them, others, girls like herself, might be so; what Mrs. Newman thought of her, others might think of her. Perhaps Carlyon himself —no, she would not think that; but had not he too expressed his conviction that her father would not oppose himself to their union? Had he then any reason to believe that he was promoting it? Was she being thrown in this rich man's way, as manœuvring mothers were said to throw their daughters? She felt the hot blood tingle to her ear-tips, at this shameful thought. And yet to whom, unless to her father, had this woman referred when she had talked of her "springing from no one knows whom or whence?" Agnes shuddered! the red rose turned to white; and she closed her eyes as though to shut out some horrible scene.

Bitter as was the cup she had now to drink, it was perhaps well to do so. Bad as it seemed, even worse might have befallen; and with that ineffectual balm she strove to heal a wounded heart.

Thus Agnes Crawford argued with herself, now yearning for his love, now fortifying her heart against him with materials from the arsenal of Mrs. Grundy, and now agitated by a nameless sorrow which, arising in the far-back past, threw forward such a shadow as seemed to make gloomy all her future.

It was while meditating on this secret grief, while sitting in her old place by the open window of the drawing-room looking out upon the empty lawn, that Richard Crawford found her one morning, and took a chair by her side. He had treated her of late with marked but unobtrusive kindness. In the absence of the man he held to be his rival he had become once more his usual self, affectionately respectful, reverent. He knew that Carlyon had been refused, and therefore that the great obstacle to his success was done away with. He had never despaired until that man came and stepped between him and his cousin from the first, taking advantage of the accident that had introduced himself to her so favorably. If it had not been for his horse, he could not have saved her; and had not *he* (Richard) been equally willing to sacrifice his life for hers? How hateful it was to think that he owed his own safety to this country squire, who held his head so high, and cared for nobody, and could make his way so easily into the woman's heart, which he — her cousin and an inmate under the same roof—had failed to win. However, this rival was now removed, and as it seemed forever. If his own place was to be only second in her affections she should still be his wife; if the other had won, it was he who should wear. As sure as the sun shone she should be his. He had been assured of that all along; but he had not been certain of securing his object by legitimate means. He would have used any had Carlyon intervened between them; but now there would surely be no necessity for proceeding to such extremities. On the other hand, there was no time to lose. He had already received a hint from his uncle, equivalent as he was well aware to a peremptory order, that he had taken holiday long enough, and must be prepared for another sea-voyage—perhaps as long as the last. Without a solemn promise from Agnes that she would be his wife, he was resolved not to go. And he was now about to exact it.

"Agnes," said he, with a grave tenderness, that was not assumed, and became the young man very well, "I have something to say to you."

"Yes, cousin." She turned her head slowly toward him, and her voice, though kind and gentle as always, had the unconcern of preoccupation in its tone.

"Something," said he, more earnestly, "for which I beg your best attention; it affects us both very nearly, but to me it is all in all."

"Yes, Richard."

A month ago she would have already begun to reprove him; but now she did not seem to apprehend to what such words needs must lead. This coolness galled him far more than his displeasure would have done; but he was very humble and quiet.

"My uncle says that I have had holiday enough, and that I must go to sea again forthwith."

"Poor boy," returned she, pityingly, almost caressingly; "and yet you do not seem to have been long at home. I think that's hard. I'll ask my father—"

"No, thank you, Agnes," answered he, coldly; "I am not a child to be begged off a day or two from school. I am a man now."

"A very young one, Richard," replied his cousin, smiling. "Nay, don't be cross; you will laugh, yourself, when you come home next, with a great beard, perhaps, to think how, as a stripling, you once imagined yourself to be a patriarch."

"Don't jest, Agnes, for I can't bear it. As to going to sea, it is my profession, and, as you know, I like it dearly. I don't mind hardships. I would not live a life of idleness, such as I lead here, even if I could. I know one has got one's work to do in the world, and I am no skulker."

"Bravely said, Richard. There is nobody who will be so proud of you as I shall be when you achieve the success you merit. We two are alone in the world, for, except my father, we have no other kith or kin; and blood is ever so much stronger that water, cousin."

Her white hand sought his shoulder and there rested; her voice had the honest ring of affectionate good-will. But neither touch nor tone were welcome to the recipient.

"Blood is nothing to me," answered the young man, impatiently. "If you sprang from the other side of the world, I should love you equally well. I wish you did, since you vex me so with 'cousin, cousin.'"

"I hope, Richard, you are not going to vex me," observed Agnes, withdrawing her hand, "with the same talk which I have already forbidden you to use. That is not behaving like a gentleman."

"What!" exclaimed the young man, passionately; "can it be wrong, when every thought within me shapes itself into the words, 'I love you,' not to utter them? I know I am young, and that there is time to spare. I do not press you to be my wife, Agnes—that is, not yet. I can be patient. I trust to show myself worthy of you before I win you. But, now that I am about to go away, I know not for how long, I want to hear from your own lips a pledge—well, then, not a pledge—I shall be content, God knows, with very, very little. Only a little hope, that is all I ask: one gleam of light to cheer me on my lonely way. Nay, hear me out. Promise me that you will never wed another, never plight your troth to another, until I come back from sea."

"That is very easily done, Richard," returned the young girl, calmly; "and I would do it gladly, but for that which such a promise would imply. You will find me as you leave me, cousin, you may be sure of that—quite sure."

Carlyon's chance was gone, of that Richard felt certain; but notwithstanding her quiet smile, there was a melancholy in her voice that jarred upon his jealous ear.

"Then, why not give me hope?" urged the young man. "If, as you say" (here he fixed his dark eyes upon her searchingly), "you do not love another—you *do!* you *do!*" exclaimed he passionately; "you are deceiving me. This fellow has not really left the place. You are only waiting till my back is turned."

"Sir," said she, with a white face, but speaking very calmly; "you said awhile ago that you regretted we were kith and kin. After such words as you have last spoken, I regret it too. A man indeed! None but a reckless boy, forgetting to whom he speaks, could have so transgressed."

"But is it not true?" urged the young man, half abashed, yet still suspicious. "Why did your color change else, when I said 'you do not love another?' Give me your sacred word, Agnes, that you have not pledged yourself to John Carlyon, and then I will believe you."

"I deny your right to ask me any such question, sir; but if it will put a stop to all such talk as this, once and forever, I will tell you. Mr. Carlyon has asked me to become his wife, and I have refused him."

"But if he were to do so, now?" inquired Richard, eagerly.

"Now, or at any future time, would be the same; I should still refuse him. You seem pleased, sir, with this news. But, let me tell you farther, since I have said so much, that what I have said of Mr. Carlyon applies tenfold to you. My purpose is to marry no man. But did I marry, I should choose a gentleman—no eavesdropper, who suspects the woman he pretends to love, nor one who sets a servant to play the spy upon her mistress—yes, I know you, sir. The next time that you propose to yourself to win a woman's heart, be honest, be open, lest, instead of love, you reap contempt, as you have reaped with me."

He had never seen her—no one had ever seen her—half so wrathful, half so moved. Erect, to her full height, she stood, and flashed her words upon his bent-down head.

"Be honest, be open," reiterated she, as she laid her hand upon the door, "that is my parting advice to you, Cousin Richard."

The words seemed to scorch his ears.

"I will take it, Cousin Agnes," said he, quietly. "You will see me from henceforth quite another man." Even while he spoke his mobile countenance grew staid and firm; his thin lips ceased to tremble. "I will, so help me heaven!"

"I hope heaven will, Richard, for you need its help."

She closed the door behind her with those words.

"Yes, I will be open enough," muttered Richard, grimly; "although not with her. She must never know what I am about to do; and, indeed, how should she, since *he* would be the last to tell her. She has only herself to thank for it; she has driven me to it. I would have won her, if I could, by any other way."

He passed out of the room and up the stairs; then took the turning that led to his uncle's chamber. A man servant, coming from that direction, met him with, "The master is scarcely dressed, sir; he can not see you yet;" but Richard pushed by him roughly, without reply, and knocked sharply at his uncle's door.

CHAPTER XIX.
IN THE SANCTUM.

"What is the meaning of this intrusion, sir?" inquired Mr. Crawford, as with his gaunt form in dressing-gown and slippers, and the hue of anger upon his withered cheek, he sternly confronted his nephew.

The scene was a curious one, independently of the striking contrast between the actors. Two small rooms, one of which could only be reached by passing through the other, were used by the master of Greycrags as a sanctum, into which none but his body-servant and Cubra, and at rare times, his daughter, were admitted. The rest of the household regarded these apartments, cut off as they were from all others, with a feeling akin to awe. In the dead of night slippered footsteps were often heard pacing to and fro, from bedroom to sitting-room, for hours at a time, albeit, in five of his accustomed strides the old man must have stepped from wall to wall. It was not the impatient tread, which the servants sometimes heard of late from Mr. Richard's room, ere that young gentleman cast himself upon his couch at night, as often as not, with his clothes on, and lay there thinking unutterable things, but one even-paced monotonous walk, such as a man might take who has not had enough of out-door exercise, during the day—a prisoner for instance; or one who is accustomed to think most deeply when in motion, with head depressed and hands folded behind his back. However late this went on, there was no stirring of coals, save in the depth of winter time, for although so old, and as he gave out, so ill, Mr. Crawford rarely allowed himself the luxury of a fire. This little sitting-room, wherein Richard had not set foot before, and which he was now regarding, notwithstanding his uncle's wrath, with most curious attention, was by no means like a boudoir; except for the absence of a bed, its bareness and unliveable look, would have better suited a mere sleeping-room. The two chairs it boasted were neither of them easy ones; the table was without a cloth; the book-shelf only contained a diary (for the old gentleman was most methodical in his habits), an almanac, and a county directory. The only article of furniture that had any pretensions to be considered ornamental, was a handsome old standing-desk of polished oak, which stood against the window. Richard, from his post of espial on the hill, had often seen his uncle writing at this desk, and watched him, with angry heart, cast ever and anon, a well-pleased glance to where Agnes and Carlyon were sitting on the lawn below. There was no door between the two rooms, but only an archway with a curtain, which Mr. Crawford hastily drew across it on the young man's entrance, yet not so quickly but that Richard perceived it to be even more sparely furnished than its twin-chamber, and in particular that it had no bed at all, but only a hammock.

"Do you know, young man, that I never permit *any* person" (this with an angry accent such as implied, "and far less *you*") "to enter my apartment unless I send for him? How dare you, sir?"

The eyes flashed fire from under those shaggy brows, and if the voice shook, like the spear in ancient Tarquin's hand, it was more through ire than age.

Upon the other hand, the young man, generally so hasty and impetuous, was very quiet and self-contained. There was a strange look of pity, too, upon his handsome features—although the other never noticed it, and it quickly passed away—and a tenderness, if not respect, in the firm tones of his reply.

"Do not be angry with me, sir," he said. "I would not have come thus unbidden, except that my business is somewhat pressing."

"It is not so immediate, I conclude, sir," answered the old man still in wrath, "but that it can wait until I am dressed, and can go down to the library."

"In the library we may be overheard, uncle, and I have got that to say which, for your own sake, perhaps, had better be told where there is no chance of listeners."

"For *my* sake, sir? That is nonsense!" answered the old man, impatiently, but he drew back, nevertheless, and eyeing his nephew askance as he closed the door, drew a chair toward himself with trembling fingers, and sat down.

"I have something to do this morning—letters, papers — and beside, I am worse than usual," muttered he; "I can give you very little time."

"I shall not detain you five minutes, uncle. That is, if you take the same view of the affair that brings me here, as I do."

"Well, and what *does* bring you here, sir?"

"My love for your daughter Agnes, uncle."

Richard had expected an outburst of wrath, but the old man only smiled grimly. He seemed to experience almost a sense of pleasure, and indeed he did so; such a feeling at least as one entertains when something befalls us which, though not welcome, is not nearly so unpleasant as was apprehended.

"Ah," said he, in the grating voice to which his nephew was so well accustomed. "Cousins should always love one another. But why interrupt my shaving to tell me this?"

"Don't sneer at me, uncle, or you will regret it." Again the quick sidelong look, and all the mockery of the ancient face giving place in a moment to suspicious fear.

"Yes, I repeat, you will be sorry for it—some day."

"Ah, I see, when you are away from home, and I begin to think over your virtues. Then I shall regret I snubbed you? Well, I am not a very sentimental person, Master Richard."

"No, uncle. You have some natural affection, however. You care for yourself and for your daughter. As for me, I know, you rather dislike me than otherwise. You have never hesitated to show it. You have been so tyrannical and overbearing to me, that I sometimes liken Greycrags to a ship, in which I am the cabin-boy and you the captain. That hammock in yonder room seems to complete the metaphor. I say, Uncle Crawford, that you have behaved so brutally toward me from my very childhood that, it astonishes myself that I venture to address you as I am doing, although I am well aware that you have a very excellent reason for keeping your temper. Shall I tell you what it is?"

"Are you come here to insult me, you ungrateful boy?"

"No; although as to gratitude, I utterly deny the debt. You have given me a home, indeed, but you have treated me like a dog, and especially at times when you knew such treatment would gall me the most. Do you remember when you beat me in your daughter's presence, and she stopped you with her tears?"

"Why, that was six years ago!" exclaimed the old man, lifting up his long thin hands.

"Yes; dogs have good memories for those who beat them. Do you not remember six years ago, ay, and twenty-six? Come, sir, you are weak, you say, and very old, but you remember what took place six-and-twenty years ago, I am very sure. You shudder, uncle; you are cold. Permit me to close the window."

The old man would have sunk back in his chair had its nature permitted of it, but as it was, he sat propped up, but huddled together, with his eyes staring stonily before him upon the empty grate, like a man that has been hanged.

"For all that has come and gone yet, uncle, I wish, however, that you and I should be good friends. We are blood relations, and we are about to be also connected, I hope by marriage."

The livid lips strove to speak and failed, but the bald white head shook, piteous to behold, in vehement protest.

"Well, I did not expect to get your consent at once. It is the point, indeed, on which I have anticipated a discussion, but I have some tolerably convincing arguments too. If I had not, this interview would have ended long ago, you know—very probably, by your kicking me down stairs."

The young man's eyes gleamed with malice; the recital of the personal indignity that had been put upon him years ago, had driven all pity from his heart; it seemed to please him to picture to himself insults even which had never occurred.

"Now, to show you, Uncle Crawford, that I am not ignorant of the nature of the ground on which I am about to proceed, let me ask you whether it is not the fact that a considerable portion of your income dies with you, notwithstanding that you seem to live on your means just as though you were a government official, or a clergyman, or, let us say, a military or naval officer. Just so. This circumstance, therefore, made you desirous to secure for Agnes a husband of independent property, such as Mr. Carlyon. You need not be ashamed of it, for it was very natural. However, that scheme has turned out a failure."

"No, Richard. He and Agnes love one another."

"Excuse me, uncle. It is an immense pleasure to me to hear you talk so tenderly, to find you so easily affected, when as you have just said, you are not a sentimental person; but let us, above all things, stick to facts; a very favorite phrase of yours, and justly so; since facts, and especially unpleasant ones, stick to us like burrs. The truth is then, Agnes does not love this man, and will never marry him. If you don't believe me, you can ask her yourself, and she will corroborate what I say. The argument of a 'previous engagement'—which I foresaw your sagacity would use—is therefore out of the question. The affections of your daughter are free, and I, sir, am here this morning to propose myself as her suitor."

"I have heard you talk like this before, Richard," answered the old man, making a great effort to speak calmly, "and you have already had my answer. It can not be."

"It *shall* be, Mr. Crawford, and it *must* be," returned the other, vehemently. "You will not surely force me to state that argument which you know lies in the background, but which may remain there unstated forever, if you only say 'Yes,' to what I ask."

"Look here, Richard," appealed the old man, slowly. "I do not want to offend you. I would spare your feelings if I could; I would indeed."

"Thank you, uncle. You are always very considerate in that respect—but I interrupt you."

"The truth is, Richard—and when I have stated it, I am sure you will not press this matter farther—that my daughter, although entertaining an affectionate regard for you as her cousin, has herself no wish to marry you. My consent, therefore, to your union, even if I gave it, would benefit you nothing. Agnes does not love you."

"I know it, uncle."

"What, then, is it possible you wish me to do violence to her inclinations?"

"Tush, tush. Like you, sir, I am not a sentimental person. If Mr. Carlyon were in my place, and your daughter only had an affectionate regard for *him*, you would strive to make it ripen into love, I think. You would exert a benign paternal influence. That is all I ask of you in my case."

"You are very young, Richard, and scarcely know what you ask," answered the other, persuasively. "When you have been this next voyage, and are more in a condition to know your own mind, then let us talk this matter over—"

"Yes, but in the mean time, let us by all means temporize, eh?" interrupted Richard, angrily. "If you are then bent upon holding your position, sir, it is necessary for me to bring up my reserve. I am afraid I shall inflict a story upon you. If I weary you beyond endurance, or if any portion of the narrative be too painful to be brought to a conclusion, you have only to say 'Stop' or 'Enough,' I shall then understand that farther recital is unnecessary—that I have gained my point."

"You are talking riddles," said the old man feebly, shading his eyes with his hand.

"If so, uncle, I think you possess the key. It is not a riddle however, which I am about to narrate, but a biography."

CHAPTER XX.

AN OLD MAN'S SECRET.

"ALTHOUGH I of course remember nothing of my infant life," began Richard Crawford; "I have been so fortunate as to meet with a person who is well acquainted with it. Through that means I learn that so soon as I arrived in England, another nurse was substituted for the one in whose charge I had come from India, and who would have been certain, as I grew up, to talk to me of my dead parents, and to inform me of certain facts which it was to somebody's interest that I should never know. All the possessions which came over with me, including even articles of garment, were destroyed by this person's direction. Nothing was left that might suggest to me in later years of whom I had sprung, except this locket."

"You are weaving a romance, Richard," observed the old man, casting a careless glance at what the other held in his hand. "I never to my knowledge beheld that trinket before."

"Perhaps not, uncle, yet you recognize this portrait." Richard turned back the little golden door, and showed the features of a handsome soldier-like man, very like those of Mr. Crawford himself, before years and sorrow and ill health had combined to sharpen them. "That's my father, is it not, sir, and your own brother?"

"It is very like him," said the old man, thoughtfully. "Yes," added he, after a moment's hesitation, "it is certainly he. It is curious enough that I should have been ignorant of the existence of such a portrait, but I am glad to see it, however it was obtained. Poor Arthur!"

"This likeness, uncle, was taken just after his marriage, and a few days before he sailed for India for the last time."

"Somewhere about that period, as I should reckon," answered the old man, gazing upon his face attentively. "This was how he looked when I saw him last, newly married, happy, and yet beneath the shadow of death. Yes, it must have been near that time."

"It was *exactly* at that time, uncle. At the back of the picture there is a date—*and a name!*"

"It is a lie!" ejaculated the old man, shutting the locket close.

"That is not the way to disprove it," replied his nephew, coldly. "If you care to do so, you can read the inscription for yourself. I was afraid that there would be portions of my story that must needs be painful to you. This is Chapter I. Shall we say 'Stop?' You are not yet convinced? It is necessary then to resume the narrative.

"I know that you never set a high value upon my intelligence, uncle, and I dare say you are very right; but all children who are not idiots, are observant, and I possessed my full share of sagacity so far. It is not love only which awakens interest; it is sometimes dislike. Where we can not be contemptuous, but are compelled to hate, we keep a narrow watch upon our foes. I noticed several things concerning you in those early days, and all your cuffs did not put them out of my head. In the first place, instead of having a home like other people, we were always moving house. Wherever we went you feigned ill-health (I could never see there was any thing the matter with you) and shunned society as much as possible. When a stranger called you shrank from him, as though he had come to bring you some woful news. I know now that what you feared was recognition.

"In the second place, you entertained a morbid hatred of the sea, and all belonging to it. The reason, as I believe, which caused you to choose this house, independently of its complete seclusion, was that through some whim of him who built it, no window looks to seaward. The least allusion to the naval calling, gave you extreme annoyance. You set yourself against my fancy for embracing it with a vehemence that was quite inexplicable. And yet, notwithstanding all this, you exhibited, when off your guard, a surprising knowledge of nautical affairs. This of course I only understood lately, since I have myself become a sailor; but it struck me, even as a boy, how strange it was that you should sleep in a hammock, and chew tobacco like old Benbow."

Here Richard paused, as though expecting either some indignant outbreak, or specious explanation, but the old man did not speak, only shifted uneasily upon his chair. "It was not until last year," resumed his nephew, "and when I was two thousand miles away from English land, that I came into full possession of your secret."

Mr. Crawford groaned.

"You are your own tormentor, uncle," expostulated the young man, parenthetically, "and compel me to turn the rack, though I have no wish to hurt you. It was on deck at midnight in the tropic seas, that the revelation was made; the companion of my watch was a far older man than I, and had seen much sailor's service. He had been, it was understood, in the royal navy himself, but had had to leave it through some breach of discipline; yet, perhaps, through a desire to avert any suspicion of such a fact—just as some men take an opposite course and shun the subject— he was forever talking of naval matters, and particularly of the incidents of that great war, which was finished long before I was born, but of which you, uncle, were a contemporary. Our talk turned upon that matter on the occasion of which I speak. Youngster-like, I was boasting of our national prowess, and of the valor which had ever distinguished our naval commanders. I averred, that in equal fight we have never been beaten, and that in no case had any British commander disgraced his flag. I knew, indeed, that there was the affair of Admiral Byng—"

"A most unjust and cruel sentence," interposed the old man, vehemently; "a wicked act that has been long repented of by a mistaken country."

"Just so," observed the young man, dryly; "but my companion spoke of other cases about which no such public stir was made. Three other British admirals were brought before courts-martial during that long war, and all for cowardice. Of these three, one was acquitted; one reprimanded; and the third—whose case, although in some respects a hard one, was by far the worst, was 'relieved of his command,' —what, in the common soldier, is termed being 'drummed out.' He retained his pension, indeed, but without his rank; but, after a little time—so at least my informant told me—he died, being of a very proud and haughty spirit, of a broken heart. I have reason to believe, however, that he is still alive, leading a secluded life, under a feigned name. His real title (for he had had a knighthood conferred upon him for past services) was—I have forgotten; but if you will press that locket, uncle—"

"No, no," gasped the old man, placing the trinket in his own breast-pocket; "you have said enough."

"Just as you please, uncle; you have only yourself to thank that you have heard so much. I have said, 'I have forgotten,' I will add, that I solemnly promise never to remember, or, at all events, not to use the recollection, if only you, on your part, accede to my request. I do not ask you to bestow your daughter, for your secret's sake, on one who will not prize the gift at its true value. I love her with all my soul; I will work for her, slave for her, serve any probation you may choose to appoint to prove myself worthy of her; but I must have her plighted word, that when that is over she shall be mine. I am not unreasonable, but I am well resolved. Mark that, old man; I will have no subterfuge. From her own lips—not yours— I must hear the promise. If you refuse to use your influence as I have desired, or if you play me false, I will not spare you. No one in Mellor but shall know what a great man is living among them. All your precautions of these five long years shall count for nothing; this place of peace, which you imagined you had found at last, remote from all that knew you, shall know you more than any other. These drones, your neighbors, shall become a nest of hornets; the very children in the village street shall point at you; and wherever you may go, thinking to find repose, you shall meet scandal and clamor. For a few days you may think you have evaded me; but rumor, noising all around, shall soon let you feel that I have followed you, like fate."

As if goaded by the very bitterness of his own language, the young man's passion rose almost to madness; his dark face glowed with lurid fire, and he hissed his words out as though his tongue was very flame.

"But first of all," he went on, "your shame shall be made known to your own household. Your daughter Agnes, she shall learn it first. Do you hear me, Admiral Sir Robert Vane?"

"Yes, yes; I hear you," answered the other, in hollow tones. "I am a very old man, and your own flesh and blood, sir; but you are not merciful. I can not bear this talk much longer."

And, indeed, no more cadaverous and death-like face was ever seen in living man, than that which Mr. Crawford now turned upon his nephew. It had hitherto been studiously averted from him, and the expression of it both shocked and appalled the young man.

"I have nothing more to say, sir," answered he, with abated vehemence; "and my passion must be my excuse if I have been unnecessarily harsh. I am only afraid that you may underrate my fixed determination—which, however, I assure you, nothing can shake; that when I leave you, you will endeavor to persuade yourself that there is some loophole by which you may escape my importunities; or even, perhaps, that I may not be in possession of the facts which I have pressed upon your attention. When I tell you, however, that I have read that newspaper slip which lies in the secret drawer of yonder desk—you perceive at once, I see, how idle in that case must be such expectation. Well, sir, I will not press you for an answer to-day. I am passionate, but I can also be patient. I can easily understand that this interview has severely shaken you. I would rather receive your promise of assistance when you are more like yourself. Will you give me my answer to-morrow?"

The old man's chin sank slowly forward, either from weakness, or in token of assent.

Richard chose to conclude it was the latter.

"To-morrow, then, uncle, you will answer me 'yes,' or 'no.'"

The young man rose, cast one long, steady glance upon his uncle, huddled together as before, and with his grey head still resting upon his breast, and softly left the room.

———

CHAPTER XXI.

TO-MORROW.

For more than an hour after his nephew left him, Robert Crawford sat silent, and motionless, helpless and prone, like a statue that has been thrown from its base. Then, feebly feeling for the locket, he drew it forth, and opened it; gazing once more at the picture, and sighing wearily, he unclasped it at the back, and there lay the inscription before him. "To Mary Caroline, from her loving husband, Arthur Vane;" and a date of more than a quarter of a century ago.

"'Did I remember twenty-six years back?' said he," murmured the old man. "He knows it all. Unnatural, cruel boy. Who could have given him this? His nurse, Cubra, doubtless. They are in league together, and have undone me. She has access to my room, and has told him of what lies in yonder desk. I was a madman to keep it there—to keep that at all, the sight of which pierced my heart. Has he stolen it, I wonder, this traitor to his own flesh and blood?" Very slowly, and supporting himself by table and chair, he made his way to the standing-desk. Clearing away a mass of papers within it, he touched a little spring, and out darted a little drawer. In it was a printed slip—apparently an extract from some newspaper—and a small colorless globule. He took out the paper, and sat with it awhile before him, like one who waits for breath. Then he unfolded it and began to read. It was headed in large letters, "*Trial of Admiral Sir Robert Vane*," and contained the usual dry bald details of a naval court-martial, beginning with the statute under which the accused was charged. "Every person in the fleet, who, through cowardice, negligence, or dissatisfaction, shall in time of action, withdraw, keep back, or not come into the fight or engagement, or shall not do his utmost to take or destroy every ship which it shall be his duty to engage, and to assist all and every of His Majesty's ships, or those of his allies, which it shall be his duty to assist or relieve, every person so offending, and being convicted thereof by the sentence of a court-martial, shall suffer death, *or such other punishment as the offense may deserve.*"

The witnesses were admirals and captains, who had acted under the accused person in a certain engagement; and the point at issue was, "Did or did not Admiral Sir Robert Vane do his best to renew the battle which had already gone in his favor?" The witnesses for the prosecution affirmed he did not; the witnesses for the accused averred that a renewal of the fight was beyond his power.

At the conclusion of the evidence, the admiral read his defense, which began by stating that he had served his country seven-and-thirty years, during which he had been honored more than once with marks of approbation from his sovereign. The sentence was as follows: "The court is of opinion that the charge of not having done his utmost to renew the said engagement, and to take or destroy every ship of the enemy, has been proved against the said Vice-Admiral Sir Robert Vane, and the court doth, therefore, adjudge him to be dismissed the service."

Party spirit ran very high at the time of this trial, which was, of course, instituted by the government, and the newspaper in question, being a government one, bore very hardly upon the accused. It mentioned the cases of Byng, and Sir Robert Calder, and insisted upon it that the present was one far less deserving of indulgence; it hinted, that but for the last line of the statute (which was printed in italics) having been added in more merciful times, the accused would certainly have suffered death. Every imputation that malignity could suggest was heaped together against the unfortunate accused; but the charge of cowardice—as being likely to wound most deeply—was reiterated again and again. This part of the newspaper, viz., its comments on the trial, bore evidence of having been much oftener handled than the account of the trial itself. It was over these that the old man lingered now, as alive to every stab as when they were first rained upon him, when he stood broken and disgraced before the world a quarter of a century ago. *Litera scripta manet;* but, how infinitely more terrible is the permanency of that which is *printed,* since it stops not here nor there, but is promulgated everywhere, and at the same time. All England knew his shame upon the same day, and while he read, the old man felt that all England would be as full of it to-morrow as it was in that far-back time. The perusal of those hateful words (probably long forgotten by him who had written them) always set those wounds bleeding afresh which time had stanched; but now, with the menace of his nephew ringing in his ears, the torture was intolerable. Probably if the unfortunate admiral had sought in the opposition journals only for *their* version of the affair, he would have found commiseration, if not comfort, instead of these venomous stings; but he nourished the serpent in his bosom, as a proud man will, and it bit very deep. If physical pain is held to be some excuse for harshness of manner or ill-temper, how much more should have been this mental agony, the existence of which was not unknown to Richard!

"A cruel boy, a cruel, cruel boy," murmured the old man, again and again, as he sat gazing on the cruel words. "He would tell Agnes, too. He would not even spare the girl that he pretends to love. He called me coward, too, like this man here. And if I gave my daughter to him—if I persuaded her to give herself—they would speak truth. He shall never hold her in his power as he now holds me. No! No!"

This resolution seemed to give him strength. He rang his bell and bade the servant bring his meals up thither, since he did not feel well enough to leave his room. He busied himself throughout the day in arranging certain papers in his desk. In the evening, "Tell Miss Agnes

I will see her," said he; for even his daughter never ventured to seek his room unsummoned.

"You are ill, dear papa," said she, with anxious tenderness, directly she caught sight of his weary face.

"No, love; much the same as usual. I have been arranging my affairs, and that has tired me. You know what a sad hand I am at business."

"But why not send for me to help you, then?"

"You could not help me in this matter, Agnes. No. You could not. Where is Richard?"

"Like yourself, he is not well. He was not at dinner; he has one of his bad headaches. I am afraid you are angry with him, dear papa; and, indeed, it was very wrong of him to come up here. But he is really scarce himself at times, poor fellow."

"You pity him, then?"

"Of course, papa. I fear he feels the effects of that sunstroke still. He is so very odd at times."

"But you do not love him? You still have no affection toward him deeper than a cousin's? You are sure of that?"

"Quite sure."

"That is well, dear child." He took her little hand within his own, and stroked it tenderly. "You must promise me that when I am dead and gone you will never marry Richard."

"Certainly I never shall, papa; but why do you ask such a thing? I wish you would let me send for Mr. Carstairs."

"No, dear, no; I am as well now as I shall ever be. But life to me is worse than uncertain, and nothing should be put off."

They sat together side by side, without speaking, and upon the other side of the old man, unseen by her, sat Death.

"Is it true that Mr. Carlyon has left Mellor, Agnes?"

"Yes, papa."

"Left it 'for good'—I mean. Is it certain that nothing would bring him back?"

The young girl blushed and hesitated.

"You may trust in me, love; tell me all. Does he not love you?"

"I can not tell; I am not sure, papa."

"Do you love *him*?"

"I can never marry him," answered she, steadfastly.

"Is it a matter of religion, then, that separates you?"

"I can not say that, papa. But perhaps, if we thought alike respecting religious matters—but I don't know, indeed."

"Don't weep, my child, don't weep. You have, doubtless, acted rightly. There is something—what is it—in the Bible about 'choosing the better part.' I do not blame you, if I ever did. It is well to give up all for God. Yes, yes," here he paused for a little, sighing heavily; then resumed: "You will not be penniless when I am gone, Agnes; there will be more than you thought—that is," added he, observing her pained look, "more than others have imagined. I know you never think about such matters. You are a good girl; and God will never forsake you. Kiss me, darling. You must go now, for I am getting tired. No; I shall want nothing more till morning. Nothing more."

There was a pathos in those last words which might have moved Richard himself could he have heard them.

"God bless you, dear papa," said Agnes, kneeling down and looking yearningly into his wan face.

"That is right, darling. Perhaps he will, since it is you who ask it. Good-night, good-night."

Mr. Crawford was once more alone, except for that grim attendant whom he had himself summoned, before he sent for his daughter, lest she should persuade him from his purpose to her own hurt. He once more sought his desk and opened the secret drawer; the little globule was no longer there, but only the newspaper slip. This he tore into a hundred minute shreds and threw them on the hearth. Then he took out his watch.

"A few hours hence, and there will be no more apprehensions, no more disgrace," said he. "To-morrow he will have his answer—to-morrow! To-morrow! What will to-morrow be for me?"

* * * * * *

In the morning, when the servant came to call the old man, he was lying in his hammock, very white and quiet, as usual, but with a ghastlier look upon his face than even it had ever worn before. The sentence of the court-martial had not been so humane as the report had stated. It was death, although the execution had been so long deferred. Those thin stern lips had spoken their last words, but to one of those who, summoned by the servants' terrified clamor, surrounded that strange death-bed, they still gave their dumb reply:—

"No, would-be traitor, no!"

CHAPTER XXII.

AT RICHMOND.

IT is autumn, and deep in autumn; still all "the quality" have not yet fled from town. They have abode within its scorching walls through June and July, amid the dust of the roaring streets. They have borne the burden and heat of the bustling day, when it lay in their power to enjoy the summer coolness of their woods and streams. And now, though the trees are putting off their green, and enclosing themselves in their most glorious garment of all—their Joseph's coat of many colors—they still delay, as their fathers did, who "preferred the smell of a link-boy's torch to all the scents of garden or field." It is to be stated, *per contra*, however, that these worshipers at Fashion's shrine have not withdrawn their patronage from the country altogether. Once a week, or even, during its balmy time, bi-weekly, these idolaters have emerged from the interior of their grilling brazen bull, and sought the glades of Windsor, the banks of Greenwich, or the wooded heights of Richmond. And now, as the latest period of their final departure draws nigh, those who have not already fled congregate like migrating birds, and take these swallow flights into the country more than ever.

There is a party of such birds of fashion, the females full-feathered, and magnificently hued, the men not so gorgeous, yet with a certain nicety of apparel quite as striking, gathered together now at one of those Richmond palaces, where you sit and eat of the best that art can provide, while nature ministers of her fairest to the eye. The popping of champagne corks, the chink of glasses, the murmur of pleasant talk, the laughter of fair women, flow forth from the open windows like streams of music into the sea of harmony without, where wood and water are vying with one another in the great Even song. The birds are caroling from park and meadow, whence uproarious mirth and robust ditties come mellowed by distance; and with the cool breezes from the river, are upborne the even pulses of the oar and all the cheery sounds of that crowded highway. Presently, their feast concluded, the revellers come forth into the terraced garden, and there is not a dame so churlish as to forbid her cavalier to light the grateful weed. In twos and threes they promenade upon the sloping lawn, or on the broad graveled walks, or lounge upon the garden seats, or lean upon the balustrades and watch the glorious picture that is spread beneath them; the river winding slow, as though over-burdened with its freight of home-bound pleasure-seekers; the wooded banks, and path-pierced meadows; and the blue hills that close the scene.

Two of these loungers are remarkable; the one is a lady of great beauty, tall as Minerva, imperious as Juno, but very well knowing how to be tender, too, as you may see by the soft glances which she casts ever an anon at her companion, and by the soft tones in which she addresses him; the other is a man near half a foot higher than the others of his sex about him, and very powerfully made.

"Yes, indeed, I should be most ungrateful if I was *not* pleased, Mr. Carlyon," replied she, in answer to some question; "so are we all, I'm sure. I never enjoyed a day at Richmond more."

"That's well. I am very glad."

"You don't *look* glad," returned she, in a tone of playful discontent; "but then you are always melancholy."

"Am I?"

"Yes." Her voice sank very low; each had had a hand upon the balustrade a little apart; but now they were touching. "If I did not know you *so* well, Mr. Carlyon—you smile, but you are more easily read than you imagine—I should say that it was the day's closing scene, the influence of the evening—"

"That's you," interrupted Carlyon, smiling.

"Tush, nonsense," continued she, pressing his hand reprovingly; "if I had any power over you, I should make you cheerful, happy. I don't like to see my friends—persons I have a genuine regard for—so hipped and serious. You are worse than ever to-night. One would think you were frightened by that foolish Captain Plasher's remark about our being thirteen at dinner, and how that one of us would die within the year."

"Yes; but your mother put him right, you know; she said that the proverb ran 'would die or else would marry.' Marriage is better than death, is it not, Edith?"

"Well, really, that depends. What a disagreeable man that is to haunt us in that manner."

Carlyon turned sharply round, only in time to see a young man sauntering slowly away with a cigar in his mouth.

"Never mind," continued she; "he is gone now: oh! pray don't meddle with him; I do hate a scene."

"He is indebted to you for a whole skin," rejoined Carlyon, quietly. "If I have a prejudice it is against eavesdropping. At the same time, the poor wretch is not without an excuse. Where Edith Treherne is, there is always a temptation to draw nigh."

"Now you talk nonsense; what a wayward will you have, to be so serious when others are enjoying themselves, and to jest, when you ought to—be—that is—but here's mamma."

A stately dame bore down upon them at this critical juncture.

"Dearest Edith, it is getting late, and I have ordered the carriage. My dear Mr. Carlyon, we have a seat to offer you."

"But not to offer Red Berild, I conclude," returned he, smiling; "thank you very much, but I ride home. Must you go so soon, Mrs. Treherne? When you and yours leave us the party is broken up indeed."

"You are engaged, however, to dine with us to-morrow, remember, Mr. Carlyon; although it will be a bathos after your charming treat of to-day I'm sure. In five minutes we shall start, Edith; indeed, directly I have found Julia. I can't think where that little puss has got to."

Mrs. Treherne could make a very tolerable guess however, for she had a sharp eye for both daughters' movements; if a glance of that organ ever expressed "make the most of your time," it did so, when she parted with her eldest hope in professed pursuit of her second-born.

"Then you won't come home with us?" murmured the beauty, plaintively. "I do think you like that horse of yours better than—" she hesitated, then concluded her sentence with "mamma."

"Well really, my dear Miss Treherne. I never should have ventured upon comparing their relative merits," answered Carlyon, smiling.

"But you must allow that Red Berild is more devoted to *me* than your lady mother is. That goes for a great deal you know."

"People don't always know how much they are esteemed, Mr. Carlyon."

"Do you think so?" returned the other, musing. "That is not the case with love, however, is it? If a woman sincerely loves a man he always sees it, does he not?"

"I think so; that is, unless he is willfully blind."

"You are right, Miss Treherne, as usual."

"What makes you sigh, Mr. Carlyon?"

"Ah, that is a long story, and our time is short. Ask me any question but that and I will answer you."

"Good," returned the girl, fixing her fine eyes upon his own, "what is it then that you always carry in your breast-pocket? We have often laughed—at least, spoken of it, at home; it is too large for a note-book, or a miniature; what is it?"

"I did not give you credit for so much curiosity about me, Miss Treherne. Here is the subject of your wonder: a plain book in a plain binding."

"Why, it is the New Testament!" ejaculated the young lady.

"Ought it then to have been the Old one?" returned Carlyon, coldly.

"No, of course not. But, excuse me, I was a little surprised at your carrying about with you such a book at all. Cousin Archibald, whom you met at the club, told us—at least, we had the impression—"

"That I was an infidel," interposed Carlyon, quietly. "Well, so I am."

"How shocking!" returned the beauty. "How very naughty of you." And she tapped him lightly on the arm with her lace-fringed parasol. "You must have been in very bad hands, sir, when you were young. That is, I mean when you were a boy. I will ask my uncle the dean to give you a talking to."

"Your uncle the dean!" Carlyon burst into such laughter as quite astonished some neighboring knots of well-bred folk.

"Well, I'm glad to hear you laugh, although it need not have been quite so loud," said she, smiling. "Now—for I am still curious—let me have the book to hold. Will you?"

Carlyon hesitated for a moment, then put the volume into her dainty hand.

"Why, there's nothing in it!" said she; "absolutely nothing."

"That is not your uncle's view, Miss Edith."

"I don't mean that. I mean that there is no name, Mr. Carlyon," returned she, gravely; "the title-page is blank. Who gave it to you?"

"I did not promise to tell you all my secrets, Miss Treherne. But why do you ask? Does it look like a *gage d'amour*—this book?"

"Well, no," answered she, doubtfully: "though some girls give very funny things for keepsakes. But there, I dare say you have quite a collection of such."

"Not I, indeed, Miss Treherne. No girl cares for me; and for the matter of that, no human creature—only Berild."

"Don't say that, Mr. Carlyon," returned she, softly. "I am sure that I—that is, mamma and I—care for you very, very much. She is beckoning to us yonder. Won't you take our vacant seat? *won't* you?"

"Not this evening, Edith—" he drew her fingers on to his arm and led her away—"how your hand trembles! The air is getting chill; I shall never forgive myself if you have caught cold."

"I am not chilly, thank you, dear Mr. Carlyon," murmured she, tenderly. "We shall see you to-morrow." Then, in her usual cold and cynical tone she added, "Mr. Carlyon will not go home with us, mamma. He prefers his horse, as usual, to our company, or that of any one else."

A few minutes more of handshakings and conventional expressions of good-will, and all Carlyon's guests, in roomy chariots and snug broughams, had rolled away. It was felt that it was a bathos to remain after lovely Edith Treherne and her scarcely less beautiful sister had departed.

Carlyon had known Edith three years before as the belle of the London season; her place had been usurped by others, younger, if not lovelier than herself, and perhaps her mother looked upon an untitled country gentleman with some two thousand a year in land with more favorable eyes than heretofore. At all events, Mrs. Treherne, having satisfied herself that his melancholy did not proceed from pecuniary losses, had welcomed him to town with unexpected kindness and hospitality. He knew but few families in London, and in those few weeks had grown proportionately intimate with this good lady and her daughters, and those who were introduced to him through their means.

His guests to-day had been almost all friends of the Trehernes; and it was understood among them that a match between Edith and himself was by no means an improbable event. Still, the cautious mother had dropped no word of it to any of them; on the contrary, had expressed her opinion that Mr. Carlyon was so strange a person—so very "peculiar in his views," too, that it was hardly likely that any girl should take a fancy to him. Her friends, of course, translated this to mean that Carlyon was a difficult fish to hook; but she did not mind that one pin. She could'nt help people "talking," but she would not permit of the existence of a peg, upon which they might hang the scandal that her Edith had been jilted. She loved her daughter—this practical, worldly old lady—after her own fashion, very dearly; but she had no intention that she should be the bride of Heaven until, at least, all hope was over of earthly suitors.

Although, as we have said, knowing but few families in town, Carlyon had a pretty large male acquaintance, chiefly men from his own county. These men were not school or college friends; his mother's love had precluded his going to a public-school; she could not bear to part for any length of time with the only being to whom she could cling, and so he had been sent to a small seminary in the neighborhood of home. His father's selfishness had refused the expenses of a university education. These men were, therefore, mainly acquaintances of the hunting field. They all liked him, and were glad to see him in town; their prejudices upon the score of his opinions were not valid there; London society is very charitable, and "the clubs" have open arms for every one who doesn't cheat at cards. The conversation that sometimes — once in a year, perhaps — turns upon spiritual matters in the "smoking-room" (generally late at night,) exhibits religious liberty upon its broadest ground. If an honest country parson could only be smuggled in quietly to listen to it, how it would open his eyes; not so much in horror, but in astonishment. Between him and the man of the world there is a great gulf fixed, not of fire, but of ice; each makes believe that it will bear—that communication is, in fact, established; but neither ventures to cross. It is not to be expected that the latter will budge a step; if they are ever to meet, it is the business of the Royal (and Ecclesiastical) Humane Society's man to make the attempt.

Well, Carlyon's club was glad to see its country member; the sporting set (with whom he was best acquainted) introduced him to the fast set. He saw a good deal of what unphilosophic persons call "Life," in a little time. He had seen it before, of course. All Englishmen of good means do see it, sooner or later. Really moral men, whether philosophers or otherwise, are as rare as respectable folks are plentiful. The Josephs are few, the Joseph Surfaces many. Some say the former are not to be found at all, which seems to have been the view of some wise and very good teachers, such as Jeremy Taylor. But it is only the heartless, the sinners in cold blood, who pursue dissipation for any great length of time; passionless vice is the longest lived of all. Carlyon had never been a debauchee in his youth, and license had no greater charms for him in his middle age. Still, he wished to escape from himself, and was in no wise particular about the means. He never gambled, however. There was very high play among some of the men he knew, and there is nothing that offers so strong a temptation to one that would forget both the past and the future as high play; but he never touched dice or cards. If he lost, would he not be robbing her to whom he had left all he had?

Thus time went on with John Carlyon, among his new friends—for almost all were new, except Red Berild, who was stabled near to his own lodgings in the Albany—much as it goes on with many a man who has a month's holiday to spend in London; only Carlyon had already spent two months there, and (so it seemed to him) had ten months yet to spend. He scarcely noted time, save by its loss. Another week gone, or a day, such as he would never see again, was his occasional reflection. Without hope or fear as to the future, the material approximation to his life's end made itself felt within him. By nature a very unselfish man—as men go—his mind, like a bent sapling, still obstinately reverted to himself, notwithstanding that he strove to bind it to other things. We may, and often do, love others better than ourselves as Carlyon certainly did; we may even merge ourselves in them, and lose our very identity therein for a season; but, after all, there is nothing that interests a poor human creature so unintermittingly and for such long continuance as his own self. Carlyon often caught himself musing, not, indeed, exactly upon his own fate, as upon what would happen in the world in relation to him after he was gone. He smiled bitterly to think what sister Meg would have to say about him when the contents of his will were made known, and how Jedediah would run through that paltry five hundred pounds, and never fill a glass to his uncle's memory. If these relatives had really stood in need of his money, he would certainly not have disposed of it as he had done. As it was, how good a use would Agnes make of it! There was no fear, too, of wealth spoiling her. And yet it would give her pleasure, since it would afford her larger opportunities of doing good.

He could not, however, strive to please her in that which he knew would have made her happiest. Her own apprehensions with regard to that parting gift of hers had been fulfilled; he regarded the little volume she had sent him, so reverently, for her sake, that he almost always carried it about with him; but he would have preferred it to have been any other book. On its own account it was unwelcome and even repulsive, for he saw in it the material bar which had kept him and her asunder. It was terrible to him to think of that. Hopeless as his love for her was, the thought of death was hideous, inasmuch as it must needs separate them forever. In other respects, the contemplation of it was more curious than painful. The notices of matters to take place at a far-distant date, when he should no longer be above the earth but under it, affected him sharply; even a friend's casual mention of some plans for the ensuing summer would overcast his brow. That he had never felt himself stronger, or in more excellent health, only intensified the strangeness of all this. Such feelings, although frequent, were however, evanescent enough. His life, as has been said, went on much like any other idle man's. He lounged, and rode, and read, in his usual desultory way; he feasted, nay, he flirted willingly, though aimlessly enough, with the beautiful Edith. Hers was a heart not easily to be broken, and there was scarcely any body but himself now left in town for the poor girl to practice upon. Why should not she be gratified with the idea that he was being enthralled? She certainly did not love him; and when he was dead, if the rumor of there having been any *tendresse* between them should get abroad, it would only make her the more interesting. He would take care that matters should never go so far as to compel her to put on mourning, which she had confided to him did not become her. She enjoyed those little dinners at Richmond immensely, and so did he, did he not? Well, asking himself this question, as he strode up and down the broad graveled terrace after his guests were gone, he could scarcely answer, "Yes." Through most of his life he had been accustomed to be alone, but he had never felt so solitary, so friendless, so desolate, as now, with the congratulations and compliments of those fair-weather friends ringing in his ears, and the soft breathings of that lovely girl warm upon his cheek.

Why had she insisted upon bringing forth the skeleton of his closet, demanding, like some foolish princess in a fairy tale, the keys of his secret chamber, when he had only wished to give her the best of what he had? Why had he let her take that precious book within her hand; she—with her "How shocking!" and "What a naughty man to be an Infidel!"—was it not sacrilege to let her do it? And, on the other hand, who was he, to play fast and loose with this poor girl, as though his fellow-creatures were his puppets? Was his life, just because it was fated to be a short one, to swallow up all others while it lasted, and make them of no consequence? Was not his morbid mind compelling him to selfish and unworthy acts, which threatened to leave behind him an evil memory? It was surely worth while to look to that if to nothing else!

Thus perturbed in mind, the doomed man strode up and down the hotel garden, amid the thinning groups of pleasure-seekers, each with their hidden care, but none with one so heavy as his own, or, at least, which sat so heavily. Their light talk and easily moved mirth jarred upon his ear, and he descended to a lower terrace, from whence could still be seen the winding river, now silent and pale in the moonlight, and the sleeping fields curtained with silver mist; and after him, like his shadow moved the man that had aroused Edith's wrath awhile ago, by hovering near them.

CHAPTER XXIII.
THE DOCTOR'S DIFFICULTY.

ALTHOUGH poor Mr. Crawford had been found in his hammock cold as a stone in a sling, Mr. Carstairs had at once been sent for; and notwithstanding that he knew his professional services were not needed, the good-natured little man had hurried to Greycrags, for the sake of her whom the dead man had left alone in the world. Of course his first visit was paid to the chamber of death. The servants, weeping from the sudden strangeness of the event rather than from sorrow, unless, perhaps, some of them were touched for their young mistress's sake, were directed to retire—except Cubra, who had been so long the old man's confidential attendant—and the doctor stood by the dead man's side alone. There lay the fellow-creature who had been his host but lately, and his patient for some trifling ailment only two days before. He had been an old man, it was true; but he had had no immediate warning of this fate; the gaunt form was wan and thin enough, but so it had always been since Mr. Carstairs had known him. There was nothing to account for so sudden a failure of the vital powers.

"Poor old man!" That was the only piece of sentiment in which the little doctor, accustomed to see death claim the aged, permitted himself to indulge. He was musing upon what he should say to the unhappy girl that was. awaiting him below; what scheme he should propose to her for her future life, for he felt that he was the only counsellor she had, when something about the lips of the corpse attracted his attention.

"Draw the curtain still more back, Cubra," said he, hastily. "Give me all the light you can."

He bent over the dead man's face—already like the work of a sculptor's chisel—and then drew back, with something like horror depicted on his own.

Any one who had been looking in at that bedroom window would also have shrunk aghast from another face—that of Cubra herself, who was staring forth upon the lawn without, with cheeks of leaden hue, and eyes rolling in their sockets.

"Do you hear me, Cubra? more light," reiterated the doctor.

"Yes, Massa Carstairs;" she obeyed his mandate, yet did not turn her gaze toward him; but her ears were strained to catch his every word and movement.

"How strange," he murmured. Then, passing to the mantel-piece, whereon stood a couple of bottles, he took out their corks and smelled at their contents. They were both from his own dispensary.

"Cubra," said he carelessly, "did your poor master take any other medicines than those I used to send him?"

"Never, Massa Carstairs, never. Poor massa never liked medicine."

"Now, look at me, Cubra; you knew your master's ways better than any body. Are you quite sure that he did not keep by him, in his desk, or in a drawer, any thing to stop pain—he suffered from toothache, you know, for instance—now, try and recollect; was there no box or bottle from which he used to take something to relieve it?"

Cubra shook her head. "No; she was 'certain sure' such was not the case. Massa did not mind pain like other folks."

Mr. Carstairs knew that this was true; for the old man, although it was his whim to be considered more of an invalid than he really was, had been a very stoic with respect to physical pain.

Mr. Robert Augustus Carstairs, F.R.C.S., had his weak professional side—a tendency not uncommon among the faculty to assign all ailments to one particular disease, and to exaggerate the effects thereof—but he was both a sagacious and a scientific man. Affecting to be convinced by Cubra's replies, he determined to ask a question or two elsewhere respecting the matter which had so much moved him. It was impossible to get any information out of this black domestic. She was faithful, no doubt, and it was to be hoped to a greater degree than any white woman, for she was certainly far stupider. If the late Mr. Crawford had really kept secreted about him any such thing as he (the doctor) suspected, it was in the highest degree unlikely that Cubra should have been made his confidant. Mr. Carstairs descended to the drawing-room, where he found poor Agnes alone. She was very sad and pale; but her tears were not falling now. She had been praying to One who wipes tears away from all eyes, and had found present comfort. Good people, as a rule (with the exception of utterly heartless folks) weep least when Heaven takes away those nearest to them. She could not trust herself to speak much; but she had ears to hear all that was necessary to be said.

The little doctor took her hand in his with fatherly tenderness, and addressed to her a few unconventional words of sympathy. "Can I see your cousin, dear Miss Agnes?" inquired he; "for it must rest with him, of course, to arrange—"

"No," replied she, shaking her head. "Richard is quite unable for such a task. I never saw him so utterly unnerved as when—" Here she broke down a little; then resumed, "No, my dear Mr. Carstairs, I must trust wholly to your kindness in this matter."

"I am sorry," mused the doctor; "not," added he, hastily, "that I grudge either time or trouble in such a service, my dear young lady, but because I had certain questions to ask of him—mere matters of form it is true—but which must be more or less distressing to a daughter, respecting your poor father's death."

She bowed her head in sign of her willingness to hear him.

"Did Mr. Crawford suffer, to your knowledge, from any chronic, or other pain, such as might have induced him to take opiates—or even stronger palliatives?"

"Certainly not. I should say that my poor dear father—considering his great age—was signally free from such maladies. He never had even so much as an attack of rheumatism."

"He suffered, however, much at times, did he not, from depression of spirits?"

"Yes."

"Was that depression hypochondriacal, or resulting from some sufficient cause; I do not of course seek to pry into the nature of it, but was there a cause?"

"There was."

"Was that cause likely to have increased with years, or to have diminished?"

"To have diminished."

At this Mr. Carstairs looked sharply up into the grave young face; but nothing save truth was to be read therein.

"There was no immediate apprehension, then, hanging over your father, such as, combined with this depression, or independent of it, might have affected his reason?"

"Oh, sir, he spoke to me last night—as wisely, kindly—" here she hesitated; "we had a long talk together, and little did I imagine that it was to be the last between us."

"Forgive me the pain I see I am inflicting, dear Miss Agnes, but, during that conversation did he mention nothing of importance which was also novel, and such as dwelling upon a mind already enfeebled, might go far even to overthrow it."

"We spoke of an important matter, but it was one on which we had talked before. There were no secrets—none—between myself and him."

"Did you agree on that in which you talked, or was there a difference of opinion?"

"We agreed."

"Nothing then has taken place, to your knowledge, since I saw your father last, to give him any sudden mental shock?"

"No."

"Nothing to disturb or distress him?"

"Richard had an interview with him yesterday morning; I suppose, about my cousin's going to sea. They were not on such good terms with one another as I could have wished —as I wish now more than ever. But my father was never put out by any disagreement with Richard, and he did not even mention that there had been such when I talked with him in the evening."

"And is Mr. Richard absolutely too ill to see me?"

"Yes, Mr. Carstairs. I am very anxious about my cousin. At times—and particularly of late—I have almost thought that he has not entirely recovered from that sunstroke which he received when upon the coast of Africa. I am not alarmed, except for himself, you will understand," added she, hastily, perceiving the doctor's grave looks, "but I do think his position precarious."

"What you have told me, my dear Miss Agnes, is only one more reason added to those which have already occured to me, why you should not remain at Greycrags."

"Oh, Mr. Carstairs; could I leave *him?*" cried she, with a piteous glance in the direction of her father's room.

"You can be of no use to him more, dear girl. You will, of course attend the funeral if you feel it well to do so; but, in the mean time you should not be here. I have already secured you rooms at Widow Marcon's, at the Brae Cottage, if you will consent to remove thither. She is a good motherly person, and has herself experienced a recent sorrow that will make her sympathize with yours. With your cousin in such a state as you describe—independently of other very valid reasons—it is only right, nay, necessary, that you should move thither at once. You will have nothing to reproach yourself with, I hope, in leaving all matters here in my hands. Cubra will of course accompany you. Come, will you give me your promise, like a good girl?"

"I will do what you will, Mr. Carstairs, upon one condition. Tell me what has killed my poor dear father."

"*Killed* him! my child—for I must be your father now—how ever can you use such words? He died of that commonest disease of all, old age. But, since it was so very sudden, it was my duty to ask those questions. Richard, if he had been himself, would have understood the necessity of them at once, although they seem so strange to *you*."

For serious, systematic, kindly lying, there is nobody that approaches your honest medical man. He will assure the husband (with the best intentions, and for his physical good, mind you), lying upon the bed, which his science tells him he will never leave with life, of returning strength; he will bid the wife, worn out with watching by his side, and to whom one refreshing sleep is priceless, to be of good cheer, for that there is healthiest hope. And, used to these pious frauds, Mr. Carstairs let fall his words as though he were dropping drops from the phial of the very quintessence of truth, and Agnes Crawford believed them.

"When we poor mortals have struggled on to eighty years," continued the doctor, "death can scarcely be said to come upon us unawares. If its approach be sudden, so much the better—that is, if we are only prepared for it in a spiritual sense; with the young and the unprepared, alas! it is very different."

Cunning Mr. Carstairs walked to the window as though he did not wish his countenance to be perused. His object was to interest his hearer in something else—no matter if it was itself distressing—than that with which her mind was oppressed; to lift, if but for a few minutes, the dull weight of that desolation which sits upon the mourner's soul and crushes the life-springs. His attempt succeeded. Agnes, always solicitous for others, inquired of whom he spoke.

"Of John Carlyon."

"What of him?" cried Agnes, starting to her feet. "He is not ill, I trust; not dying—oh, no, surely, sir, he is not dying?"

The doctor had overshot his mark. With clasped hands, and suddenly tearful eyes, the young girl stood before him, the very picture of despair. In closing one channel of grief he had opened the flood-gates of a deeper woe.

"Mr. Carlyon is not in any immediate danger, that I know of, my dear young lady. But his is not a good life. I mean, he has a disease—heart complaint—which may carry him off at any moment, and with which it is not to be expected that he can live long."

"How long have you known this, Mr. Carstairs?"

"Not long. Only since that day when he saved your life upon the sands."

"Oh, would to heaven that I had known it, too," cried Agnes, passionately. "I might have tried more earnestly to move him than I did. He is not fit to die, doctor."

"Few of us are, my dear young lady. Yet he has a noble soul, and a kind heart."

"He has, I know it. That such a one should be lost is only the more terrible." Here she paused a moment. "Does Mrs. Newman—does his sister know of his sad state? I mean, as to health."

"Yes; I thought it my duty to acquaint her with it, in order that some reconciliation might be effected. But she would not move in the matter. She said that she had washed her hands of him. She is a hard woman. Carlyon once remarked that she had made a religion for herself out of the worst parts of Christianity, and certainly she is one of those who makes its profession repulsive. He has gone to London, and will not return to Woodlees any more. They will never meet again in this world, those two—be calm, my dear young lady; be like yourself, and bear with patience what God himself permits to be. I can not, I dare not, leave you in this state. You will come to the Brae, like a good girl. I have a close carriage at the door."

He spoke to her as though she were a child, and, like a child, she listened, and obeyed him.

"I suppose you are right, doctor," returned she, feebly; "as I am sure you are kind. Yes, I will go with you. But first let me take leave of *him* for the last time."

"No, my dear young lady," replied the doctor, firmly; "that must not be. It may seem cruel, but I am only doing what he would wish could those cold lips speak. Think of him as you saw him last."

"I understand, sir. Alas, alas!"

"A good girl, a wise and dutiful girl. I will ring for Cubra, and she will get ready such things as you may require. Mrs. Marcon quite expects you both."

"You will see Richard, sir, before you go."

"True, I had forgotten him; I will look to him at once."

"Tell him, please, with my kindest love, Mr. Carstairs—his cousin's love—that I do not feel equal to wishing him good-by to-day. In a day or two—after the—"

"Yes, yes, I will manage all that," returned the doctor. "Of course you can not see him. Here is Cubra—that's well."

The black woman put a key into his hand, and whispered a few words, unobserved by her young mistress, who lay back on the sofa with closed eyes, conscious of nothing save her bereavement.

"I will ring for them when they are to come up," resumed he, in the same low voice. "Get together what your mistress will require for the next few days. You must go with her to Widow Marcon's at once. The sooner she gets from this house the better. Where is Mr. Richard?"

"He has gone out, sir."

"Gone out? Where has he gone?"

"God A'mighty knows. Gone for a long walk, he said; his head was bad. He take poor massa's death to heart so much."

Mr. Carstairs nodded, and left the room.

"That's strange," muttered he. "He was in the house when I came, for I saw him at his bedroom window. I wonder why he doesn't wish to see me." Once more the doctor sought the chamber of death; once more bent over the dead man—and, as he did so, his countenance grew graver than ever. "This is horrible," murmured he. "It would kill her to think that he killed himself, and would benefit nobody. But if there has been foul play—yet that is impossible." He rang the bell, and summoned the man-servant, while he set his seal upon the desk, wherein he knew lay the dead man's will. For Mr. Crawford had been more communicative to the doctor of late than to any other person. Then the chamber was again given up to those who minister the last rites to poor humanity.

Mr. Carstairs saw the carriage depart containing the unhappy Agnes and her attendant; then followed close behind it on his pony.

"At all risks, I will spare her if I can," murmured he. "It will be time enough to make a stir when the will is read, and if any body but herself is found to derive benefit from the old man's death. I wonder why Richard would not see me."

CHAPTER XXIV.

TOWED ASTERN.

MONTHS have passed away since the events recorded in the last chapter. In the will of Mr. Crawford no other name save that of his daughter was mentioned. Richard's little property had been somewhat improved while in his uncle's care, and was found more than sufficient for his own very simple needs. He had had an interview with Mr. Carstairs after his uncle's funeral, in which he had behaved with unexpected calmness and good sense. He was very solicitous about his own state of health, and seemed to be well aware that there was danger with respect to his mind. He owned that he still felt the effects of the sun-stroke received two years ago, although only on occasions of excitement. He spoke of his uncle with respect, but without any hypocritical regret. He felt sorry, he said, now that Mr. Crawford was dead, that they had not been better friends; but confessed that they never had got on agreeably together. Any lingering suspicion which the doctor may have entertained of "foul play" in the matter of the old man's death was entirely done away with, and whatever views he still entertained with respect to the untimeliness of his decease, he attached no blame to Richard. He was much ashamed of himself at having ever harbored so groundless a prejudice, and felt a kindly interest in one he had so gravely wronged in thought. He cordially approved of the young man's proposition to mix with the world for a little before going to sea again, and Richard accordingly set out for London.

Agnes was greatly pleased at the unexpected good sense exhibited by her cousin. When he came to bid her good-bye, he showed no trace of that willfulness and passion he had been used to exhibit, and which had caused her to regard him of late (although she did not own it to herself) with less of affection than alarm. Perhaps, out of regard for her recent bereavement, perhaps, because he felt that he had really no chance of winning her heart, he made no direct allusion to his love for her, and even the hint he dropped was so slight that it did not strike her with any force until long afterward. He said that he felt it was better for him to leave Mellor for the present, but that he should see her again—she might depend on that—before he undertook another voyage. When she spoke of writing to him in the mean time, he answered, "No, Agnes; I had rather there was silence between us for the present. I shall hear about you, and of every thing you do—that is, Mr. Carstairs has promised to let me know." He was manifestly making a gallant effort to shake off his hopeless passion, and at parting she was more deeply moved, or seemed to be so, than he. She mentally blessed the kindly little doctor for his good offices which, while releasing her from a most embarrassing attachment, had left her an affectionate well-wisher and friend in her only cousin.

So Richard Crawford, like John Carlyon, was swallowed up in the great world of London, where men do, even more than elsewhere, what is right in their own eyes; and Agnes was left in her little world at Mellor—shrunk to small dimensions indeed by their secession—at Widow Marcon's cottage, "The Brae."

A very pretty little dwelling it was, on the very margin of the bay, down to which the small garden, with its couple of tiny terraces and Lilliputian arbor, sloped. A toy palace, fit for a queen (of Titania's nature), with a very limited court. The widow, finding herself but ill provided for at her husband's death, had taken the place with a speculative eye. Such a bijou of a villa residence could not fail to attract some elderly spinster or widow like herself, or even two sisters (if they did not mind occupying the same sleeping apartment, for there was but one "best bedroom"), it was such a lovely spot, and so adapted for persons of elegant tastes and limited incomes. There was a dining-room, in which one could not quite give what is called a dinner-party, but three could sit down in it very comfortably, and even more, if the fourth didn't mind getting up from her seat to let the servant pass round the table. This room opened upon a lawn, soft as a carpet (and not at all larger than are the common run of carpets)—the only naturally level piece of ground in the whole fairy demesne. The dining-room opened upon "the hall," upon the white stone floor of which you might have eaten your dinner, so far as cleanliness was concerned, and provided you did not have more than one dish up at a time, for there would not have been room for more, and, on the other side of the hall—a good long step (for a short person)—lay the drawing-room, quite a stately apartment by comparison with the rest, and capable of accommodating six persons—four in the body of the room, and two in the bow window, which was built in a bower of honeysuckle and roses, and looked, from the outside, like a bird'snest. The rent of "The Brae"—which, considered as a model for a habitation, was really perfect, however absurd as a real dwelling-house for grown-up people—was small even in proportion to its dimensions; but then Miss Crawford was such an eligible tenant for "not giving trouble," and for "putting up" with the widow's shortcomings and ignorance confessed of how "the quality" require to be served; and also, in all probability, "you see," said the widow, in confidence to her gossips, "she would be for a permanency."

Thus, though the income hitherto paid to her father, notwithstanding his change of name, by the good-will of the Government, had, of course, ceased, what with her very moderate outgoings in respect to lodging, and her inexpensive habits of living, Agnes, so far from being poor, was able to make more considerable investments even than before in that stock which, though it pays but little more to its debenture holders at present than the London, Chatham and Dover Railway, is spoken of by the clergy and others as likely one day to return an immense percentage. If giving to the poor is lending to the Lord, as there is good reason to believe, Agnes Crawford was laying up for herself much treasure in heaven. And yet she was not happy. That the prosperity of the wicked (unless prosperity means happiness) should offend us almost beyond reconcilement, appears unreasonable, compared with the distrust inspired by the unhappiness of the godly. *That* (as it seems to me) is a matter that much more requires an obedient, unquestioning faith. It is certain that Agnes Crawford was not happy. Unlike that pious gentleman who deemed it a cause of thankfulness (to himself and the elect) that there were "babes a span long in hell," she not only wished that no little one should perish, but, if it were possible, not a single soul, and especially not John Carlyon's soul. What a short time had he to live, and in the midst of life how near was he to death; and yet what could she do? Many a night she lay awake in her

sea-bordered home, while the great winter tides swirled in and out, and the wind moaned and shrieked like a lost spirit, thinking with aching heart of him who saved her from the roaring flood, but whom *she* could not save. What was he doing, what was he thinking, what was he believing, during those precious unreturning months? Mr. Carstairs had heard from him once or twice, but only with respect to certain business matters of a nature to be entrusted to him rather than to Mr. Scrivens. He was setting his house in order in one sense, yet there was no sign of carefulness for the most important matter of all. How often were her small white hands wedded in vicarious supplication—how often was his name whispered to God through those pure lips! Many men have intercessors of this sort (besides the Great One), who, innocent themselves, little know what sins they would have shriven; and Heaven grant such prayers may not be altogether unanswered. Let us trust there must be something good in the object, however unworthy, that can provoke such supplications.

Winter, then, has come and gone, and it is Spring. The grass is green upon her father's grave, and his memory has faded away wholly, save from one loving heart. It is warm enough slowly to and fro to pace the tiny terrace of "The Brae," or sitting in the harbor, book in hand, to let it idly fall upon the lap, and watch the red-sailed fishing-boats putting out to sea with the flood, or the carts with their freight of cocklers, crossing the *eau* to their work upon the sands, with the ebb. In the morning, Agnes sits there before she sets forth upon her ministrations among the poor and the sick, and those (saddest of all human wayfarers) who are at once both sick and poor; and in the evening, when her labor of love is over.

It is morning now; the beginning of a bright and cheerful May day, with a wind that has lost the sting of March, not keen, yet blowing free. The air is clear, and objects can be seen afar which are often hidden by the hazy veil of Summer. The tide is running out like a mill-race. If yonder fishermen, who have been fishing beyond Greycrags, be not wary, there is danger that their boat will be left aground. Agnes knows this from long acquaintance with the treacherous bay, as well as from her constant watching of the sands and the sea during these latter months. She knows, too, the men who are in the boats; they are the Millets, father and son. If old Stephen (not improved in morals, poor fellow, although still proposing to be so—ashamed, but not reformed) were alone yonder, she would be alarmed for his safety; but William is with him, agile, sagacious, cool. Still, why do they delay? By the line of sea-wall that is showing on the island, by the dark crests of rock that are rising here and there out of the yellow foam, she knows that they have already lingered longer than is prudent. True, the head of their boat is pointing seaward, but they are not yet in the main current, and their progress is very slow—slower than it ought to be, considering that one has the oars out, and the other is pushing his hardest with the punt pole. She makes out so much through a little telescope; but she can not make out what is the dark object they are towing astern, and which impedes their movements. She is not afraid, as one only acquainted with the dangers of the bay and not with its peculiarities, might be of its being a drowned man. Such are rarely found in the locality in question, and never until the tide has retired. By great exertions, and with frequent and inexplicable changes of their course, the boat is at last got into the main stream, and hurries toward the village fast enough; the sole difficulty now lies in stopping in at what is called, by courtesy, the landing-place—a few narrow yards of planks laid upon a bed of shining ooze. Now, she can make out what it is they have behind them; it is a horse, fastened to the boat's stern by a bridle.

Agnes threw down her book, and hastened through the little garden to the landing-place. Some accident must have certainly happened when a saddle-horse is found in that terrible bay; it is not long before they find the rider. Her mind at once reverted to Red Berild, and to him with whom it was so often occupied, his master; but John Carlyon and his steed were far away, she knew. Whose horse was this, then, exhausted, half-dead, hurried along by the rapid stream without any motion of its own, and at times half-rolling over, so as to show its girths, as though it were dead indeed? In a village like Mellor, one knows not only each inhabitant, but every horse and dog, yet she did not recognize this horse. Without wasting time in questions, however, she stood ready, as the fishing-smack drew near, to seize the boat-hook which William Millet was holding out, for there was nobody but herself at "the point," as this place was called, where a jut of land turned the main course of the *eau* and formed a little bay behind it. Into this bay the boat was drawn, with the poor animal towing behind it —a small black mare, with heaving flanks, and frightened eyes, who could scarcely keep her feet in the shallow water, although the sand beneath was tolerably firm.

"A bad business, miss, I fear," observed William, when they were safe in port.

Old Stephen, to whom, probably, conversing upon such a subject with Agnes was personally distasteful, contented himself with touching his cap and shaking his head.

"Where was it found?" asked she. "Poor creature, how it shivers!"

"Under the lee of the island, miss. A game little thing is that mare; she must have been in the water these four hours, swimming round and round, and round and round, with not an inch of firm ground for her feet."

"And the rider, William?"

"The Lord have mercy on him, whoever he be," answered the young man, reverently.

"You don't know, then, to whom the horse belongs?"

"Yes, I do, miss. But it may not have been the owner who was upon her, you see. Heaven forbid that it should have been."

"Why do you say that, William?"

"Well, miss, we're none of us fit, but Mr. Scrivens, he never loved God's people, and was a hard man to the poor."

"Hush, William; do not say things like that. We are no man's judges. Is it Mr. Scrivens's horse?"

Two or three men had gathered together at the landing-place by this time, and were helping with the boat; one of them, the hostler at the Mellor Arms, here interposed.

"No, miss," said he, "it's was than Lawyer Scrivens, or at least it comes nigher to Mellor. That's Mr. Jedediah's horse."

"What, Mrs. Newman's son?"

"Yes, miss. He bought this mare of Mr. Scrivens only three days ago. I saw him cross the sands upon her yesterday, and spoke with him; he said he should not be back last night, for that there would not be time. He must have tried to come back, poor lad, and so been drowned."

Agnes turned deadly pale, and grasped the hand-rail of the little wooden pier; her limbs trembled beneath her.

"What is to be done, William?"

"I must get a horse and search the sands, miss, and you must go up to the Priory as was, and break it to his mother."

CHAPTER XXV.

MY JED.

THAT would have been a terrible office for any woman, no matter of how dutiful a spirit, which William Millet laid upon Agnes Crawford, when he said, "You must go up and break it to her"—the almost certain death of her only son, to a doting mother; but it was far worse for Agnes than for any one else. Mrs. Newman and herself had never met since that angry parting at Greycrags, months ago, and she knew that Carlyon's sister had not grown less bitter against her in the mean time. It was impossible for Agnes, because contrary to her nature, to shrink from any duty, but it was no wonder that in such a case she should procrastinate.

"We can not be sure, William," said she, meekly, "that this awful catastrophe has happened. We do not know for certain that any one is drowned, and far less who it is."

William shook his head, and answered, quietly—

"Very good, Miss Agnes. As soon as the tide runs out, I will take horse and search the sands."

"This here mare won't be fit to carry a man within this twelve hours," observed the hostler; "even if she gets over this at all. A nice bit of blood, too, she is; and a pretty price, I'll answer for it, poor Mr. Jedediah paid for her."

Poor Mr. Jedediah. How that word shot through Agnes Crawford's heart. She knew the young man by report only too well; knew of his evil doings among her own little flock; a wolf, he had been, to more than one pretty lamb. And, lo, he was now cut off in the midst of his sins!

"What horse have you up at the inn, Jim?" asked old Stephen.

"Not one," returned the hostler. "The greys are gone to a wedding out Northbrook way, and a gent, as come to our house last night, has just taken out the strawberry mare, meaning to call at Woodlees on his way home. I believe he wants to buy Squire Carlyon's house."

Marrying and buying, how the world runs on, though death is ever so busy among it! thought Agnes.

"Is there no other horse?"

"None as I knows of, ma'am; no, not one in the village, excep—" and the hostler hesitated and looked at William.

"Then it's all the more necessary, Miss Agnes," said the latter, interpreting his glance, "that you should see Mistress Newman quickly. It's Mr. Jedediah's own horse as is wanted; there's none else. I am sorry to put such a burden on you, Miss Agnes, but you must ask her to lend him to me, you must indeed."

"Ask for her son's horse to search for his dead body! I can not do it!" exclaimed Agnes, wringing her hands.

"You need not say it's her son as is lost, miss," observed old Stephen, cunningly. "You can say as *somebody's* a-missing; there will be no lie in that, for, as you were saying, it *may* not be Mr. Jedediah after all."

The children of this world are, in their generation, wiser than the children of light; and the old man's proposition was welcome to Agnes, by comparison with the unrelenting straightforwardness of his son; it put off the evil moment, and even afforded some flicker of hope.

"I will go at once," said she, quietly. "You will come with me, William?"

"Certainly, miss. You see," continued he, as they left the landing and took the road together toward the Priory, "that I couldn't go myself to Mistress Newman's. I am out of her favor, although through no fault of mine. I thought it was only right to tell her something the other day, respecting—something about her son, as it was her part to look to; and she was very angry, very. Therefore, she might think (which Heaven forbid), that I brought this sad news to her in the way of a judgment like. You, who have never given her offense, and are a lady like herself, are much more fit to tell her."

"I see, William, I see," answered Agnes, mechanically. Her brain was busy with what she should say to this unhappy woman, not dreaming of the desolation that had befallen her, filled with petty thoughts, and probably even hostile and aggressive toward herself. What *should* she say?

Up the hill, and beside the ivied wall to the gate of the old house, which every body, save its tenant, still called the Priory. It was getting very near now, that terrible interview; and nothing had been given her to speak. The page looked astonished when he opened the door; perhaps because she was a stranger to the house, perhaps because of her companion, William. On either supposition it was natural enough, and yet it seemed to add to her discomposure.

"I wish to see Mrs. Newman."

The boy lingered, as though some explanation were necessary; very likely he surmised that something was wrong; "on very particular business," added she. He led the way at once up stairs; she did not notice that he gave William a sign to remain below; she had counted upon his presence and support, but she was ushered in alone.

Mrs. Newman, early as it was, had already breakfasted, and was seated at a window of the drawing-room, from which she had doubtless watched her approach; she rose and gave a cold and haughty bow. The room was cold and without fire; the atmosphere and the frigidity of her reception combined to chill the unhappy visitor. Mrs. Newman was the first to speak.

"To what am I indebted for the unexpected honor of a visit from Miss Crawford?" The tone was studiously constrained, but there was no mistaking the expression of the speaker's face. It was the very concentration of rage and loathing.

"I come, dear madam—"

"Spare the 'dear,'" interrupted Mrs. Newman, harshly. "Pray avoid all unnecessary hypocrisies; I assure you that no words you can make use of will impose upon me."

"I have no wish to impose upon you, madam. I come as a Christian woman in the cause of charity, just as I would come to any one else."

"Thank you. I have my own poor to attend to; and all that I have to give away has been given. I am not so rich as some folks, and have no such expectations, but I do my best."

"God forbid, madam! that it should not be so, or that I should doubt it; but you misunderstand me."

"Indeed! I only drew my conclusions from the person who accompanied you. An impudent, low-bred fellow, who has himself insulted, although he has not injured me as you have."

"I, madam?"

"Oh, you have a very innocent face, but it does not hide your scheming heart from me, young lady. And let me tell you this—in order that you may not stay here from the idea of your being welcome—that I hate the very sight of you. You the are vilest and wickedest girl I know—there is not a hussy in the parish—"

"Mrs. Newman," interposed Agnes, in a trembling voice, "there is a man drowned in the bay, and I want your horse—the loan of your son's horse—in order that William Millet may search the sands for the dead body."

"There are horses at the inn, which you may hire, for you have plenty of money now, I make no doubt. Let the backbiting, impertinent knave, who seems to be your friend, take one of those. I will not lend him—him, least of all people—my dear son's horse. Jedediah is very particular about his horses."

"Those at the inn are all engaged, madam. Pray lend it."

"I will not. Is there any thing else that you have come here for? If not, you have your answer."

"Oh, Mrs. Newman, pray forget that it is I who ask you, and lend William your horse. You will be sorry for it, else, some day, you will indeed. Think of the father, or the mother, who may be awaiting the return of this lost man, and in vain—"

"Yes, or the lover," interposed Mrs. Newman, scornfully. "The young woman that adores him, but who will be comforted a little, perhaps, if he has left her all his money. You feign astonishment, Miss Crawford, remarkably well. Do you mean to tell me"—here her voice rose to a shrill scream—"that you do not know that my brother, John Carlyon, has left you—you, you minx—doubtless for value received—all his money? has beggared his natural heirs for your sweet sake? Do you dare to tell me that you do not know that?"

"God is my witness, Mrs. Newman, that I have never heard one whisper of this thing before."

"Well, then, you hear it now, let us suppose, for the first time; mind, I say, let us suppose? Do not imagine that you will hoodwink me any more. Months ago, I confess, when I taunted you with some such design, though not one half so bad and base as what you have effected, your pretended indignation almost imposed upon me. I was nearly regretting having called you husband-hunter, fortune-seeker; but I am not to be deceived now. However, supposing you hear for the first time of the disposition that this man has chosen to make of all his fortune—save a beggarly five hundred pounds left to my son—what is your opinion as to its character? Is it just? Come, though I am speaking of your lover, and to you who profit by his insane doting, is it honest?"

"Mrs. Newman, if what you say be true, I am as astonished as yourself, and almost as sorry."

"Are you ashamed, miss?"

"Yes. Ashamed to have been the involuntary cause of warping a just man's judgment."

"But when he is dead, and you get the money, you will keep it?"

"Not an hour—not a moment. I would not touch one shilling. So soon as the lawyers can do it, you will have every penny paid over to you, as though it had come to you directly, and all I shall ask in return will be that you forgive your brother."

"Come here, girl; more to the light, that I may see your face. Is it possible that you speak the truth?"

"God knows, madam."

So quiet, so gentle of speech, and the fair face so grave and peaceful, as it looked up at the morning sky, not even a miser could doubt her.

"Agnes Crawford, I do believe you."

"I hope so, madam, else you do me wrong indeed."

"Stop, girl," cried Mrs. Newman, with a suspicious glance; "the way that we find out whether persons are really sorry who have committed theft—not that I call you thief, although my brother's will is robbery—the test of sincerity, I say, is restitution. You promise to restore what you may come by, but will you set that promise down in writing?"

"Very gladly, madam. Write any form of words down which you please, and I will sign it now, at once. Or get a lawyer to do so, if law there be for such a thing. In any case it will be some hold upon even the most shameless to have her written words to hold up against her, and that hold you shall have."

"Good; you do your best, though only what is right, girl," said Mrs. Newman, sitting down, pen in hand. "You have behaved like a lady and a Christian woman. You will understand that for myself I am quite content with your word. If it were only *I* concerned in the matter, it should rest here. But the interests of my son are bound up with mine. To me, an old woman, and given, I trust, but little to the world's vanities, money is nothing; but my Jedediah—he, dear boy, is on the threshold of life. I should like to see him settled well before I die; married, perhaps, to some good girl like yourself—for I believe you to be good, I do indeed—and living on the old estate. He is a fine lad, and loves his mother; you must not listen to what some folks say against him."

"The horse, dear madam. You will let William have the horse?"

"Certainly; I will ring the bell and give orders." Here she did so. "He must be very careful with it, however, for it is Jed's favorite. The other, upon which he rode to Castleton yesterday, is a new purchase. Mr. Scrivens—" Mrs. Newman blushed and hesitated. The fact was that, so desirous had she been to get the truth concerning her brother's will out of the lawyer, that she had given a large sum for the animal solely to loosen Mr. Scrivens's tongue; and in this she had succeeded. Never was such bad news bought at so high a price. However, all was well now.

"It was a black horse, was it not?" asked Agnes, very gravely.

"Yes, dear. Did you see it? How well Jed rides, and how well he looks on horseback; don't you think so? You have not seen him lately, perhaps; let me see, in three hours' time

—he would be here for lunch, he said—he will be coming home. The tide has almost run down." There was a clatter of horseshoofs in the road, and Mrs. Newman flew to the window. "How stupid of me," said she, with disappointment; "of course it couldn't be Jed. There goes William Millet on the grey, and I hope he will be very careful. I don't know how I should look Jed in the face, if any thing— What's the matter, Miss Crawford? What's the matter, Agnes?"

"Nothing: at least it may be nothing; but dear Mrs. Newman, I have bad news for you."

"What—what?" interrupted the other, seizing her by the arm. "My brother is dead: say it is that. Say any thing but— It's not my Jed. No, no, it's not; it can not be my Jed."

"Let us hope, let us pray, for the best, dear lady. But it was the black horse—your son's horse—that was found in the bay this morning with saddle and bridle on him, but without a rider."

The pen fell from Mrs. Newman's fingers; her face stiffened; her eyes gazed upon Agnes in a sort of stupefied wonder. The sorrow was too great for the poor soul to realize. "Let us go," murmured she, "up to my room. Help me up to my room."

Agnes knew what she meant; her bedroom was on the floor above, and commanded from its window a wide sweep of the bay, now getting bare and brown. So, leaning heavily on the young girl's arm, Mrs. Newman made her way up stairs, trembling in every limb, and murmuring to herself, with a pathos beyond all tears or moans, "My Jed—my Jed!"

The two women took their seats at the window, watching the wide waste of sand growing and growing with the outgoing tide, while the sense of desolation grew and grew in the widow's heart. Her lips had ceased to move, but ever and anon she returned the gentle pressure of the young girl's hand with a sharp grip. Her eyes followed everywhere the movements of a dark and distant speck, that was a man and horse, moving so swiftly, that it seemed to flit over the sands. As the day went on, the usual busy scene began to present itself in the wave-deserted bay, but the women's eyes never wandered elsewhere. Suddenly they lost sight of this object of their anxious gaze.

"I don't see him, Agnes," exclaimed the elder lady, hurriedly. "I don't see William Millet. Oh, where is he?"

"He is behind the island, dear Mrs. Newman." Another clasp of the hand was her reply. Minutes went by, that seemed hours; then other tiny specks, that were cocklers, seemed to make toward the island, and disappeared behind it. There was evidently something unusual thereabouts that was attracting them. Presently all emerged together—quite a thick black block—round the rocky promontory of the little isle, and moved toward the village, very slowly—like a funeral.

"Shall I go and meet them?" asked Agnes, tenderly; for her companion's suspense seemed to be growing insupportable.

"No, no; I shall know it soon enough— soon enough. I am not childless yet, Agnes —not my Jed, oh, God, not my Jed!"

But it was her Jed, poor soul! William had found the body of the unfortunate lad upon a spit of sand, quite near the island, but separated from it by what was in flood-time a raging river. He was lying upon his back, with his handsome face very pale and quiet, looking up at the sky, and the water (a usual sight in such cases) coming out of his mouth, as one who saw him said, "like barm."

Jedediah had attempted, it seems, being somewhat in liquor, to cross the sands the night before, dangerously late, in respect of the tide, yet not so much so, but that one well mounted, and who knew the road so well as he, might have effected the passage. But his new purchase, the black mare, unaccustomed to the unstable track, it was supposed grew restive, and carrying him much eastward of the proper course, there threw and drowned him.

CHAPTER XXVI.

A NEW SISTER.

AGNES CRAWFORD not only remained at the Priory to comfort the wretched mother all that day, but at Mrs. Newman's earnest entreaty, took up her abode there until after the funeral. Her unselfish goodness, evidenced by a thousand daily acts and words, worked its way into Mrs. Newman's heart, as the continuous falling of the pearl-like water-drops will eat into the grimmest stone; and well for the widow that it was so. Certain sad truths respecting her dead boy—fiercely combated by her at first, but which, at last, she could not resist—were presently disclosed. Mrs. Newman had to confess to herself that her idol had not been all she had fondly supposed him to be. She was not less devoted to his memory upon that account—what mother could have been?—but the knowledge that her son had sinned, sowed in this seed of good, that she grew to be less bitter against sinners. There must, she felt, be mercy for them such as she had not dreamed of, since it was needed for her dead boy.

Not a day now passed but Agnes came up from the Brae, and sat an hour or more in the bereaved woman's company. She never stayed to dinner, because she saw that her hostess did not wish that; for, as time grew on, the old habit of saving, of parsimony, not unobservable even during that interregnum of bereavement, resumed its sway over the forlorn widow. Sad as it was, Agnes smiled to see it, for it was a sign that although the heart-wound might not have been healed—and, indeed, could never do so—it was cicatrized. When the poor lady began once more to sniff at her cook, and bully her page, to count the cutlets that left her table, and pursue the half-pence in her grocer's book with wrapt attention, it was as healthful a sympton as the return of motion to the limbs of the paralytic. Yet, thanks to the influence of her new friend, she made some struggle against this infirmity of her nature. The first time she felt herself able to walk to church she dropped something more than small silver (of which she always had a great store) into the collection plate; it was not, indeed, a coin of the realm; but it was gold, and had been valued as such by her for many years, and kept in a locked drawer in her cabinet. Mr. Puce called the next day at the Priory with a polite speech about her having made a mistake and given a much more rare and costly gift than a common sovereign; but she only said that she was glad such was the case, and bade him keep it for the good purpose for which it had been intended; it was only right that she should suffer for her carelessness. So Mr. Puce had to give the poor a pound out of his own pocket, and add *per contra* to his collection of curiosities at the rectory, a Spanish moidore of an inscrutable epoch, and with a large perforation in its middle.

Nay, though the widow's loss bore heavily upon her night and day, she absolutely made use of it to excuse little economies and retrenchments; "now that her dear Jed had been taken from her," this and that were no longer necessary. Perhaps it was partly due to these proceedings (for any new act of thriftiness had always tended that way, as "a good stroke of business" mollifies the city man) that her voice grew softer, her manners more gentle even than before; but something of this was doubtless owing to Agnes. Mrs. Newman's household outgoings for the day having been reduced to a minimum, that lady would welcome the young girl to her breakfast parlor with the sweetest smile, apologizing for not taking her to the more ceremonious apartment upon the ground that the sun spoiled the carpet, for which reason the shutters were kept closed; or, quite as often, as time went on, the widow would walk down to the Brae, and spend "a nice long morning" with Agnes, which was always made to extend over the dinner hour. It fortunately happened that, although she had given orders for that meal to be prepared at her own house, it consisted of cold meat, which will be "just as good to-morrow, my dear, as to-day." This frequent hospitality, so cheerfully and ungrudgingly afforded, and the consequent disappearance of a few items from her own butcher's bill, completed her young hostess's conquest. An individual that is always glad to see and feed one, and who never looks for any thing in return, is formed to be a miser's friend; nor was this unhappy woman's perceptions so dull but that she understood the motives which actuated her new ally. She knew that these were pity for her forlorn condition, and the pleasure of returning good for evil.

"It is very kind of you, Agnes Crawford," said she, as they sat together one afternoon in June in the little dining-room of the cottage; for the drawing-room was avoided upon such occasions at the Brae, as it was at the Priory, although for far different reasons. Agnes would not compel her guest to look out upon those sands which had been her son's untimely grave. "It is very kind of you, dear, to let me drop in here, and eat you out of house and home in this manner. I am afraid I am a great expense to you."

"Not very great," returned her hostess, smiling; "you don't eat much more than my pet bird yonder, to whom I give my breakfast crumbs; and if you eat, as you complain that good Mr. Carstairs does—"

"Well, so he does, my dear," interrupted her guest, laying her work down upon her lap, to allow of greater emphasis; "the last time he dined with me—that is, let me see, just nineteen months ago—he eat of every dish, and finished every one. I call it most ungentlemanly. And because there was nothing in two of the silver dishes—put for ornament, my dear, of course—and because there were flowers in the champagne glasses and no champagne—the idea of giving a village doctor champagne!—he was really quite rude."

"Mr. Carstairs is a very good, kind man," said Agnes.

"I don't deny that, my dear; I only say he is a most inordinate eater."

"And I say that you eat like a robin, and are, therefore, no judge," rejoined Agnes, smiling. "As for my expenses here, they are not much more than if I were a doll in a doll's house. Cubra, it seems to me, eats nothing but rice, so that I almost suspect her of being a ghoul; and Mrs. Marcon, I am sure, is the most honest and economical of landladies."

"Ah, well, that is as it may be; every body seems honest to *you*, dear. You judge people by yourself. And that brings me to the thing which I wanted to say to you. Every day, when I go to my desk, this writing reproaches me—look at it. It is what I wanted you to sign with respect to Mr. Carlyon's will."

"Your brother's will," observed Agnes quietly.

His name had never been mentioned between them since the day of Jedediah's death. Agnes had deemed it injudicious to press that he should be asked to his nephew's funeral; but she did not think it right to pass by his sister's mention of him by his surname.

"Yes, he is my brother, of course; although his conduct has not been brotherly—that is, in this matter," added she hastily, in answer to the young girl's glance. "I don't say that I did all I could to win him. But as to disinheriting my Jed, that was a shameful thing, and—and—"

"Hush! my dear Mrs. Newman, hush!"

"You don't know what I was going to add," said Mrs. Newman, tremulously, "and yet—I was about to say—with respect to that will, now that I know you, I do not so much wonder at it. That is what I feel bound to confess. He loved you—how could he help it?—better than all else, and he strove to show it. And I can't blame him—that is, not now." Here she paused, thinking of the "might have been," with all its radiant hues, extinct forever, and the tears rolled down her thin but not uncomely cheeks. "You have not signed it, Agnes, have you, yet?"

"I *will* sign it, dear Mrs. Newman, gladly."

"No, you have not, and you shall not. And what is more, if John, my brother, dies before me, I shall not take this money. He meant it for you, and you shall have it."

Agnes smiled sadly. "What is the use of money to *me?*" asked she.

"Of much use. Of use to every body, my dear," answered Mrs. Newman, with vehemence: then added, tenderly, "take it; do good with it. Kiss me, Agnes."

She tore up the paper as she spoke, and rising, threw her arms about the young girl's neck. She had overcome, perhaps, the greatest temptation of her life; but the struggle had been severe and long, and she felt the effects of it.

"There, I have done it now," cried she, "and I feel all the happier. If you like to give me any thing *out of it*, you know, my dear," added she, cheerfully, "why that is a different thing; you may let me have Woodlees, my old home—for it is not sold, I hear—to live in rent free. But I want every thing to be yours to do just as you like with. That's all."

"I hope none of it will ever be mine, Mrs. Newman. I trust Mr. Carlyon may be spared long years—and to God's glory—to possess it. His is a noble life, although it has hitherto been passed in darkness."

"You know his state of health, I suppose, Agnes, and what Mr. Carstairs thinks about him? He heard from him only last week, and he was saying—"

"Oh, yes—yes—do not speak of it. At least, not in that way. I know all."

"I am sorry to have distressed you, my dear."

The two women sat for some time in silence. The hostess stitching at some baby clothes destined to cover some expected little stranger in the parish, for whom there was small welcome, the guest darning an old glove.

"Agnes," said Mrs. Newman, presently, in a very gentle tone, "I have been a hard woman all my life—except to one who is gone—but I am not hard to you. I can not bear to see those tears. What can I do to comfort you? Nothing? Yes, a little, surely. When I pray to God to-night, I shall pray for somebody else. Not for you, for you do not need my prayers. Can you guess for whom?"

"Yes."

"Mind, I do not mean in my old way, as you are thinking. I shall not thank heaven that I am not like him, unregenerate, wicked, predestined to eternal death; but as one fellow-sinner for another, as a sister for a brother."

"I am, indeed, rejoiced to hear it: at the same time, as a Christian woman, it is only your bounden duty."

"True, but one I have not performed for years. And why shall I do so now, Agnes? Because I really love him? No. Because I honestly wish to be reconciled with him? No; I can not even say that yet. Why shall I do it, then? Can you guess?"

"For God's sake, I hope, dear Mrs. Newman."

"No; for *your* sake. And why do I say for your sake? You need not answer me, my dear; I know all about it. How very much you forgot when you sought me out and brought me comfort; how very much you forgave, which even if it had been committed against yourself only— There, lean upon me; I am your elder sister now, since John Carlyon is my brother once again, and you, my poor girl, love him. It is poor comfort that this can bring you, dear. A forlorn woman, vexed with petty cares, is a sad substitute for such a bridegroom; but it is something. The man that made the breach between us two shall henceforward be the link between us. I shall love you all the better, and you will, at least, despise me less, Sister Agnes."

CHAPTER XXVII.

THE MIDNIGHT VISITOR.

IT was night, and Agnes sat alone in her little drawing-room at The Brae. Mrs. Newman had left her hours ago; not long indeed after she had expressed herself in such unexpected terms, with regard to her brother and Agnes. The latter was genuinely glad and grateful that her guest had confessed herself so changed for the better; that her mind was so conciliated, and the bitterness of so many years against her now only relative had been cast out. But so far as Mrs. Newman's demonstrativeness affected Agnes herself, it was no subject for congratulation. She felt humiliated, nay, almost ashamed. How had this woman guessed the secret which she had striven so hard to hide even from her own self? By what outward sign had she shown that she loved John Carlyon, when her own heart had been forbidden to whisper it? And yet how she did love him! How sweet it was to hear the poor folks talk of kindly Squire John! How welcome to her was the gratitude that prompted them to tell of his open-handed, generous ways; of his cool courage! With what pleasure she hearkened to their speculations regarding the next comer to Woodlees, always ending as they did, with, "Well, he will not be a better gentleman than the young squire, whoever he be." Better to *them* of course they meant: but was not that something? To have been good to the poor; to have been ready to risk his life for theirs; to have associated with them without one touch of Pride.

His lack of Religion, so far from deteriorating from such virtues, heightened them rather. If, not being a Christian man, he so behaved out of the mere excellence of his own nature, how much the nobler was that nature. How she had treasured the few commonplace phrases of Mr. Carstairs respecting Carlyon's health, listening as though they had no particular attraction for her ears. The good doctor had spoken quite openly about his patient. He had no idea that this girl who, to his own knowledge, had rejected the young squire, was any thing more than "deeply interested" in her discarded suitor. The letters he now and then received from him were not of a private nature, and their contents were freely communicated to whomsoever they might concern. There was always respectful mention of herself and inquiry concerning her well-being; for the rest, a little business and a good deal of gossip composed the whole of these communications.

"He is no better, Miss Agnes," the doctor would observe in answer to her questions, "simply because it is impossible he should get better. You can't stop a hole in your heart as you would a leak. He doesn't mention his health, because he knows this as well as I do. He is leading a gay life, which is the very worst for a man in his situation to lead, and I am surprised that he has lasted so long. If I had known he was going to racket about in London, I would not have given him so long as a year to live; and I should not be the least surprised if my prophecy come true yet. The Ides of June have come, but they have not yet gone."

To all this Agnes had listened with a grave but quiet face, and without revealing the torture of her heart. Successful in this, she had deemed concealment was easy under all less crucial tests. And yet this woman—to whom she had never since their intimacy breathed Carlyon's name, in whose presence she had studiously avoided speaking of him, although from no fear of such a consequence—had guessed the secret of her love. Agnes, though not insensible to Mrs. Newman's good intentions, was far from thanking her for this. Henceforward, then, the sweet solace of an unshared sorrow—for there are sorrows as well as joys wherein no stranger may intermeddle, and with which even a friend's sympathy is intolerable—was to be denied her. How far, too, might not this discovery extend? Would vulgar eyes begin to watch her with unwelcome pity, vulgar tongues to utter words of thankless comfort? It seemed hard that, though unrepining, she should not be permitted to bear her cross alone; yet she was far from repining even now.

God knew what was best for her as for every body. Perhaps it was to show the powerful temptation of worldly love that it was decreed she should be held up as an example of a Christian woman whose heart was given to a Godless man; for it had been given, that was certain, and was John Carlyon's still. Her very being seemed to confess it when the life-blood rushed to her cheeks, as though in protest against such a reflection as she had just made.

Carlyon Godless? Impossible! God had suffered him to revolt for a while, but would presently beckon to him with forgiving finger. That was all. Presently? It must be very soon then. It is impossible to describe in words the mental agony which that last thought engendered. We grieve, we weep, all hope and health seem to depart from us, because our loved one has died, and has left us forever. That one dread sentence, "He is Dead!" seems to comprehend in it the death of all that makes our life enjoyable, nay bearable. But how much more terrible to the truly religious soul is the fear—nay, the conviction—that our departed brother is not only Dead, but Lost.

The narrow-minded foolish folk who make up those spiritual cliques and coteries which do their very best to draw Religion into contempt, under pretense of fostering and protecting it, feel nothing of this. In their heart of hearts they either do not, for the most part, believe the fearful dogmas they enunciate, or they do not realize the effect of them. Otherwise, being men and not fiends, the sense of the eternal condemnation of the majority of their friends and acquaintances (of which they affect to be convinced) would be ever present with them; it would take away their appetites (which it certainly does *not*), would destroy their sleep, would thrust itself between them and even the most innocent pleasure: they would never cease, like Solomon Eagle, from crying "Woe, woe!" As to the few who do realize what must happen if their creed be true, and yet have learned to regard it with calmness if not satisfaction; the human wheat who are not disturbed by the doom of the tares growing up around them; who say quietly, "They will burn, but we shall be in the garner"—let them beware, lest instead of being the Elect, their cruel feet are set on the very road to Perdition. Very literally they apply the homely saw,

Of all our mother's children we love ourselves the best,
As long as we're provided for, the Devil take the rest.

But it is doubtful if their selfish complacency will be rewarded exactly as they expect.

Agnes Crawford's religion was not of this sort. She believed and trembled, but it was for others, not for herself; and for the man she loved, above all. As in some frightful nightmare we sometimes see one very dear to us blindly walking toward the brink of a sheer precipice, yet can not raise hand or voice to warn him, so Agnes beheld the coming doom of John Carlyon. It was rarely out of her thoughts, and shadowed them, even when unrecognizable there, with habitual and deepening gloom. She was thinking of it now, as she sat by the open window in the summer night, looking forth upon the fast-filling bay. There was no moon, and the sky was islanded with many a cloud, but by the dim starlight she could see the sweep and swirl of every white-lipped wave, as it licked up the sands. What hope there was for any tide-caught traveler 'twixt where she sat and yonder hidden shore, so little and no more was for John Carlyon dying in his stubborn pride. Upon one yet uncovered spot, not many yards from land, stood up some object bare and tall; the mast of a fishing-vessel the hull of which was already buried in the quicksand beneath; to not less certain—perhaps to scarce less speedy doom—was John Carlyon doomed. Across the sea and through the misty veil that hung above it, flashed down on land and wave the revolving Pharos light; now hid, now seen; it was placed there for man's guidance and salvation; but if one were so blind or willful as not to heed it, but steer right on into the gaping jaws of Death?

All things she saw supplied the unhappy girl with images of her beloved one's ruin. The waves sighed at her feet, the night wind wailed above her in unison with her own sad thoughts. Even now while she was thinking of him, praying for him, he might be dead and—

"Agnes!"

The chill of fear seized all her frame, relaxed and enervated with sorrow, and froze it so that every limb grew rigid. She could not have stirred a finger to save her life. What was that voice, unlike to any that she knew, that had murmured her own name, close by her, in the very room? No thought of danger, of physical peril, crossed her mind; she was terror-stricken with a nameless awe. Was it then true, as some good Christian folks had averred, that the spirits of the departed are sometimes permitted to return to earth and reveal their fearful doom to those they have left behind them? Was John Carlyon speaking to her, but not in the flesh? What was this cold current sweeping over her, that made her shiver so, as the air of the vault did where they had laid her father months ago?

"Agnes!"

She knew the speaker now; yet her terror did not abate, but was exchanged for apprehensions of a different sort. The current she felt was the draught of air caused by the unheard opening of the door behind her. Her midnight visitor was one of flesh and blood; yet scarcely to be dreaded less than a spectre. How had he gained admittance to the cottage without her knowledge? And how had he dared to present himself, unannounced, at such an hour?

The voice was Richard Crawford's voice, but with a difference. Even when she recognized it as her cousin's, she could not fail to mark that. Why did he stand yonder motionless—an undefined shadow—and not greet her, if self-conscious of no harm after so long an absence? What could this sudden visit mean, paid to her in her solitude, at midnight, by one that had parted from her with such studiously respectful mien and words? One answer only could be given to such a question, and her fluttering heart returned it, in many a hasty beat—"This man is mad!"

CHAPTER XXVIII.
WAS IT FACT OR FANCY?

AGNES was the first to speak, for her cousin, like a very ghost, now stood silent and motionless, as though waiting to be interrogated. "Why don't you shake hands with me, Richard?"

The young man came forward quickly into the starlight, and held out his hand. She took his feverish fingers in her own, and holding them fast, looked long and steadily into his face. It had grown very thin and haggard. His eyes, more bright and prominent than she had ever seen them, moved uneasily in their sockets, as though seeking to escape her gaze. Upon his cheeks there was an unwonted flush, which, with his wild air, gave to his beauty an almost lurid tinge.

"Where are you come from, cousin?"

"London."

"And what brings you here, so suddenly and so late?"

"You."

"Well, but I shall be here to-morrow. Why not come to-morrow? Go to the inn and sleep to-night, for I am sure you are in need of sleep."

"I never sleep," returned the young man, slowly. "I lie awake and dream—that's all. I dream of you."

"How foolish that is of you, Richard: when you could have come and seen me, if you chose, or at all events have written to me: I have heard nothing of you, you know, for many months."

This was true, but it had not distressed her, for Mr. Carstairs had assured her that the longer her cousin remained away, and the less communication between them in the mean time, the better it would be for the young man's mental health. She knew that he would visit The Brae sooner or later; for he had left his sea-chest, containing his professional apparel, in charge of Cubra, to whom he had written once or twice, short, quiet, sensible letters, which had spoken of himself as well and cheerful; and the change in his present appearance was the more startling upon that account.

"No; I have not written, Agnes, but I have heard of you; and that is why I came down here. Look you," here he raised his voice, and struck the table with his clenched fist, "you have become friends with that man's sister. Why is that?"

"Because I choose, cousin," answered Agnes, firmly. "Mrs. Newman has suffered much of late; she has lost her only son. He was drowned in crossing the sands."

"Her son? I did not know she had a son. Poor soul! I wish it had been her brother."

"Richard! Do you then wish him dead who saved your life in yonder bay? For shame—for shame!"

"Yes. All cowards deserve to die; and besides, I hate him."

"That you hate him, merely shows that you are ungrateful, Richard. As for the rest, John Carlyon is courage itself."

"What! when a man will not take an insult when it is offered?—will not accept a challenge when it is given?"

"That depends upon who insults—who challenges. Have you been seeking the man's life who saved your own—wicked, ungrateful boy?"

"I let him know what I thought of him, that's all, and I gave him the opportunity of resenting it. I say that he is a coward."

"But you do not think so, Richard. If you have come here only to tell me falsehoods, I have no wish to hear them."

"I am come here for something else, Agnes. Do not let us quarrel." Here his voice, erst harsh and sullen, sank and softened. "I am come to claim your promise, claim my bride."

"My promise, Richard?" The blood rushed to her face, and her breath came so short and quick that she could scarcely frame the words. "I don't know what you mean."

"Ah! who is speaking falsehoods now? My pretty one that will not hint of love, except by these twin-roses in her cheeks. My life, my own, my all!—ah, how I love you!" His eyes had lost their shifting light, and beamed with ineffable tenderness; his face, so sunk and hollowed, seemed to have regained its look of youth; his fingers played with one bright tress of hers that had wandered from its fellows, as a child's hand with a flower. "How beautiful you are, Agnes! Let me hear the music of your voice."

It was plain that he might have been governed by her lightest word, did she but choose to humor him. If she had but said, "Go, love, and come to-morrow," with a meaning smile, he would have obeyed her. It would have been easy to hoodwink one already so half-blind with passion. But Agnes shrank from a treachery which to many would have seemed a pardonable *ruse*. She would not play fast-and-loose even with a madman.

"Cousin Richard, you have long ago had my answer to the question you would put. It is unmannerly, and most unlike a gentleman, to press me thus. I will never marry you, because I do not love you; and more, Richard, if you continue to persecute me in this unmanly fashion, I shall forget that you are my cousin—the only relative I have in the world—and—"

"You will not marry me!" interrupted the young man, vehemently; "and because you do not love me! That is not true. It is because you love another man far better. Now, listen; I will tell you something about that man, whom you think noble, pure, and truthful."

"Are you speaking of the man you strove to kill, Richard?"

"Well, that was a lie. I did but say it to prove you—to see whether you could love him still, even if he were a coward. I *wished* him dead a thousand times, 'tis true, but then—why he saved my life. My curse upon him. If I had known, when we two stood upon the lessening sand yonder, and he was breasting the swift tide in hopes to save us—if I had known what was to come of it, and how this man should steal away your heart, I would have flung my arms about you, Agnes Crawford, and perished with you in the roaring flood, before your hand clasped his. I would, so help me Heaven!"

"Heaven will not help you, Richard, if your thoughts are such as these."

"And you shall never win him now—be sure of that," went on the young man vehemently.

"You hope so—yes, you do—but that hope shall bear no fruit. I tell you he is not worthy of you—he is neither pure nor true."

"Is that 'to prove me,' also, Cousin Richard?" said Agnes, pitifully.

"No," answered the other with vehemence, "as God is my judge. I know this Carlyon well. I ought to know him, for I have been his shadow for these many months. It has been my life's work to dog his footsteps. Yes, a spy; why not? I would have done worse things than that to gain my end."

"And what was that?"

"To find him false to you."

"There is no bond between this man and me, Richard, as I have told you long ago. He can break no faith who has not plighted vows."

"Then I suppose it is the starlight which makes you look so pale," answered the young man, bitterly; "it is the night air which chills your limbs and makes your voice tremble. Otherwise I should have almost thought you were afraid to listen to the tale of this man's guilt. If I had been loved like him—nay, though you loved me not, and only because I loved *you*, all women have been nought to me for your sweet sake; no face, however fair, has striven within me for one moment for the mastery with the remembrance of yours; nay, if I have been base, as your cruel eyes told me awhile ago, it has been all for love of you. But this man, though freighted with all the treasure of your heart, is blown about with every whisper from a wanton's lips. I have seen him, side by side with a bold beauty, her plastic hand in his, murmuring—"

"What I do not wish to hear, sir," cried Agnes, haughtily. "You may speak truth or falsehood. But if you lie, you can not be more vile than to have gleaned this shame and thought to have furthered your own aims by pouring it in my unwilling ears. I despise—I loathe you."

In the silence that followed close upon her angry words, she heard the handle of the chamber-door turn. The air, that had been flowing freely through the room throughout the interview, suddenly ceased, a third person, then, had either just entered or just quitted the apartment, closing the door behind him. She knew not who it was, but the consciousness of not being utterly alone inspired her with the courage that she was about to need.

"You despise, you loathe me, do you, while you persist in believing this man to be all that is chivalrous and noble? and you dare tell me that to my face."

"Yes, I dare."

"That is because you are angry, Agnes. A woman will say any thing when her blood is up."

"Come here, to-morrow, Richard Crawford, and I will tell you the same."

"How beautiful she is," murmured the young man, tenderly. "The passion which mars most women's charms only heightens hers. She loathes me, and yet, ah Heaven, how I love her!—You will never be my wife, Agnes, that is certain?"

"Never, never."

"Then sure as Heaven is above us, no other man shall wed you. Look you here."

From his breast-pocket he drew forth a sheathless knife and threw it on the table with a clang. The starlight shone upon the long and pointed blade, and glimmered on the stones that formed its handle.

"That is no steel for common uses, Agnes." This young girl had no fear of death, nor even of untimely death; but thus to die, stabbed by a kinsman, struck terror to her inmost heart.

"Oh Cousin, would you kill me?"

"Kill *you?*" returned the young man with a bitter laugh. "You must have told me truth indeed, when you said awhile ago that you despised me. *I* hurt you? I would not harm one shining hair of that bright head, although such sacrilege should cause the Devil to forego his rights and so should win me Heaven. I only said no other man should wed you."

"No man is going to wed me, Richard."

"But there is one who would wed you, if he could, and whom you love. A man, says Mr. Carstairs, doomed to die early. And I say the same. You will never see him more, be sure of that."

"What, wretched boy, will you then be his assassin?"

"I shall stab him: yes. In two days from this, or three at farthest, John Carlyon will be dead, and it will be your love that killed him."

* * * * * *

He was gone. Or, had he not been there at all, and was it a mere hideous dream? The sun was shining full on the window of the little drawing-room, but she was cold and shivering. How long had she lain upon the floor, whereon she had found herself when she awoke? And did she wake from sleep or swoon? No sign of her late visitor was to be seen. Upon the little table lay her books and work-box, but the shining dagger was no longer among them. Had it never been there, or had it indeed been taken away in fulfilment of that horrible threat? The deep silence of the early morning smote her heart with fear; she dared not be alone, but seized and pulled the bell-rope. The little bell, tinkling violently just outside the door, roused the inmates of that pocket-dwelling as effectually as any alarm-bell tolled backward from cathedral tower.

Mrs. Marcon, beheld for once without her widow's cap and weeds, hurried into the room.

"Lor, Miss Agnes, why what *is* the matter? How early you have got up, and how pale you are! I am sure you must be ill."

A moment after her entered dusky Cubra; her attire not presenting any very striking difference to that she wore in the day.

"Gorramighty bress us, Missie Agnes, what the matter?"

"There is somebody in the house. Some man."

"Robbers!" cried the widow clasping her hands; "Heaven preserve us, this is what I always thought would come of being a lone woman!"

"No, not robbers," said Agnes, gravely, and casting a suspicious look at Cubra.

"Lovers!" exclaimed the widow, with a shudder of disapprobation and surprise, "Lor, who'd a thought it with one of her color!"

Cubra did not deign to reply to this remark, whether she considered it as a compliment or an innuendo.

"Are you sure you locked both the doors last night, as usual, Mrs. Marcon?" inquired Agnes.

"Oh yes, miss, I am always particular about that; but it's very easy to see for yourself."

This suggestion that her lodger should satisfy her own eyes did away with the necessity of any solitary exploration upon the widow's part which she would probably not have undertaken, notwithstanding the broad day-light, for millions of money. Upon the other hand, she was exceedingly averse to be left alone in the drawing-room; so the three women accomplished the tour of the house together, the whole inspection—which was a very thorough one—occupying about as many minutes. It was impossible that even a mouse could hide itself in that diminutive dwelling, and indeed they found one in occupation of the kitchen. Both doors were securely fastened on the inside, as the widow maintained she had left them.

"I suppose I must have been mistaken," said Agnes, when the search was over; "I am very sorry to have disturbed you: but I certainly heard a noise."

"And got up and dressed yourself, without calling us! That was very wrong, Miss Agnes. Now do go to bed again, and try and get some sleep."

They did not suspect then that she had been up all night; and there was no need to tell them. Alone in her little chamber, she strove to recall what had happened in the drawing-room. Every motion made, every sentence uttered, recurred to her with a distinctness very unlike the remembrance of a dream. And yet how could Richard have possibly concealed himself in such a house, on the preceding evening, or how escaped through the locked doors? Her agitation was such that she could not bring herself even to lie down, but having disarranged the bed to give the idea that she had slept there, she once more passed into the drawing-room. Yes, in yonder corner he had stood in shadow, and then again by the table, where he had rested his hand upon that very volume. Strange and unaccountable as were his coming and going, she could not disbelieve the evidence of her senses. A sudden thought caused her to lift the sash, which the widow had closed and fastened, and lean out of the window. Yes, it was as she suspected. Upon the little margin of flower-plot that lay immediately beneath, between the window and the box-fringed gravel-walk, there were two foot-marks, with the toes turned towards the cottage. Her late visitor, stepping over her prostrate form, as she lay in a swoon, must have escaped by this means, letting himself drop—as he might very easily have done—from the window-sill. She had no farther doubt about the reality of what had occurred; of the imminence of the peril that threatened John Carlyon; but it was necessary that others should have none. She felt convinced too that it was by Cubra's connivance that her cousin had obtained entrance to the cottage, or had been harbored within it, the preceding evening. It must have been she who had informed him of her growing intimacy with Mrs. Newman. Every moment was precious, yet unwilling to arouse the suspicion of her black attendant, Agnes waited until she heard the latter—who was a very early riser—leave her room and busy herself in the kitchen. Then she stole quietly into the vacated apartment, and opening the chest where Richard's marine apparel was stored, took out a pair of shoes, and placing them in her pocket, sought the garden. Kneeling upon the gravel-walk she compared these carefully with the foot-marks on the mold, and found them—making allowance for the fact that the latter were the impressions of high-heeled boots—to correspond exactly. Then hastily putting on bonnet and shawl, she let herself out at the garden gate, and after hesitating a moment at the turning that led to the Priory, passed on through the awakening village, and rang the bell at Mr. Carstairs's door.

CHAPTER XXIX.

THE IDES OF JUNE.

IF Mr. Carstairs's audacious prophecy regarding John Carlyon's lease of life is to prove true, it must do so within the next twenty-four hours, for after to-morrow he will have lived his year. In the mean time the doomed squire feels physically as well as ever, though mentally much depressed. London life does not suit him: the pleasures of the town have long ago begun to pall.

His existence at Mellor had indeed been aimless enough, but it was at least natural, and plentifully sprinkled with kindly acts and words to those about him. He missed the homely honest faces which had always a grateful look in them when they met his. True, in London his hand was as ready to give, his heart to feel—and there is no place where the poor have greater need of help—but the charity which takes the form of subscription, although as advantageous as any personal aid to the recipient, has no such healthy effect upon the giver. He felt the bond between himself and his fellow-creatures loosening day by day, and with a sense of loss. And yet it seemed impossible for him to resume his old mode of life in the country, with its long periods of inaction, wherein his thoughts must needs revert to his lost love. He thought of her now, in spite of all distractions: how different she was from even the best of the fine ladies with whom he was acquainted; how superior to Edith Treherne, for instance, with her grand airs and shallow feelings. And what was it made her so? Agnes was beautiful, indeed, but he had seen faces quite as fair; her mind was not uncultivated; she had the accomplishments of her class; but he knew girls more intelligent and more talented than she was. What was it then that made her charm so magical? It was her goodness, without doubt. But how did she come by that?

Vicious persons are, as a rule, much better than they seem, just as Puritans are much worse; among even profligates there is benevolence, kindliness, and even occasional self-sacrifice. Amid the whirl of fashion (worse than what is called "the vortex of dissipation," because it may last for a life-time, which the latter rarely does) there are sometimes little quiet eddies of well-doing. Its votaries not unfrequently do good by stealth, and would blush to the roots of their hair if they found it fame. But regarding the company he was now keeping in the most favorable light consistent with truth (and this he did), Carlyon was obliged to confess that not only in extent and permanence, but in kind, the goodness of Agnes Crawford was of quite another sort than that of generous impulse. There was certainly something about it—supposing that the word really had a meaning—which one calls Divine. If it indeed was so, there was no wonder that Agnes could not and did not love *him*. If she had done so, if she had but consented to bear with his spiritual deficiencies, and let him learn from her own lips the whole secret of her happiness—but she had not liked him enough for that; and he would have no other teacher.

He had, now and then, of late months—thinking "this would please her if she could know of it"—found himself in a church, and listened without much profit. He had been taken thither too by Edith Treherne, to hear her uncle, the "snowy-banded, delicate-handed, dilletante dean, intone," with more amusement to himself than advantage. Edith was going to be married, by the bye, by that very dean in a few weeks, and to a most eligible suitor—a wealthy baronet of very ancient lineage, and who himself was upward of seventy years of age. The match had been somewhat hastily arranged—the bridegroom feeling perhaps that he had not any time to lose—but the happy pair were "engaged," and the fashionable newspapers of the previous week had found themselves in a position to inform society of that fact. So far from this disturbing Carlyon, it rather pleased him. His conscience had somewhat pricked him as to the part he had played with that young lady, and he was glad that it had not ever so slightly interfered with her prospects. Now if he should hear that some one was about to marry Agnes Crawford, he felt that it would well-nigh drive him mad. And yet, not only had there been no such tender "passages" between himself and her, as between him and Edith, but science had declared him to be a doomed man. The grave, and not the bridal-bed, was waiting for him. His lease of life seemed likely, indeed, to be longer than was expected; but it must at all events be very short. "The shorter," thought he, with bitterness, "the better." He should be sorry to prove Carstairs a false prophet; the little man's reputation was dear to him, he knew, and he had pinned it upon this very point. It would be quite a pity to disappoint him, and *cui bono?* What vista stretched before him—though indeed but for a short distance—in case he should live on? A little more of this wearisome London life, so self-indulgent, yet so unsatisfying. No; he would at all events quit *that*. He would just stay in London twenty-four hours longer, in order to give Carstairs his chance, and then if he did not exchange his snug rooms at the Albany for some snugger chamber in Kensal Green, he would be off to the Continent. As though Black Care, which sat so immediately behind him upon Red Berild in Rotten Row, would not be ready to cross the Channel, nay, to fly with him to the ends of the earth!

If Carlyon had been a younger man, it is probable he would not have succumbed to these melancholy reflections, as it is certain that he would have escaped from the fascination of a hopeless attachment; but as matters were, the companionship of his own thoughts was growing less and less tolerable. In society, on the other hand, he had got to be almost boisterously gay, and was voted by men (for he rather avoided drawing-rooms now) uncommon good company. When he left them, the life of the party was said to have departed from it; but it was only a galvanic sort of life, that expired with the artifical stimulus.

It was late even for roysterers; the hum of pleasure that succeeds the roar of commerce was quite hushed. The streets were so silent that the slow-pacing policeman made stiller by his tread their quietude. The stars were shining brightly, although the moon was young. Far as the eye could reach the broad thoroughfare of Piccadilly was tenantless, as Carlyon moved leisurely along it homeward. His cigar was yet but half consumed— and it is curious how men, no matter how extravagant, object to throw away a good cigar; it was doubtless on account of this economical habit that he loitered, almost as the guardian of the night— whom he could hear coming up behind him, at a great distance—loitered and halted, shaking the area gates and throwing his bull's eye into the key-holes of the doors. A cigar, with solitude and starlight, will make most men contemplative. Carlyon bethought him of the generations that had trodden that broad street before him, who had come and gone, finding even Piccadilly no continuing city; upon whom those eternal stars had looked down as they looked at him, so purely, so pitifully. And to what end? Were not the gas-lamps equally useful, and much more to be relied on? As for beauty, the pyrotechnic display called gas-stars had in that respect clearly the advantage over the heavenly bodies. And yet there was surely something in the latter which the former could not boast of. Edith Treherne was a gas-star, but Agnes Crawford was just like one of these: as pure, as pitiful, and as far removed from him and men like him.

"Hullo, you, sir!"

This exclamation was drawn from him by the sudden stepping-forth of a man from a narrow alley on his left, who placed himself directly in his way. "There is room for you and me to pass one another in Piccadilly to-night," continued Carlyon, sternly, "without rubbing shoulders, and you had best take your own side of the pavement.—Oh! I beg pardon; I see, it is Mr. Richard Crawford."

There had been a tacit antagonism between these two men from the very first; but they had always been frigidly polite to one another. The recollection of what he owed to Carlyon had restrained any expression of the young man's antipathy, and the squire on his part never forgot that Richard was Agnes's kinsman, and one who was dear to her. But they each knew that they were rivals; and the one of them that the other had been successful where he himself had failed.

Carlyon would have held out his hand, perhaps, and said a few ordinary words of civility, but the look and manner of the other forbade that. His face, contrasting with the coal-black hair, was white as marble; his eyes burned with the steady glow of hate; the iron steadiness of his arm, as it barred Carlyon's way, was a menace.

"It is late, I know, Mr. Carlyon," said Richard, hoarsely; "but I have waited for you here these four hours, and I must insist upon having speech with you."

"Insist, sir? However, we will not quarrel about a word. Your business must be urgent since it has put you to so great an inconvenience, although how you knew that I was about to pass this way to-night is beyond my guessing."

"I knew it, Mr. Carlyon, and much more. I have watched your every movement for these many months. In town and out of town, you have had a companion whom you little suspected."

"Indeed!" returned Carlyon, scornfully. "True, now I think of it, I remember that once or twice of late it has struck me that some fellow dogged my footsteps."

"It was I."

"Well," rejoined Carlyon, calling to mind something that Mr. Carstairs had written concerning this young man; "it is fortunate for you that you have said as much. A gentleman that stoops to play the spy is in the same category as one who, being wealthy, plays the thief. He is not the master of his own actions; and therefore—"

"Out of your charity he may escape the horsewhip," interrupted the young man, bitterly. "Thank you. I owe you my life, Mr. Carlyon, and you draw upon the bank of my gratitude without fear of its breaking, I perceive."

"Indeed, sir, I had forgotten the circumstance to which you allude," returned Carlyon, hotly; "and I beg you will forget it too. I wish to have no relations with you which are not of the most conventional sort. Pray release yourself from any thing that may seem to link together you and me."

"I wish I could," replied the young man, sternly. "There is something else than the saving of my worthless life that set me on your track, and brings me here. You pretend to love my cousin Agnes."

"Silence, sir!" cried Carlyon, in a terrible voice. "Let me pass, I say."

"No. You may vapor as you please, but you shall hear me out. You told her, I say, that you were her lover, and she believed you. Nay, *I* believed you too until I came to know you. Till I found you with that girl—Edith Treherne—at Richmond, I thought you might have loved my cousin—not indeed as I love her, indeed no—but with an honest heart. I knew you were unworthy of her—who is not?—but I did not think to find you false to her. And yet how glad I was to find you so! If you had married that girl, I could have blessed you, deemed you the best friend that man ever had. But when I found her plighted to another, I hated you worse than ever, because I knew that Agnes would love you still."

"That Agnes would love me still!" repeated Carlyon, mechanically, but in low and gentle tones, like one in his sleep that dreams a pleasant dream. Then she did love him after all; for whose evidence could be so trustworthy as that of his rival? His anger was clean gone; he began to pity this unhappy youth, who saw in him, it seems, a more favored suitor.

Richard marked the change in his countenance at once, and assigned to it the right cause. He had unwittingly been the means of giving this man hope in the very matter wherein he would have had him despair. Mortification, jealousy, hate, seized upon his soul together, and he was no longer himself. His fixed intention upon leaving Agnes two days before, had been (as he had told her) to kill Carlyon; but his better nature had in the mean time revolted at such an act of ingratitude, more perhaps than at the crime itself. All that he really wanted was to detach his rival's affection (the strength of which he greatly underrated) from its object. If he could do that, there would be some comfort for him, even although he could never call Agnes his own. The idea of any other man's possessing her was intolerable to him, and he was well aware that she really loved Carlyon. He had also hitherto imagined that Carlyon knew this, and it had been his purpose in seeking the present interview to work upon his rival's pride with the same weapon which he had used with so fatal an effect in the case of his uncle. He had meant to tell him that if he were to marry Agnes he would wed the daughter of a disgraced and outcast man. If this should fail—well, he had persuaded himself that it would not fail. He had not dared to look the alternative that had suggested itself to him in the face; and although the sight of his rival had set his very brain on fire, he had until this moment intended to confine his arguments to words. But now that he found he had actually let Carlyon know for the first time that he was beloved, and the possible consequences of such a revelation flashed upon him, he forgot all his scruples.

"You need not smile, sir," cried he, passionately, "nor wear that look of triumph. If Agnes Crawford ever loved you, she does not do so now. She knows that you deceived her, played her false, and wooed another."

"What, did you tell her?" exclaimed Carlyon, seizing him by the collar.

"Yes, I told her all."

"Tale-bearer, coward, spy—"

The two men struggled together, each holding by the other's throat; Carlyon's giant strength had already made itself felt, when Richard drew from its hiding-place the long keen knife, the sight of which had of late so terrified his cousin, and struck his antagonist two violent and rapid blows. Carlyon, with his hand to his heart, staggered and fell. Richard, transported with fury, would have thrown himself upon him, and stabbed him a hundred times; but the policeman whose footsteps had been growing more and more distinct throughout the interview, now hastened up at the sound of their struggle, and the assassin, throwing the bloody steel upon the pavement, fled from him at utmost speed. The former having given the alarm, proceeded to attend to the wounded man. He was quite insensible, but the contents of his card-case showed he was within a very few doors of home, and as soon as assistance arrived, he was taken to his own lodgings.

"I doubt it's a bad job," observed the first policeman, to his fellow, as they emerged from the gates of the Albany; "them snug chambers will want a tenant before long."

"Ah! likely enough. Did he speak e'er a word when you fust found him?"

"Yes, and a very queer thing it was he said —a pint to remember when the time comes, perhaps, though it's dark now. *Curstairs was right*," said he, "*after all.*"

CHAPTER XXX.

NURSE AND PRIEST.

NOTWITHSTANDING the early hour at which Agnes had made her visit to the village doctor, he was already up and away, having been sent for to one of his numerous but ill-repaying patients in a neighboring hamlet; so she turned her steps whither she had originally half resolved on going, namely to the Priory. But here, too, she was doomed to meet with disappointment, for the disheveled page who answered her summons, informed her that his "missus" had been bad all night and that he himself was under orders to run down to Dr. Carstairs to ask him to step up. Agnes knew that Mrs. Newman was not one to send for medical advice at five shillings per visit, except from urgent need, and hence, not without grave misgivings, at once repaired to that lady's chamber. She found her flushed and feverish, after a sleepless night, consequent, in reality, although she ascribed it to other causes, upon the mental conflict and emotion of the previous day—her determination to be reconciled with her brother, and her heroic resolve to give up all claim upon his property—and if not seriously ill, at all events much too indisposed to receive the information which she had come to convey concerning Richard's visit and Mr. Carlyon's danger. There was nothing for it therefore but to wait at the house with as much appearance of unconcern as she could put on, until the doctor came, which did not happen for some hours.

After the interview with his patient, Agnes unfolded to him in private all that had occurred during the past night, and besought his advice and assistance. He did not for a moment doubt (as she had almost apprehended he would) the actual facts of her narration; he had too high a respect for her common sense to ascribe any of them to hallucination; but from the opinion which he had himself formed of her cousin's character, he thought it exceedingly improbable that he would be as good or bad as his word.

"In the heat of passion, my dear Miss Agnes, and smarting under the bitter sense of disappointment, I can imagine this unhappy young man making use of any menace, and meaning, while he spoke, to carry it into execution. But any interval of time with him would produce first irresolution and then repentance. He is quite incapable — unless his nature has altered much for the worse of late—of seeking out a rival with the intention of slaying him in cold blood."

"But if he is mad, Mr. Carstairs—if he is downright mad?"

"Mad he could scarcely be to have spoken so rationally as you represent him to have done. That his brain is liable to be affected by any violent emotion I do not doubt; but that, on the other hand, he has nothing of the crafty and malicious scheming of the madman about him I feel positively certain. Do not alarm yourself, my dear young lady. Believe me there is no such danger as you picture to yourself, but at the same time I will take care to put Carlyon on his guard. I will write to him by this afternoon's post. There—will that content you?"

"I suppose that is all which can be done?" returned Agnes, sighing. "But how frightful a peril, how hideous a crime, is this which you talk of with such calmness. May God have mercy upon him, and turn his heart while there is yet time."

"Nay, Miss Agnes, if what you fear be true, there is no question of God's forgiveness in the matter; it is his own hand which has afflicted him."

Agnes's white cheeks flushed to the forehead: the surgeon had misunderstood her; her last words had referred to Carlyon; but she did not reply. Mr. Carstairs regarded her fixedly, at first with wonder, then with a look of pity.

"He shall be warned this very day, I promise you," reiterated he. "I will go home now and write the letter."

And he did so. That letter came to John Carlyon, only to remain unopened on his desk, because six hours too late to give effect to its contents.

Upon the afternoon of the third day, while he still lay fevered and unconscious, the nurse that waited upon him was called out—he being fast asleep—to see two strangers; one an elderly gentleman, who announced himself as an intimate friend of the sick man, the other a young lady, very beautiful, but with an air of intense mental suffering.

"You need not tell me who this is, sir," said the garrulous old woman, dropping a conciliatory courtesy; "it's Mr. Carlyon's sister. And very pleased I am to see you, mum—not like some nusses as might be jealous of not being let to do every thing for the poor dear. I was the fust to say you should be sent for; not as I feared the 'sponsibility—"

"How *is* your patient, woman?" broke in the male visitor, unceremoniously. "I am a medical man myself, so you may speak the truth in as few words as possible."

"I ax your pardon, sir, I am sure," said the nurse, humbly, and with an evident effort to curtail her loquacity; "better, sir, better; but he has had a bad time of it, and is not his own self in his head yet. It is his sister here as will do him the most good, as soon as he begins to come round. He has done nothing but call for you, mum, when he's awake, and moan about you in his sleep; it's 'Agnes! Agnes!' with him from morning to night."

Agnes started and trembled violently, but Mr. Carstairs promptly came to the rescue.

"Very proper — very natural, nurse," said he: "but, you see, you make the young lady nervous, and since she has come to help you nurse him, that will not do. At what time does Mr. Martin make his visits?"

"Well, sir, he has been here this morning, and he will come again at four or so; that is, in about an hour's time. But there is no reason why you should not come and see the poor gentleman at once; unless indeed the young lady is not used to a sick-room."

"She is as good a nurse as there is in London, my good woman," answered Mr. Carstairs. "Mr. Martin and I are old friends, and I am sure he will make no objection to my presence, so you may lead the way."

His three days' fever, although intermittent and at times leaving him quite conscious of what was passing, had wasted Carlyon's giant form to a mere shadow. His eyes, fast shut, reposed in two hollow caves. His head moving uneasily from side to side, was shorn of its brown curls. One large hand lay motionless upon the coverlet, bleached and thin; the other was thrust beneath his pillow.

"You find your brother sadly altered, miss, I don't doubt," whispered the nurse; "but, bless you, he'll come round yet. The wound is healing very nice. It is deep enough indeed, but it runs crosswise, no thanks to the villain as stabbed him. What saved his precious life was the little Bible as he carried in his breast-pocket; that stopped one blow altogether and turned the other toward the collar-bone. The doctor has the book, with half the leaves stuck through, against when the trial comes on, if they have the luck to catch the scoundrel, which I should like to pull his legs myself upon the gallows' tree. But see, the poor dear is waking up a bit."

With a weary sigh that told more of oppression than relief, the sick man opened his eyes. Unexpressionless and dim enough they looked, but they had lost the glitter of the fever-fire.

"He is coming to hisself," whispered the nurse to Agnes, who mechanically had shrunk behind the curtain at the bed's head. Mr. Carstairs, on the other hand, was standing by the fire, in full view of Carlyon. The latter, however, took no notice of him, taking it for granted probably that he was his usual medical attendant. With difficulty the sick man drew forth the hand that lay beneath the pillow, and looked piteously at the empty palm.

"That is what he always do when he wakes," whispered the nurse, with that triumphant zest which the ignorant exhibit when imparting information. "It's a sign that he wants to have his hands washed."

"Well, Carlyon, my good fellow, don't you know me?" inquired Mr. Carstairs gently, as he approached the bed. "You have had a bad bout of it, but we shall soon set you up again. I have come up to London on purpose to see it done."

"You're a good soul, Carstairs," murmured the sick man, smiling feebly. "Take my hand and shake it, for I can't shake yours. God bless you!"

"Those are pleasant words to hear from your lips, my friend; they give me hope that He has blessed you."

"I hope so. At all events, I have given up the fight against him, Carstairs. He was too strong for me, and I have made my submission. Perhaps I should have done it earlier, but for—" Here he paused, and a look of unutterable tenderness stole over his haggard features. "Where the bribe is very large, an honest man turns his head the other way, and keeps it so as long as he can; and oh, my friend, what a bribe was offered *me!*"

"Nay, nay; I must go away if you excite yourself thus, Carlyon. I do not come here to do you harm, but good. You may smile in that lackadaisical manner, and shake your head as much as you please, but I say 'good;' and good for evil, too, considering that you have already made my prophecy of no effect, and intend, I dare say, for contradiction's sake, to get as well and strong as ever."

"Not so, my friend, do not deceive yourself," returned Carlyon, gravely; "nor do I wish to live."

"Very well, we will talk about that when you are convalescent, and can argue the matter on fair terms. When a man is so ill as you have been, he sometimes feels like one who accidentally finds himself near a place he means some day to visit, but had no present intention of doing so; it is not worth while, he thinks, since he is so nigh the grave-mouth, to return. Such thoughts, however, do not become a man of courage. You were looking for something beneath the pillow, my friend; what was it?"

"A very little matter, Carstairs; a very foolish matter, as it will seem to you. But there is a little note in yonder desk—it lies on the right-hand, just as you open it—which I like to have under my pillow."

Mr. Carstairs gave it him, and as he did so, could not but notice the handwriting of the address.

"You know from whom it came, my friend," said the sick man.

"Yes."

"All the world might read it. When next you are asked to dinner, it will be in the self-same phrase; and yet this is the dearest thing

F

I have. They are the first words and the last—save one, which you have seen—that I ever had from her. God bless her!"

"If she were to come and nurse you, Carlyon, in your sister's place, but at your sister's special wish, what would you say then?"

"I would say that heaven had wrought a monstrous miracle, and sent an angel with the devil's own credentials—"

"Hush, hush, Mr. Carlyon," said Agnes, stepping from behind her screen; "do not wrong your sister thus. God has touched her heart, as I had hoped he had touched yours, and she loves you and prays to Him for you."

Carlyon's face was lit up with a great glow of joy, and he strove to raise himself to greet her; but the effort was beyond his strength, and he fell back with a feeble groan.

"Remember, young lady," interposed Mr. Carstairs, firmly, "you are Mr. Carlyon's nurse, and not his priest, here. I must have no such talk as this—at least, not now."

And Agnes obeyed him; "Sister Agnes," as Carlyon called her throughout her mission, and as Mr. Martin came to call her when he found how well she deserved the title.

A breezy, jocund, health-diffusing man was the doctor—an old friend and fellow-student of Mr. Carstairs, as it happened—who, living close by, had been called in by happy chance to the wounded man.

After a day or two, the country practitioner went home, feeling sure that he had left his friend in safe hands, and leaving behind him Agnes and Widow Marcon, who had accompanied the former to town, since her suspicions of Cubra's having some confederate hand in the recent calamity, forbade her taking her own attendant. It was, doubtless, very "bold," and "dangerous," and "indecorous," in the eyes of some people (although Mrs. Newman had both approved of and pressed her doing so), that she should help to nurse Carlyon every day; but I do not think Agnes was much distressed by that consideration—having a Great Adviser whom she was wont to consult in all matters—even if she entertained it at all. And indeed such misgivings were totally out of place. It was true that the sick man grew stronger, and bade fair to make a complete recovery from his wound; but he still considered himself, as did Agnes likewise, as a doomed man. His heart had troubled him of late so incessantly that he could not forget that his days were surely numbered; and she, so soon as he could bear it, had pressed the claims of religion upon him with the earnestness inspired by the same conviction. Their behavior was very far from that of lovers. She read to him from that same book whose resistance to the cruel steel had saved his life, and he listened like one upon whose favored ears fall the very harmonies of heaven; but all her influence, all her charms, were made to serve that cause alone to which Carlyon was slowly but surely being won; she

had no thought, no dream of winning him, except for God.

He had received a letter from Mrs. Newman, the contents of which, perhaps, penetrated him more than all else with the sense of this young girl's goodness. He had reproached himself somewhat with not having written to his sister upon the occasion of Jedediah's death; that opportunity passed, it seemed well-nigh impossible that they should become friends; and lo! now the overture of reconciliation had actually emanated from her. Who but Agnes could have brought this about, and by what other means than those to which she herself attributed it—that faith by which miracles were said to have been wrought of old?

Agnes told him of Mrs. Newman's revelation to her concerning the disposal he had made of his property by will, and of that lady's subsequent self-denial.

"I could not have believed it," said he, gravely, "from any other lips than yours. What a pang it must have caused poor Meg!"

"Yes, Mr. Carlyon," said Agnes, with an answering smile; "but you must not inflict it a second time. Under no possible circumstances should I have taken or would I take one shilling of that which she so highly values, and which should naturally revert to her; but the gift must come directly from your hands, and not through mine."

"What, must I make another will then, and leave you nothing?"

"Certainly. What right have I to what you have to leave? Nay, even what need of it?"

"You will let me bequeath you Red Berild, however, the horse that saved your life to bless mine—the horse that you sketched on Greycrags lawn in those happy summer days, Agnes?"

"Yes; you may leave me Red Berild, Mr. Carlyon, if my acceptance of it will please you," said she, softly. "I have been to see him since I came; Mr. Carstairs took me; the noble creature looked so wistfully for the master that we could not bring."

"Poor Berild! You will ride him for my sake, Agnes; he is very quiet, and after a little you will find that you may guide him—as you did his owner—with a word."

So, like two children in a church-yard, into whom enters no natural thought of mirth and play, because of the open grave close by them, and of its expected tenant, Agnes and John Carlyon spoke not of earthly love and scarce of this world at all.

CHAPTER XXXI.
A CONSULTATION AND ITS RESULTS.

WHEN Carlyon was well enough to lie on the sofa, and take his meals with the enthusiasm incident to a convalescent after fever,

Mr. Martin announced his own occupation to be gone. "I never stay where I am not really wanted," said the cheery surgeon, "but if you like being doctored, I will send you a man who will stick by you, and give you pills as long as you choose to take them. In my opinion you are cured."

"Cured of my wound?" returned Carlyon, slowly. "Yes, thanks to you, sir, I feel that I am. This is not the first time that I have been deeply indebted to your profession."

"Ah. Well, I hope you'll never need to see any one of them again."

"Thank you," returned the patient, smiling. "I shall be always glad, however, to see *you* again, Mr. Martin—that is, at dinner; and likewise our good friend Carstairs."

"Ah, capital fellow, Carstairs," assented the surgeon, cheerfully, at the same time walking to the door and opening it as though to make sure that the nurse was out of ear-shot. Agnes had been sent out by his own edict that afternoon for a "constitutional" with Mrs. Marcon, in the park, for the recent change from her usual active habits at Mellor had begun to tell upon her somewhat. "A capital good fellow is Carstairs, and a man of science too, but crotchety; between ourselves, sir, infernally crotchety. We were students together at Guy's."

"Were you, indeed?" rejoined the sick man, languidly, and thinking to himself how long Agnes had been away. "What an immense time ago it seems."

"Eh! well, it's not so long, sir," rejoined Mr. Martin, sharply. "I don't suppose either of us are fifteen years older than yourself. But what I was going to say is, that even then Carstairs was very like some sexagenarian physician, who has devoted his whole energies to one branch of disease, and has got to believe that all mankind, either directly or indirectly, dies of it. With doctors who are ladies' doctors, this creed is of course restricted by the sex of their patients (to which, by the bye, it is my opinion that some of them assimilate in time, and become old women), but otherwise this fanaticism has no bounds. With a young practitioner, however, it is not usual to make one disease swallow up all others, like so many Pharaoh's serpents; and yet Carstairs, even as a student, entertained this curious notion. We used to call him Angina Carstairs."

"Ah, indeed," said Carlyon, dryly. "He was effeminate, then, as a young man, was he?"

"Not a bit of it, sir, but he thought every body was sure to die of *angina pectoris*—he believed every body—even those who had *no* hearts, like our hospital porter, who was a savage—had disease of the heart."

For the first time since his wound, Carlyon sprang up to a sitting posture, supporting himself by one hand, while the other was pressed tightly to his side.

"Oh, sir," said he, "do not hold out to me a false hope; even now I feel that Carstairs has told me nothing but the truth."

"What, that you would be a dead man a fortnight ago! That, Miss Agnes tells me, was his cheerful prognostication, and yet you have eaten a very tolerable breakfast for a '*post mortem.*'"

"Do you mean to say, Mr. Martin, that I have not heart disease?"

"By your change of color, my dear sir, and the pain you are evidently feeling in that side, I should be inclined to think that you have," answered the surgeon, quietly. "If I chose to use the stethoscope, I could undoubtedly tell you for certain; but that is not my line. If the young gentleman's dagger had gone through your heart, it would have been my business to pronounce you dead. No physician—who had any respect for himself, and the profession—would have ventured to have done so. But this is no surgical case. If you take my advice, you will allow me to call in Dr. Throb. He knows more about heart disease than any man in Great Britain; and there is this great advantage about him, that even if you have not got it he will prescribe for you as if you had. I am sure it will be a great satisfaction to your feelings to procure the opinion of a man like Throb. And besides, my dear sir, you will be witness of a consultation which, of itself, is quite as good as a play—although, to be sure, it's a little dearer."

"If you think a consultation will be of any use—" began Carlyon.

"I don't think it will," interrupted the surgeon, irritably. "A duel is no sort of use, for instance, but every body calls it a satisfaction. It settles the matter one way or another, at all events. Come, let me call in Dr. Throb."

To this proposition, Carlyon, not very eagerly, gave assent, and Dr. Throb condescended to make an appointment at the Albany for the afternoon of the day after the morrow. That great man, so far as physical stature went, was a very little one; much smaller than Mr. Carstairs, and round as a ball; but his grey eyes were large enough for a policeman's lantern, and roved fiercely about under his shaggy brows, as though in search of the villain who might venture to contradict him. Even the presence of Agnes failed to soften that terrible glance, although he gave her a re-assuring nod, as if to guarantee her personal safety, menaced by his tremendous arrival. He had been previously closeted with Mr. Martin—for a medical consultation is uncommonly like one of those children's games wherein two little folks go out of the room and whisper together, and come in and guess, and then go out and guess again—and perhaps that gentleman had softened the bashaw's heart toward the poor girl. But he had not softened it at all toward Carlyon. Dr. Throb marched in, like a drum-major at the head of an invading army; glared upon his patient—indignant perhaps at his being so large; shook his learned head, like a terrier with a rat in his jaws, and then turned to Mr. Martin and said "Yes," decisively, although the surgeon had said nothing whatever. The great man had previously addressed the salutation "Humph!" to Carlyon himself, so that there was no necessity for any farther courtesies, and he proceeded at once to business. To see him cast himself, stethoscope in hand, upon his victim, was to witness a gladiatorial exhibition; but in reality his every movement was directed with the utmost nicety and skill. This examination ended, Dr. Throb put certain questions to the patient regarding his own symptoms, exactly as though he were himself the chief inquisitor, and Carlyon, a heretic, doomed, upon the slightest show of hesitation, to the thumb-screws, rack, and stake. Then pursing his lips, and giving that mysterious nod to the surgeon, which the lady of the house gives to her principal female guest before leaving the dinner-table, the physician led the way to the consulting-room. As the door closed, Agnes stole to the sofa and took the sick man's hand. There was something in this Goth of a doctor's manner which had given her hope.

"I feel," said she, calmly, "an uncommon confidence in that man's judgment."

"So do I," answered Carlyon, smiling. "But indeed, if his opinion is not to be relied upon, he impugns the beneficence of the whole scheme of creation. Such a terrible Turk would otherwise scarce be permitted to live."

"If his verdict should agree with that of Mr. Carstairs," said she, in trembling tones, "you will not receive it as you did his, I know."

"No, Agnes. Thanks to you, it will no longer be with dogged submission. I shall say —and honestly feel it—God's will be done."

She had scarcely time to resume her former position when back stalked the little doctor, with drums beating and colors flying, and a triumphant flourish of trumpets. The chamber had evidently been given up to pillage; but was the life of its tenant to be spared?

"Humph!" said he. "You have heart complaint, Mr. Carlyon."

"I quite expected to hear you say so, Dr. Throb. My friend and medical adviser in the country gave me to understand—"

"Pooh," interrupted the great man. "He pledged his 'professional reputation,' didn't he, that you wouldn't live six months?"

"He said a year, sir."

"He might just as well have said a fortnight. Medicine is not an exact science like mathematics; and he was wrong, you see. He has forfeited his professional reputation — which most country practitioners would be very glad to do, and start afresh. He ought to be under great obligations to you—this Mr. Whatshisname —Farstares."

"But he was right so far as my having heart complaint?"

"Of course he was; no man with ears could be wrong about that, sir. You *have* heart complaint; but what of that? You may die of it, of course—you must die of something, I suppose—but you may also live with it for a quarter of a century, and die of drink at last. I have known a worse case than yours where the patient lived for longer than that, and was eventually hung. Good-morning, sir; good morning, ma'am." And away marched the little doctor, with a nod of great severity, to fresh fields of conquest and subjugation. But when he reached the outer door he turned round sharply to Mr. Martin, who had reverently followed him so far, with—"I say, my good fellow, can *he* afford *this?*" and he took out a crumpled note, which he had received in fee from Carlyon, by a most dexterous backhanded evolution, and without moving a muscle of his face. But it was one of this great man's weaknesses to object to take large fees from persons of moderate means, or any fee at all from poor folks.

"Oh, yes, he can afford it," said the other, laughing.

"I am glad to hear it, for both our sakes," returned the little man, with a significant action of the left eyelid.

With his professional brethren, and when removed from the observation of patients, Dr. Throb unbent a good deal. He was whispered to be invaluable at medical dinners—the only festive occasions he ever patronized—and there was even a story current, among the more audacious students of his hospital, that he had once sung a comic song.

When Mr. Martin went back to his patient he found him as sad and silent as though the sentence of Dr. Throb had been for his immediate execution, rather than a dismissal upon his personal recognizances, to come up when Justice More chose to send for him—as it really was. Agnes too was paler and more thoughtful than she had looked throughout the consultation. His entrance seemed to be a relief to both parties.

"Nice, agreeable, affable person, Dr. Throb, is he not?" inquired the surgeon, cheerfully.

"Very much so," said Carlyon, absently.

"I dare say he is very clever," observed Agnes, evasively. "I feel a great confidence in his judgment. If you will be so good as to ring for nurse, Mr. Martin, I think I will go to my lodgings, as Mrs. Marcon will be anxious to hear what his verdict is."

She cast a glance at Carlyon full of unspeakable emotion, but he had closed his eyes and lay back on the pillow, as though overcome by weakness. She rose softly, and left the room as the nurse entered it. Mr. Martin followed close upon her.

"As Mrs. Marcon has not yet come for you," said he—that respectable old lady being in the habit of calling for her every evening at six o'clock with the regularity of clock-work, "you must allow me to see you home, Miss Agnes."

"I am not afraid of going home alone, Mr. Martin, and I know your time is valuable," answered Agnes, quietly.

"You would also rather be alone just now,

would you not, my dear young lady? That's the very reason why I am going with you. I have got something of importance to say to you upon the road."

When they had fairly started, and she had placed her fingers lightly on his arm, the surgeon patted them in a re-assuring manner, and began as follows:

"You are trembling, my good girl, and all in a flutter, and it is not about me, I know. If I was twenty years younger, and did not happen to have a wife already, that reflection would distress me, but as it is, I am only distressed about yourself. You said just now that you have confidence in the judgment of Dr. Throb; and, as generally happens, you are quite right. He is a very wise man in his vocation, and can tell by the look of a young lady, without even so much as feeling her pulse, whether there is any thing the matter with her heart. Now as we were in consultation together, when (between ourselves) we doctors talk about almost any thing except the patient, he remarked that there was something the matter with yours. It's not my line of business, you know, but I'm bound to say that he only corroborated my own observation. There, don't cry—or, if you must cry, put your veil down. The symptoms are obvious; a general practitioner in the country (as Throb would say) could scarcely make a mistake in your diagnosis. You are in love with my poor patient yonder. Now, my dear child, I am old enough to be your grandfather, so that there is no occasion for embarrassment with me; but if you tremble in that way I shall be obliged to call a cab, and I can never hear a word that's said in a cab. You are in love with John Carlyon, I say, and I needn't tell you that he is in love with *you*. Well, why did you say 'no' when he asked you to marry him, some ten minutes ago? I don't, of course, wish to pry into private matters, but if it's religion — or rather (as you wrongly imagine) the want — of it in him—"

"No, sir, it is not that, sir, now, thank God," interrupted Agnes, earnestly.

"Then what the dickens is it?" inquired the surgeon, with irritation.

"Sir, there are two reasons, since you force me to speak so openly," said Agnes, with firmness; "but I deny your right—"

"Of course, my good young lady, I have no right," interposed the surgeon, briskly, and once more patting her fingers; "but it's my privilege. You'll find it in all the diplomas. Now, what are the two reasons?"

"One is, sir, that I can not marry the man whose life has been attempted by one of my own blood, the only relative I have in the world."

"Oh, I see. You make your relative's quarrel your own. Since your cousin has failed to kill this man, you will, at all events, deny him all that makes his life worth having. That is the true Corsican fashion; but I should doubt whether it has the approbation of the Christian Church."

"I mean, sir," explained Agnes, gravely, "Mr. Carlyon has never spoken to me about Richard; never hinted at whose hand laid him upon what might have proved his death-bed; but there are times when I feel that I have almost been his murderess."

"Tut, tut; you could not help two men falling in love with you—I dare say a dozen have done it—nor could you prevent one of them going mad after sun-stroke. The rest of the circumstances I have had only at second-hand, but *that's* a medical fact, and I can speak of it with certainty. This mad cousin of yours too has left the country, has been traced into a ship bound for the Indies, whither he has gone under the agreeable idea that his rival is disposed of. There will be, therefore, no necessity to ask him to the wedding, or otherwise inconvenience yourselves by his attentions. To suffer this poor lunatic to blight the life of a man like Carlyon is mere wanton cruelty under the guise of sentiment. I am sure you will not do this, Miss Agnes. I hope, for the sake of your reputation for common sense, that the second reason for saying 'no' is more valid than the first."

"Yes, sir, it is, indeed. Forgive me, Mr. Martin, but I can not pursue this subject farther, except to say this much—I am sure that your questions have been dictated by a desire to do good, to diffuse happiness. The second objection I can not reveal. It is a family secret. True, there was a time when it did not seem to me so insurmountable an obstacle, but that was because a still more formidable impediment—that of Mr. Carlyon's opinions—lay in the way. Now he is no longer a godless man, I wonder how I could have ever overlooked the barrier of which I speak."

"There is madness in her family," thought the surgeon, his mind recurring to her cousin's frenzied act; but the next moment he recollected that his aberration had been produced by the tropic sun.

"My dear young lady," answered the surgeon, tenderly, "I have no intention of prying into this unhappy matter; I only charge you, as you are a Christian woman, not to embitter this man's life without great cause. If any disgrace"—he felt her shudder through every limb—"has ever happened to any of your kith and kin—for that it has not done so to yourself, I am very sure—see that it affords not only a reasonable but a sufficient ground on which to reject a brave man's love. I do not say that there may not be such a disgrace; it is my opinion, however, that you should reveal it, whatever it is, to his own ears, and then abide his decision."

"I could never tell him, sir," replied Agnes, in half-choked tones. "It reflects upon the memory of one that is most near and dear to me, and who is gone to his rest after long years of trouble."

"Poor dear! poor dear!" ejaculated the surgeon, tenderly; "I have only then one alternative to propose. However sad may be this secret you speak of, however insuperable a difficulty it may present to your eyes, you can not gauge this man's love and say it is not sufficient to overcome it. Since you shrink from speaking with him on the subject, write the whole matter out, and let me place it—sealed—in his own hands. He will certainly make no bad use of the information; at the worst, it will remain with him a sacred trust. If it strikes him as it does you, you need never see one another any more. If, on the other hand, he writes back, 'Come,' that will be a sign that he prizes you at a value, from which nothing can materially detract. See, here we are at our journey's end. Let me exact this promise of you. Let me call for this writing in a few hours, for such a matter is best done at once, and done with. Say 'yes,' my dear Miss Agnes, I adjure you. At least let this man's future life be marred by no misunderstanding, no meaningless repulse. It is better for a man to be denied than to be evaded."

"I will do as you request, Mr. Martin," said Agnes, sighing; "but you do not know the heaviness of the task you lay upon me. The paper shall be ready within two hours."

"That's a brave, good girl," said the surgeon, with affectionate earnestness. "I shall call for it myself, and it will never leave my hands till it reaches his. God bless and strengthen you, my dear."

The next moment the door of her lodging opened, and Agnes hurried in.

"Now, if I were in that fellow Carlyon's place," mused Mr. Martin to himself, as he turned away, "I would marry that very charming young woman, no matter what might be urged against her family, and although both her parents had perished on the gallows."

CHAPTER XXXII.

CUTTING THE KNOT.

"WHEN you have read this, write to me," were the words which Agnes had appended to the secret statements confided according to promise to Mr. Martin's care, for Carlyon; and now it was the second day, and yet she had received no answer. For the first and last time in her life she had written "Agnes Vane," at the foot of what was an honest narration of her unhappy father's misfortune. The old man had not concealed it from her, although her cousin had taken it for granted that he had. The threat, therefore, employed by Richard of revealing his uncle's secret had been quite without weight so far as Agnes was concerned, however it may have told with respect to others. But Mr. Crawford, naturally enough, had estimated his nephew's worth, or rather the want of it, by the baseness of the menace, and had judged his unfitness to become her husband by the very means which the young man relied upon to insure his acceptance. Whether rightly or not, we can not tell. To secure Agnes for himself, it was true that the wretched youth had stooped to every baseness, and even to crime; but with relation to all other things he had behaved himself with honor and probity. Strange as the comparison may seem, the love of her was to him like the one vice, such as gambling or drinking, which so often deforms an otherwise noble character. If Richard Crawford had been her accepted lover from the first, perhaps he would never have strayed from the broad road of right.

By reflections upon this matter, however, Agnes was not disturbed. She was filled with remorse at having revealed, even to one single person, that disgrace which her dead father had been so solicitous to conceal. True, she could not have permitted this man to marry her while the secret remained untold; but why had she not sacrificed her own wishes (for she no longer attempted to conceal from herself that her heart was another's) to so sacred a trust? Had not Carlyon himself set her an example in preserving his own father's memory from obloquy? How weak and wicked she had been! No wonder Carlyon had sent her no reply; offended, no doubt, less by the nature of the family disgrace than by her own selfish disclosure of it. And yet, surely he might have written to her too, even if it had been that word "No," with which a year ago she had driven him from his home at Mellor.

She could not read; she could not work; she could only sit with her hands before her and think, and think, and listen. Was that the postman's knock? No. And yet it could hardly be any visitor. Nobody had called upon her since she had been in town, for scarcely any of her acquaintance knew of her being there. Doubtless, this arrival concerned the lodgers who occupied the dining-room floor. Any thing that diverted her mind from its present melancholy, even for a moment, was welcome, and she listened with attention. There must be many visitors—more than one or two—to judge by the time that they took to enter the house. Why, too, should they delay in the hall instead of— But now it was certain that they were ascending, although very deliberately, to the drawing-room in which she sat. The slowness of their movements and the frequent halts that they seemed to make, suggested that one among them, at least, must be very old or feeble —as old as her poor father, perhaps, whose secret she had so fruitlessly betrayed. The door opened, and in walked Mr. Martin, with a gaunt man, very white and shrunken, leaning heavily upon his arm.

"Mr. Carlyon!" cried she, with an involuntary cry of wonder.

"The same, miss, and no other," returned the surgeon, quietly; "and he would be obliged to you if you would offer him a chair."

In the extremity of her astonishment she had forgotten how much this exertion must have cost the invalid; but in a moment she was herself again, and had wheeled round the sofa and arranged the cushions as she had done so often for him in his own chamber.

"I thought it was better, Agnes, that I should come and see you myself—"

"*I* didn't; mind *that*," interrupted the surgeon. "I thought it was madness."

"Better to tell you what I had to say by word of mouth, than to offer any explanation by letter," continued Carlyon, feebly. "You must have thought me very brutal, Agnes, these last two days."

"Brutal, Mr. Carlyon! Why so? I blamed myself, but not so much as I do now, seeing that I have caused you to be so imprudent as to venture hither."

"I should have come yesterday, if Mr. Martin would have let me out; he kept me prisoner against my will, until I threatened to apply for a writ of *habeas corpus*. Sit down here, Agnes, close by me, for my voice is weak."

"Mendacious hypocrite," muttered the surgeon; "he bawled at my coachman to drive faster, until I expected the man would have given me warning on the spot."

Agnes took her seat, as Carlyon requested, very white and quiet. He had come, she thought, like a brave man as he was, to tell her face to face, that he was too proud to marry a woman who, because of a family disgrace, bore a name that was not her own. How rightly was she about to be punished for her selfish conduct!

"Our excellent friend, Mr. Martin yonder, has placed in my hands a document written by yourself, Agnes, and relating to certain private affairs connected with your family. He did so with a good motive, I am sure; but he did not know me."

"It was I myself who told him to give it to you, Mr. Carlyon."

"I know it. It was not unnatural, perhaps, that one, with so delicate a sense of duty, placed in your position, should have done so. Otherwise, and supposing you had been in his place, you would have known me better; you would have said, as I hope and believe, 'John Carlyon will never read it.' Here it is, Agnes, with the seals unbroken. If the secret it contains be any misfortune which it is within my power to remedy, or mitigate; if it be any sorrow, which may be lightened to yourself by another's sympathy, I will hear it from your lips. If not, let it remain unrevealed. Of whatever nature it may be, the knowledge of it could no more weaken my devoted love for you, my ardent hope (presumptuous as it seems) that you may become my wife, Agnes, than some small stream of brackish water newly set a flowing could alter the saltness of the sea into which it runs; but I do not wish to hear it. If the telling of a secret be the proof of some women's love, let the keeping of one be yours for me. Take it; burn it. And when it is burned, be sure that the evidence of its existence is thereby not more surely destroyed than any—the least misgiving of what it may have been has vanished from my own bosom. Agnes, dear Agnes, you have blessed me beyond all that words can tell; but I still ask for more. Say, tell me: Will you be my wife?"

There was no verbal response; but nevertheless she answered with her lips.

"Really," murmured Mr. Martin, after he had stared discreetly out of the window for a considerable period, "I am hanged if they have not forgotten I am in the room.—Mr. Carlyon," exclaimed he, aloud, "I have got other patients besides yourself and this young lady (for I consider that I have prescribed for her, and with considerable success), and I can't afford to keep my horses standing still here all day. It is time for us to be off. My dear Miss Agnes, whom I beg leave to most heartily congratulate, you can not use your newly-acquired supremacy to better purpose than to order this sick man home."

"My good friend," remonstrated Carlyon, coolly, "I tell you what you'd better do, if you really *have* got other patients to attend to. Go and see them, by all means, and then come back and call for me. I assure you I feel much better since the morning, and in perfectly safe hands."

So the good surgeon, laughing very merrily, left patient and nurse together, and started off on his professional round.

"He looks quite another man already," chuckled Mr. Martin, when he found himself alone in his brougham, with its pockets stored with cases of horrid implements; "upon my life there may be something in physicians' prescriptions after all. I never saw such a satisfactory result from a mere external application of lip-salve before."

CHAPTER XXXIII.
ALL'S WELL THAT ENDS WELL.

THE first person to whom Carlyon wrote to tell of his approaching marriage with Agnes was sister Meg; and she wrote him back a letter, filled half with good wishes and half with good advice, the last solely with reference to the economy of a household; "for," said she, "with respect to your spiritual welfare it is impossible that you can have a better teacher than she whom you have chosen; whereas, as respects pecuniary expenditure, she is culpably lavish."

To Mr. Carstairs, the convalescent, out of the exuberance of his spirits, could not help sending a mourning card with,

JOHN CARLYON.
Friends will please accept the intimation,

on one side; and on the other,

Of his marriage in September next.

In return, he received the most disinterested congratulations from the kind-hearted doctor, and a budget of country news. "I am sorry to say," wrote he, "that these insatiable sands of ours have been devouring more victims. Old Stephen Millet and his son were both lost some nights ago during a dense fog; the former, they say, was not himself—having fallen of late more than ever into his old habits—and that William perished in the attempt to get him home. Heaven only knows how it was; but a nobler or more self-sacrificing soul than that young man never drew breath. I have just seen them laid in the same grave. There is another vacancy among us here, which, in my opinion, is by no means to be so regretted. Mrs. Newman and I agreed to keep it to ourselves while Miss Agnes was in trouble about other matters; but there is no reason why she should not be told now. The second morning after her mistress left Mellor, Cubra suddenly disappeared. As she never goes upon the sands, I did not apprehend any danger from that source; after much inquiry, I came to the conclusion that she had been sent for by that unhappy young man to accompany him in his flight; and on application to the shipping-office, I find that a person answering to her description embarked in the same vessel as Richard Crawford. Thus, the poor old woman has been faithful to her young master to the last, according to her lights, sad will-of-the-wisps though they were. I am glad for both your sakes that they can now lead neither him nor her so dangerously astray; and for poor Richard's sake, that he has some one who will cleave to him whithersoever he has gone."

Poor Richard! That was how Carlyon and his wife always spoke of her unhappy cousin—never with anger or uncharitableness. To believe him mad was the most consoling creed which they could hold.

The newly-married couple did not make their home at Mellor. There was an association connected with that place that made it painful to Carlyon to do so. Though he was far from entertaining an un-Christian despair respecting any man's future, though the more he experienced of God's love and mercy (and he experienced much) the less was he prone to plumb their depth, and say "It ends here—or here;" yet, he could not now regard that tombstone in the church-yard with "Gone to join the majority" upon it, with the old sardonic indifference. It was curious enough that *that* should be the bitterest drop in Carlyon's cup after all; but so it was.

He and Agnes made their home in another part of the country; but paid a yearly visit to Mrs. Newman, now installed at Woodlees, which he had settled upon her—the gloomy place having fortunately found no purchaser—for life. She gave one dinner-party in their honor on each of these occasions; but it cost her a great deal—not in money, indeed, for it was the reverse of an expensive entertainment, but in many a mental pang.

Robin and the rest of the household suffered for it when the Carlyons went. Having at last reduced her expenditure to a minimum, this good lady determined to give the public the benefit of her experience, and has occupied her spare time of late in composing those well-known and useful little volumes, "How to live on forty pounds a year—and passing well;" and "Enough is as good as a Feast; or how to make a leg of mutton last a week."

Carlyon put in his protest once or twice for Robin's sake; but sister Meg only replied, "My dear John, you have no idea what that old man eats, although he has not a tooth in his head." Where, however, her brother made a resolute stand and carried his point, was in the stable arrangements. Red Berill had his two feeds of corn per diem, while at Woodlees, in spite of all her protestations; and generally received them, scarcely less from affection than for security, from Agnes's own hand.

As years went on, two little children—first a girl, then a boy—began to hold as the highest treat a ride upon the good old horse, which, they were told, had saved dear mamma's life years ago from the hungry tide. There is no fear of the faithful creature's not being affectionately cared for in his old age, even though his master should die before him. As to that, John Carlyon was no worse when we last heard of him than during that period when Mr. Carstairs put so exact a limit to his days. That gentleman, however, holds to his own opinion that the squire ought to have died years and years ago, and that he owes his present existence only to the heretical nature of his disposition.

"He flew in the face of Providence in his youth," says he, "and having been converted from that error, he now flies in the face of Science."

He has the magnanimity to add, however, "Long may he fly."

And all who are acquainted with John Carlyon as he now is, have good cause to say Amen.

THE END.

www.ingramcontent.com/pod-product-compliance
Lightning Source LLC
Chambersburg PA
CBHW020307090426
42735CB00009B/1258